CORE CONCEPTS.
A STUDENT'S GUIDE TO CORPORATE AND PARTNERSHIP TAX

ANNE L. ALSTOTT
JACQUIN D. BIERMAN PROFESSOR IN TAXATION
YALE LAW SCHOOL

EDITORIAL STAFF
Editor: Barbara L. Post, Esq.
Production: Jennifer Schencker
Cover Design: Laila Gaidulis
Interior Design: Patrick Gallagher, Laila Gaidulis

This publication is designed to provide accurate and authoritative information in regard to the subject matter covered. It is sold with the understanding that the publisher is not engaged in rendering legal, accounting, or other professional service, and that the authors are not offering such advice in this publication. If legal advice or other expert assistance is required, the services of a competent professional person should be sought.

ISBN: 978-0-8080-5536-5

©2020 CCH Incorporated. All rights reserved.
2700 Lake Cook Road
Riverwoods, IL 60015
800 344 3734
CCHCPELink.com

No claim is made to original government works: however, within this Product or Publication, the following are subject to CCH Incorporated's copyright: (1) the gathering, compilation, and arrangement of such government materials; (2) the magnetic translation and digital conversion of data, if applicable; (3) the historical, statutory and other notes and references; and (4) the commentary and other materials.

Do not send returns to the above address. If for any reason you are not satisfied with your book purchase, it can easily be returned within 30 days of shipment. Please go to *support.cch.com/returns* to initiate your return. If you require further assistance with your return, please call: (800) 344-3734 M-F, 8 a.m. - 6 p.m.CT.

Printed in Canada

Introducing Business Taxation

Every few years, corporate tax avoidance hits the front page. In 2018, for instance, Amazon and Eli Lilly were among the sixty of America's largest companies that paid zero federal income tax. A casual observer might assume that these companies are bad actors — tax evaders who should be punished. But the reality is more complicated. Outright tax evasion certainly exists. But many business tax breaks (like accelerated depreciation) have been enacted by Congress. And then there is the legal borderland of tax shelters, where the IRS and taxpayers battle over the interpretation of uncertain legal rules.

This book aims to introduce students to the complex world of business taxation. Through cases, problems, and explanations, we will explore the rules that aim to impose taxes on business income – and the tax-planning strategies that businesses use to reduce their taxes.

Business taxation is a specialized field, typically covered in advanced tax courses on corporate and partnership taxation. These courses can be a bear for students, because the transactions are intricate and the law is complex. The basic course in taxation is good preparation, but business taxation takes complexity to a whole new level. Most people do not have keen intuitions about technical questions like whether a stock redemption should be treated as a distribution or an exchange.

Still, business taxation should not be reserved for tax specialists, and it needn't be impenetrable to students. In my earlier book, *Taxation in Six Concepts*, I showed how the rules of the income tax reflect six conceptual problems. In this book, I take a similar approach. It turns out that even advanced tax problems are driven by a handful of conceptual problems. And in a stunning coincidence, the concepts that star in this book are the same as those examined in the earlier *Six Concepts*. The core problems of *valuation, realization, net income, tax deferral, income shifting*, and *substance over form* all help explain most of the core problems in the taxation of business income.

This book arose from necessity. There are a several excellent student treatises on corporate and partnership taxation, but they tend to delve into the details of tax rules. That's totally sensible. But I found that students also wanted something a little different: a short, readable introduction to business taxation that connects to what they already know. And so this book makes use of the six concepts to sketch an overview of the major issues in corporate and partnership tax. The six concepts help unify the two subjects, revealing connecting threads that we often do not see, because most professors do not teach these materials side-by-side.

Here, as in the original *Six Concepts* book, the six concepts help illuminate the hardest problems in corporate and partnership tax. The six concepts are the six major pressure points in the law: the places where policy makers just can't get it right, no matter how hard they try. And it's those pressure points, those inevitable gaps in the law, that motivate tax planning by taxpayers – and responses by Congress and the IRS.

To take just one example, the corporate income tax imposes a two-level tax on corporate income. But the basic structure reflects a problem of *valuation* and *realization*: if the IRS could observe the value of corporate stock every year, we wouldn't need a separate corporate tax at all. The impracticality of mark-to-market taxation led Congress to adopt an entity tax plus a distributions tax. But this corporate double tax is far from perfect. Taxpayers can use it to achieve *tax deferral* and *income shifting*, and policy makers have adopted rules that attempt to use *substance over form* to curb tax planning. Nevertheless, the tax law offers rich fuel for tax planning for mergers and acquisitions, stock buybacks, and other corporate deals.

This short book cannot, of course, cover all the technicalities that will be discussed in the tax courses on corporate and partnership tax. But you'll find most of the big legal topics covered here, with an explanation tied to one – or, often, several – of the six concepts.

Even more so than basic tax, business taxation considers complex transactions and deliberate tax planning. Just as in the *Six Concepts* book, I've provided illustrations drawn from the case law and real-world transactions. And to help students understand the transactions, I've included two new features. First, most chapters now include at least one problem with a detailed answer, which I've found essential to digesting the complexities of business taxation. Second, many chapters also include a new feature, called Business 101, which introduces business forms and common deal structures. So even if you are not quite sure what a corporation is yet, we've got you covered. By the end of the book, you'll throw around (and even understand!) terms like redemptions, reorganizations, and substantial economic effect.

To begin, I draw on one of the six concepts – *substance over form* – to show why business taxation is so complicated. Business entities, of course, are purely formal constructs. Corporations aren't people. They don't exist, except as a stack of contracts in a conference room or on a computer disk. Corporations don't make loans or invent new technology or fly airplanes. People do all those things. And so, when the tax law attributes those activities to corporations, the law is privileging form over substance.

We can say exactly the same thing about partnerships, which are just another legal form that sets the rules for relationships among human beings. Whether it's a small law firm or a big hedge fund, a "partnership" is just the word we use for the contracts that set the terms on which human beings (and their money!) come together to do business. The partnership itself is nothing more than a stack of documents sitting in a file (or stored in computer memory).

Now, legal formalities like corporations and corporate residence can be useful for individuals and for the economy. There are whole fields in economics (industrial organizations) and in law (business organizations) that seek to explain the many benefits of permitting individuals to conduct business through firms (rather than by ordinary contract).

But when it comes to the income tax, formalism is a dangerous game. When tax rules diverge from economic reality, the law will predictably create traps and opportunities with a distinctive pattern. In fact, the pattern is so distinctive, and so often repeated throughout the subject of business taxation, that it deserves a text box of its own:

> **Formal Rules Create:**
> **Traps for the Unwary**
> **Opportunities for the Well-Advised**

Now, policy makers know all this just as tax experts do. So lawmakers sometimes fight back, crafting rules and standards that try to reintroduce substance into all this form, closing off both the traps and the opportunities.

But let's be real. Sometimes, policy makers *like* the hidden traps and opportunities. From a politician's perspective, the tax law is a good hiding place for goodies for business constituents. Most ordinary people have no reason to know the ins and outs of the tax code, while most sophisticated business players will have every reason to do so. The result is that politicians often talk one game ("Soak the rich!") and play another (accelerated depreciation, anyone?).

All of these dynamics come together in an ongoing tax conflict that resembles one of those mega-battles in multiplayer video games. Business interests tend to like formalities, not least because big business loves the tax-planning opportunities that arise when the rules deviate from economic reality. The IRS, for its part, tries to import substance into the tax arena, but sometimes its efforts create complexity without accomplishing much in the way of reform. The Congress is a rogue actor in all this, because it sometimes fights on the side of business and sometimes on the side of the IRS.

If all this sounds complicated, then you've got it! A relatively straightforward conceptual problem – *substance over form* – motivates a great deal of the legal complexity in business taxation. We will see that the law seesaws back and forth between substance and form, but that there's rarely a perfect outcome, a stable rule, or a lasting compromise.

About the Author

Anne L. Alstott is the Jacquin D. Bierman Professor in Taxation at the Yale Law School. She has held the Bierman chair from 2004-2008 and again from 2011 to the present. From 2008-2011, Professor Alstott was the Manley O. Hudson Professor at the Harvard Law School.

Professor Alstott has taught tax law, tax policy, and social welfare policy at Yale, Harvard, and Columbia since 1992. She has won the annual teaching award at Yale Law School four times and at Columbia Law School once. The Yale Law School graduating classes of 2013 and 2017 elected her to speak at Commencement.

Professor Alstott's books include *Taxation in Six Concepts* (2018, Wolters Kluwer), *The Public Option* (2019, Harvard University Press) (with Ganesh Sitaraman), *A New Deal for Old Age* (2016, Harvard University Press), *No Exit: What Parents Owe Their Children and What Society Owes Parents* (2004, Oxford University Press), and *The Stakeholder Society* (1999, Yale University Press) (with Bruce Ackerman). Her scholarly articles have been published in the Harvard Law Review, the Yale Law Journal, the Columbia Law Review, and the Tax Law Review, as well as in many other journals and in books.

Professor Alstott was born in Indianapolis. She has two children and two rescue dogs.

How to Use This Book

This book introduces the central issues in corporate tax and partnership tax by showing how each issue relates to six concepts in the income tax: *valuation, realization, net income, tax deferral, income shifting,* and *substance over form*. You probably recognize these ideas from your basic course in taxation, and they will provide welcome signposts as you take on the complex material covered in advanced classes in business taxation.

This book isn't a casebook, although it discusses major cases, and it isn't a treatise, although it does explain the law. Casebooks and treatises have to convey a large amount of material, and the result is that they are long and detailed. This book takes a different tack: it aims to boil down the complexity by showing how difficult topics (stock distributions, anyone?) relate to the six concepts that you already know. (In case you need a refresher on the six concepts, you might have a look at my other CCH publication, *Taxation in Six Concepts*, which connects the concepts to the topics and cases studied in the basic course on taxation.)

This book is organized to help supplement your course readings. There are separate sections on corporate and partnership tax, and within each section, each chapter addresses one or two types of transactions. These will map onto the typical progression of subjects in a corporate or partnership tax course. For instance, if your course is just about to cover corporate distributions, you could read Chapter 7 of this book to introduce you to the major issues and connect them to the six concepts.

You might even want to go back and re-read the relevant chapter from this book again *after* you've read your casebook, just to be sure you've grasped the essentials of corporate distributions (or whatever). Keeping a firm grasp on the basics is not an easy task in advanced tax classes where the trees can definitely keep us from seeing the forest.

The book's chapters include a number of problems, all with lengthy answers, to help you apply what you've learned. Appendix C provides more advanced problems, which mirror the kind of issue-spotters you might see on an exam, along with full answers.

Finally, when final exams come around, this book has additional material that may be useful. Appendix A provides general advice on exam writing, and Appendix B lays out a specific method for spotting issues in an advanced tax exam.

Contents

Introducing Business Taxation iii

About the Author vii

How to Use This Book ix

Part I: Taxing Business Income 1

Chapter 1 *Valuation* and the Challenge of Taxing Business Income 3

¶100 Introduction 3
¶101 The Challenge of *Valuation* 4
¶102 Compounding the Problem with Multiple Tax Rates 5

Chapter 2 Income Shifting, Tax Deferral, and the Choice of Business Entity 9

¶200 Introduction 9
¶201 The Basics of Entity Taxation:
      Corporation versus Pass-Through 10
¶202 Quantifying the Value of *Income Shifting* and *Tax Deferral* Using Entities . . . 13
¶203 Problem 2.1: Corporate versus Pass-Through Taxation 16
¶204 Business 101: What Is a Corporation? 17
Appendix 2-1 The Math Behind the Madness of Entity Choice 18

Chapter 3 Entity Choice and the Limits of *Substance Over Form* 21

¶300 Introduction 21
¶301 The "Check-The-Box" Rules 21
¶302 Problem 3.1: The Check-The-Box Rules 22
¶303 *Bollinger* and the Limited Reach of *Substance Over Form* in Entity Choice... 23
¶304 The Use of Substance Over Form in Business Taxation 25

Part II: Taxing Corporate Income 27

Chapter 4 *Substance Over Form* in Corporate Tax: Debt Versus Equity 29

¶400 Introduction 29
¶401 Debt Versus Equity: The Impact of Taxes 31
¶402 *Indmar* and *Substance Over Form* 34
¶403 Problem 4.1: Debt and Equity 38
¶404 Business 101: What is Debt? 39
¶405 Advanced Problem 41

Chapter 5	*Tax Deferral* and Corporate Formation	43
¶500	Introduction	43
¶501	Incorporation and *Realization*	44
¶502	Section 351 and *Tax Deferral*	47
¶503	Problem 5.1: Section 351	49
¶504	*Substance Over Form* in Incorporations: *Intermountain Lumber*	51
¶505	Business 101: What is Corporate Control?	53
¶506	Advanced Problem	55

Chapter 6	Limitations on *Tax Deferral:* Boot and Services in Corporate Formation	57
¶600	Introduction	57
¶601	*Tax Deferral* and Boot	57
¶602	Nonqualified Preferred Stock	60
¶603	Compensation for Services	61
¶604	Problem 6.1: Section 351 and Boot	64
¶605	Business 101: What is Preferred Stock?	65

Chapter 7	*Realization*: Corporate Distributions and Redemptions	67
¶700	Introduction	67
¶701	*Realization* and the Distribution Rules	68
¶702	Problem 7.1 Distributions and Dividends	69
¶703	*Income Shifting* and the Dividend Rules	71
¶704	*Substance Over Form* and Redemptions	74
¶705	Problem 7.2: Redemptions	75
¶706	Business 101: What is a Dividend? What is a Stock Buyback?	78
¶707	Advanced Problems	79

Chapter 8	*Substance Over Form*: Disguised Dividends and Stock Dividends	81
¶800	Introduction	81
¶801	Disguised Dividends	81
¶802	Stock Dividends and *Eisner v. Macomber*	84
¶803	Stock Dividends and Code Sec. 305	86
¶804	Problem 8.1: Disguised Dividends and Stock Dividends	89
¶805	Advanced Problem	90

Chapter 9 Realization and Tax Deferral in Corporate Acquisitions 91

¶900	Introduction	91
¶901	The Basics of Taxable Acquisitions: Just Two Structures	92
¶902	*Realization* and Taxable Acquisitions	93
¶903	*Tax Deferral* and Reorganizations	96
¶903.01	What Qualifies as a Reorg?	97
¶903.02	How Does a Reorg Award *Tax Deferral*?	98
¶904	Problem 9.1: Taxable Acquisitions and Reorganizations	99
¶905	Business 101: What is a Corporate Acquisition?	101
¶906	Advanced Problem	103

Chapter 10 Substance Over Form and Corporate Reorganizations 105

¶1000	Introduction	105
¶1001	Reorgs and the Problem of *Realization* in *Marr*	106
¶1002	Continuity of Proprietary Interest	108
¶1003	How Much Continuity?	110
¶1004	Problem 10.1: Continuity of Interest and Corporate Reorganizations	111
¶1005	Advanced Problem	113

Part III Taxing Partnership Income 115

Chapter 11 Valuation and Realization in Partnership Taxation 117

¶1100	Introduction	117
¶1101	A Little Bit of Terminology	119
¶1102	*Realization* and the *Net Income* of the Partnership and Its Partners	120
¶1103	*Basye* and *Realization*	124
¶1104	Problem 11.1: Partnership Tax Basics	126
¶1105	Business 101: What is a Partnership?	127

Chapter 12 From Two Levels of Tax to One: The Basics of Partnership Taxation 129

¶1200	Introduction	129
¶1201	Each Partner (Not the Partnership) Pays the Tax	130
¶1202	Partners Must Report Income Even Without Distribution	131
¶1203	Partners Adjust Their Bases to Ensure Income is Taxed Only Once	132
¶1203.01	Partners' Outside Basis Increases to Reflect Allocated Income	132
¶1203.02	Partners' Outside Basis Decreases to Reflect Distributions	134
¶1203.03	Contrast the Corporate Tax Results	135
¶1204	Problem 12.1: Partnership Tax Basics	135
¶1205	Advanced Problems	136

Chapter 13 *Tax Deferral* and Partnership Contributions 137

¶1300   Introduction 137
¶1301   *Tax Deferral* and Partnership Contributions 138
¶1302   *Tax Deferral* at the Partnership Level 139
¶1303   Problem 13.1: Contribution Basics 141
¶1304   *Income Shifting* and Contributed Property: The Role of Sec. 704(c) 142
¶1305   Problem 13.2: Section 704(c) and Its Limitations 145
¶1306   Advanced Problems 147

Chapter 14 *Income Shifting* and Partnership Allocations 149

¶1400   Introduction 149
¶1401   *Valuation* and Partnership Allocations 150
¶1402   *Income Shifting* and Partnership Allocations 151
¶1403   The Logic – and Limitations – of Code Sec. 704(b) 153
¶1404   Advanced Problems 156

Chapter 15 *Substance Over Form* In Partnership Tax 157

¶1500   Introduction 157
¶1501   The Partnership Anti-Abuse Rule 158
¶1502   *ACM Partnership v. Commissioner* 159
¶1503   *Castle Harbour* 162
¶1504   Advanced Problem 165

Appendix A The Basics of Writing an Issue-Spotter Exam 167

Appendix B Advanced Strategies for Business Tax Exams 173

Appendix C Advanced Problems 177

Corporate Tax 177
Partnership Tax 182

Case Table 187

Table of Code, Regulations and Rulings 189

Index 191

PART I
Taxing Business Income

CHAPTER 1

Valuation and the Challenge of Taxing Business Income

Introduction	¶100
The Challenge of *Valuation*	¶101
Compounding the Problem with Multiple Tax Rates	¶102

¶100 INTRODUCTION

Suppose that Amanda, Bill, and Calla have decided to found a new chain of high-end boutique hotels. The three have been friends since college, and they differ in their skills, assets, and plans for the future. Amanda, who used to work in a consulting firm, has a good eye for properties and financial analysis. Bill has ten years of hands-on management experience in the hotel industry. Calla has just graduated from college and has no prior experience, but she has inherited some money and wants to use it to found and run her own business. Together, they believe, they can reap the synergies of their knowledge, skills, and assets.

The first question for the three friends is the opening question for this book: How should they structure a business venture together, and how might taxes affect their decisions?

The A-B-C hypothetical seems simple, but it represents the classic business venture: some parties to the venture contribute knowledge; others provide labor; others bring capital. The economic theory of the firm suggests that firms exist precisely because there are profits to be made by combining knowledge, skill, and money – gains that cannot be captured by off-the-rack market investments (such as stocks, bonds, and mutual funds). Put another way, it must be the case that A, B, and C believe that they can earn more money with this business than by investing in stocks and bonds in the marketplace. Otherwise, they'd do that instead.

Quite apart from tax, there are many legal and business issues that the co-venturers must work out, because each has preferences about risk and return and different time horizons. For instance, Amanda may have a short time horizon for this project, because she has a five-year plan that includes going back to business school. Bill may be looking for a medium-term commitment for full-time employment at a secure wage. And Calla may be in this for the long run; she's looking to build a life-long business out of her inheritance.

The key point is that there is no reason to suppose that a one-size-fits-all business agreement will meet the needs of all three participants. So they will ideally want the legal flexibility to negotiate different terms, while also keeping the deal simple and transparent enough that they can all understand what everyone is getting.

To add to the mix, each party should also pay attention to the others' incentives. Things may be happy at the outset, but the course of true business never did run smooth,[1] and each person should be confident that the other parties have every incentive to contribute more know-how, work harder, or contribute more capital if need be. The co-venturers should also specify exit options if things go south or if one person (or the whole group) just wants to wind things up early.

¶101   THE CHALLENGE OF *VALUATION*

So what does all of this mean for tax? The key point is that the income tax aims to tax the economic income of A, B, and C. In principle, income should be measured by the change in fair market value of the wealth of each party. In practice, of course, the tax system won't meet that ideal. Still, you will see that the tax system retains some allegiance (as it must) to taxing according to the economic situation of each individual. Thus, the income tax must in some way register the specific contractual arrangements, time horizons, and payoffs to each party.

As you've probably spotted, the tax system confronts a major tradeoff between accurate measurement of income and administrability. A, B, and C are unique individuals, and they should (for the reasons above) negotiate detailed economic arrangements. Multiplying A, B, and C by a few hundred million Americans, it would be unwieldy for the IRS to try to document every detail of every deal. And it is definitely not possible for the IRS to observe the (changing!) fair market value of each person's entitlements. So practicality is going to push for simpler rules and less differentiation among A, B, and C.

But there's the rub.[2] An income tax cannot abandon entirely the project of taxing individuals according to their economic situation – or else it isn't an income tax any more. The ideal of taxing ability to pay requires the IRS to take notice of ability to pay – and that requires attention to business arrangements.

This tradeoff between accurate *valuation* and practicality run throughout this book. The corporate tax, we will see, imposes a more standardized tax burden on investors, while the partnership tax rules accommodate (nearly) limitless flexibility. To foreshadow: each approach has its benefits and its flaws. The corporate tax is so standardized that it opens up opportunities for investors to profit by shifting income and deferring tax. The partnership tax is so flexible

---

[1] With apologies to Shakespeare. William Shakespeare, A Midsummer Night's Dream Act 1, Scene 1.
[2] Sorry, again, Shakespeare, but quotations from Hamlet are ubiquitous in our everyday speech. William Shakespeare, The Tragedy of Hamlet, Prince of Denmark Act 2, Scene 1.

that sophisticated parties can (and do) structure clever tax shelters that are hard for the IRS to detect.

¶102 COMPOUNDING THE PROBLEM WITH MULTIPLE TAX RATES

Now let's add a key wrinkle to the backstory for why taxing business income is so hard. The A-B-C example takes place in an ideal-ish world: we assumed that the goal of the tax system is just to tax everyone's Haig-Simons income (income that is used for personal consumption or added to savings). But real-world tax policy is far more complicated because Congress has multiple goals, all pursued at the same time.

Sometimes, Congress is pursuing economic policy. Fast depreciation, say, might be intended to spur the economy by increasing private capital investment. (There is a large empirical literature attempting to discover whether that policy works.[3]) Other policies seem to be frankly political, directing spoils to political allies and favored industries. The result, as you know from the basic course in tax, is that the law is complicated, with lots of different tax rates for different investors and investments.

Congress is, if anything, even more active in the sphere of business taxation, where major rules and tax rates change with dizzying speed. The result is that the Code often applies different tax regimes to businesses, depending on their activities, location, and capital structure.

The complexity of these regimes is, yes, another major theme of this book. We will investigate the (very different) tax rules that apply to corporations and partnerships. At every stage, we will see that the Code draws sharp, and sometimes nearly inexplicable, distinctions among very similar businesses.

For now, let's begin with a (relatively) straightforward example that shows how quickly things get complicated. As you know, taxpayers typically make decisions based on marginal tax rates. Put another way, business people are interested in what they can keep after taxes, and so they evaluate profits and costs on an after-tax basis. In the basic course on taxation, we usually treat each individual as having one marginal tax rate, based on her income level in a progressive rate system. But in business taxation, where multiple tax regimes can apply, determining the marginal tax rate that applies is much less straightforward.

> **EXAMPLE 1.** Darren earns $500,000 per year from his business. He is considering earning an extra $100,000. What is his marginal tax rate in the following cases?

---

[3] *See, e.g.,* Jane Gravelle, Cong. Research Serv. R43432, Bonus Depreciation: Economic and Budgetary Issues (2014).

(a) Darren operates a small rental-car business as a sole proprietor (i.e., the business is not incorporated).
(b) Darren earns a salary as the manager of a local branch of Hertz, a large corporation.
(c) Darren runs a small law firm as a sole proprietor.
(d) Darren is the sole shareholder of an incorporated car-rental business.

The answers, in case you just can't wait, are (a) probably 29.6%, (b) probably 37%, (c) probably 37%, and (d) some combination of 21% and 20%, depending on the firm's distributions to Darren. (Why "probably"? Because there are additional facts, not specified in the example, that could change the outcome. The discussion below identifies some of these.)

Now let's unpack all this. Begin with the basics. The federal income tax law divides the business world into two types of entities: corporations and partnerships. Corporate income is taxed twice, in the following sense: Code Sec. 11 imposes a flat tax rate of 21% on income earned by corporations, and Section 1 then imposes a second level of tax on dividends received by shareholders. In general, for U.S. corporations, the rate of tax on dividends is the same as the rate on capital gains; thus, a shareholder may pay 0%, 15%, or 20% on dividends.[4]

Partnership income is taxed on a pass-through basis, meaning that each partner is taxed at her own marginal tax rate on each item of partnership income. Thus, a partnership generating ordinary income would allocate that income to each partner. Each partner would include the allocated income on her tax return, where it would be taxed at her marginal tax rate (ranging, under Code Sec. 1, from 0% to 37%).

But wait, there's more! Section 199A provides a special deduction for income from some (but not all) unincorporated businesses. Qualifying taxpayers with qualifying income from qualifying businesses (say that three times fast!) can deduct 20%. Put another way, Section 199A, when it applies fully, reduces the taxpayer's marginal tax rate by 20%, so an individual in (say) the 37% bracket faces a rate of just 29.6%.

Section 199A is notably complicated, but, boiling things down quite a bit, Section 199A has three key features. First, it applies only to unincorporated business income and never to wages or salary from a job. Second, it applies to most business income earned by taxpayers with total taxable income under about $426,000 (for a married couple) or $213,000 (for a single person).[5] Third, for taxpayers with income over those amounts, the rules get very complicated very quickly. Among other rules, the Code denies the 20% deduction entirely for "specified service businesses," including law firms, investment banks, and consulting firms. (Take that, BigLaw!)

---

[4] *See* Code Sec. 1(h)(11).

[5] These thresholds are updated for inflation each year. *See* Rev. Proc. 2019-44, 2019-47 IRB 1093, at https://www.irs.gov/pub/irs-drop/rp-19-44.pdf.

Stepping back a bit, you can see why the title of this section refers to the problem of "multiple tax rates." The tax rules expressly favor and disfavor different businesses based on entity choice, income level, and type of business. Applying all this to the Darren example, a basic analysis looks like this. To begin with, we know that Darren's income of $500,000 puts him in the highest marginal tax bracket for single individuals.[6] So his marginal tax rate on an extra $100,000 would be the top rate of 37% *unless* some special rule applies. Going through the different scenarios, we see that there are several different special rules:

(a) In this case, Darren runs an unincorporated rental-car business. He may qualify for the Section 199A deduction, reducing his marginal tax rate to 29.6%. (To be sure, we'd need more facts, since Section 199A has additional requirements.)

(b) In this case, Darren is a salaried manager. Section 199A doesn't apply to employees, so his marginal tax rate is 37%. Putting (a) and (b) together, we can see that Darren pays a lower tax rate if he goes into business for himself than if he holds a job.

(c) In this case, Darren's income is from running a small law firm, which is a "specified service business," disfavored under Section 199A(d)(1). In (c), then, Darren's business income isn't eligible for the 29.6% rate. His additional $100,000 will be taxed at the full 37% marginal tax rate.

(d) In this case, Darren has incorporated his business, and that changes everything. Section 199A doesn't apply to corporations. But the special "double tax" rate structure does. His business income would be taxed at the corporate level at the flat 21% rate of Section 11. He would pay no further tax until he pays himself a dividend, at which point he'd be taxed at his capital gains rate (20%, given his his income level).

* * *

As you may remember, one of the themes of the basic course in taxation is that tax complexity tends to benefit well-advised taxpayers, who can engage in tax planning to choose the most favorable transactions and rules. The same is true in business taxation: we're about to see that the challenges of *valuation* and the availability of multiple tax rates make business taxation very, very hospitable for tax planning.

---

[6] Code Sec. 1(j)(2)(C).

CHAPTER 2

Income Shifting, *Tax Deferral*, and the Choice of Business Entity

Introduction . . . . ¶200
The Basics of Entity Taxation: Corporation versus Pass-Through . . . .¶201
Quantifying the Value of *Income Shifting* and *Tax Deferral* Using Entities . . . .¶202
Problem 2.1: Corporate versus Pass-Through Taxation. . . . . ¶203
Business 101: What is a Corporation . . . . ¶204
The Math Behind the Madness of Entity Choice. . . . . .Appendix 2-1

¶200 INTRODUCTION

Income shifting is one of the simplest and most familiar tax strategies. The basic idea is to lower your tax rate without changing the economics of what you do, what you own, or how you operate. That's kind of the definition of amazing tax planning: change nothing, but lower your taxes!

We will see that *income shifting* lies at the heart of business tax planning. That idea might sound really odd at first, because in the basic tax course, we encountered *income shifting* mostly within the family. Now, it's possible that you have had a few other things on your mind since you took Basic Tax. So, to refresh your memory, *income shifting* takes place when a high-bracket taxpayer can shift her income to a lower-bracket taxpayer *for tax purposes*, without losing control of the money. Presto! Lower taxes with no practical effect on access to resources.

To see the point, imagine that you have a two-year-old child. (Her name is Molly, and she's very smart, by the way.) You'd probably be completely comfortable with shifting formal legal ownership of a chunk of your money to her. After all, you are Molly's legal guardian, with full control of her money. And since the two of you live together, and much of your income goes to support her anyway, the shift in formal, legal title wouldn't change anything you do day-to-day. It's not as if little Molly is going to demand that you change your spending choices or investment strategies. She may demand cookies or refuse to sleep, but she isn't really interested in making money decisions.

The key to *income shifting*, of course, is that the two taxpayers have to have different tax rates. There would be no point in shifting from 37% to 37%. So, the example of the two-year-old works only if Molly (a) is a separate taxpayer from you and (b) has a lower marginal tax rate. These conditions were, in fact, true from the inception of the income tax until 1986: every individual, no matter their age, was a separate taxpayer. And every taxpayer was required to pay only the marginal rate on her own income—even if she was a child.

Congress knew all about this kind of *income shifting*, and in 1986, the "kiddie tax" mostly ended the game. The kiddie tax, found in Code Sec. 1(g), taxes children's investment income at the parent's marginal tax rate, making it difficult or impossible to save money by shifting income to kids. (Sorry, Molly.)

Finally, here's our jumping-off point: *income shifting* isn't just a gambit for families. Instead, *income shifting* motivates a great deal of business tax planning, and it is a far richer game – for both taxpayers and their tax lawyers. That's because businesses can multiply themselves, using entities like partnerships and corporations.

To see how *income shifting* works in this context, imagine that you own a business. Let's make it a fun one, say, winemaking. You own a big vineyard in Napa and earn a hefty income. Now, if you just earn the money as yourself, you'll be in the top income tax bracket and will pay 37% on your earnings.

But if you incorporate your vineyard as Napa Wines, Inc., then from a tax perspective you aren't just you any more: you've multiplied yourself into (a) you, the individual, and (b) the Napa Wines corporation. You can now see the possibilities for *income shifting*. If the corporation has a lower tax rate than you do, then you've found an excellent way to shift income. After all, you own Napa Wines, Inc., and you control everything it does.

We haven't yet said whether this kind of *income shifting* is legal. Complicating matters, Congress and the IRS know all about *income shifting*, and they seem to be of two minds: sometimes the law clearly permits shifting, but sometimes the law attempts to limit it. And then there are the gray areas. We will see that the problem of *income shifting* underlies many of the business tax rules we will study throughout the book.

In an important sense, *income shifting* is just the opening wedge for business tax planning, because it often combines with other strategies, notably *tax deferral*. We will also see that *income shifting* can be difficult for the law to counter because of *valuation* difficulties. And we will see that the IRS, the Congress, and the courts have only a limited capacity to deploy *substance over form* principles to limit these gambits.

Most of this won't be clear until much later. For now, let's begin with how *income shifting* and *tax deferral* interact in the most basic choice in business taxation: the choice of entity.

¶201 THE BASICS OF ENTITY TAXATION: CORPORATION VERSUS PASS-THROUGH

Let's stick with the Napa vineyard example, since it's such a pleasant one. You and your tax advisor are sitting on the shady porch with a view of the vineyards.

You recount that you've built up your business from scratch, and now you're making millions, and finally you're ready to think about taxes. One of the first decisions to make (and, really, you should have done this much sooner, but your tax advisor is too polite to say so) is what kind of legal entity, if any, you should use for your business. A corporation? A partnership? An LLC, whatever that is?

We will explore (and explain) these choices in a moment, but before we dive in, make sure to look for the continuing storyline. The critical point is that *by using business entities, a taxpayer can multiply her tax options.*

Now, state law often recognizes a variety of entity forms. Sole proprietorships, corporations, partnerships, limited liability companies, and so on. But the federal tax law is – for once! – very simple. For tax purposes, there are just two business entity choices:

(1) Pass-through entity: these include (most) partnerships and limited liability companies.
(2) Corporation: these include state and federal corporations and, at the taxpayer's election, a wide variety of other entities (discussed in ¶205 below).

This list omits a couple of options that you might have questions about. For one, the list doesn't include sole proprietorships. That's definitely a business option, and it's the one our hypothetical Napa entrepreneur has used. I don't include it in the business entity list for the obvious reason that a sole proprietor isn't an entity but an individual. As an individual, the business income is taxed directly and currently to the owner, without any *income shifting* possibilities. For a combination of tax and business reasons (see Business 101 in ¶205 below), most businesses of any size use some kind of business entity, so we won't spend further time on the proprietorship form.

This list also omits something you may have heard of (or may hear of at some point): the S corporation. The term "S corporation" is one of the most misleading tax terms of all times. An S corporation is basically a tax category for an entity that is a state-law corporation but is treated as a pass-through (and not a corporation) for most tax purposes. And it's called an "S" corporation because the relevant tax rules are in Subchapter S of the Code, while the normal corporate tax rules are in Subchapter C. Clear? Probably not, but no worries. We won't devote more time to S corporations. They are taxed, more or less, like pass-throughs, and they are less and less likely to be used these days.[1]

Returning to Napa, the business owner's choice of entity will, of course, take into account business and legal considerations as well as tax planning. Business 101, in ¶205 below, goes through some of the major business and (non-tax)

---

[1] S corporations once appealed to a specific niche audience: small-ish businesses that wanted the limited liability of incorporation but without double corporate taxation. Today, a business owner can get the same result, with fewer organizational constraints, by using a limited liability company, thanks to the check-the-box rules discussed in Chapter 3 below.

legal factors. The big takeaway is that many (though not all) businesses will find that they have a great deal of flexibility in choosing their entity form and, thus, their tax status.

From a tax perspective, the two choices – pass-throughs and corporations – have both advantages and disadvantages. A pass-through entity bears that name because it doesn't pay entity-level tax. It may be recognized as a separate legal person for some purposes (say, liability and contract under state law), but it's "transparent" for federal income tax purposes, so that income flows through to the owners of the pass-through entity. In our Napa example, there's one owner – you. So, 100% of the income, deductions, losses, and credits will be passed through onto your tax return and taxed at your own marginal tax rate.

Complicating matters, some pass-through entities qualify for a special lower tax rate under Section 199A, which we introduced in Chapter 2. As you may recall, the basic idea is that some pass-through businesses are taxed at 80% of the owner's marginal tax rate. Since the maximum individual tax rate right now is 37%, eligible businesses are taxed at a maximum of 80% of that, or 29.6%.

EXAMPLE 1. (Regular rates) Napa Wines, LLC, is a pass-through that earns $100 in 2019. The owner has a marginal tax rate of 37%. After paying taxes, the owner has $63 left.

EXAMPLE 2. (Section 199A applies) In this case, the pass-through income is eligible for the special 29.6% tax rate created by Section 199A. The result is that the owner pays $29.60 in taxes and, afterward, has $70.40 left.

By contrast, corporations are separate legal persons for tax purposes as well as for other legal purposes. They file their own tax returns and pay a corporate-level tax under Code Sec. 11, now set at 21%. When corporations distribute their earnings to shareholders, those distributions are usually called dividends. (If you want to know more, Chapter 7, ¶706, explains what dividends are.) Dividends are also taxable, but this time, taxable to the shareholders, not the corporation. Thanks to Code Sec. 1(h)(11), dividends from U.S. corporations are often taxed at the capital gains rate, now a maximum of 20%.[2] But, importantly, dividends are not capital in character; they are ordinary income that is taxed at a special, low rate.

You can now see why people sometimes call the corporate tax a "double tax" or "two-level tax." Think about the Napa business. If it becomes Napa Wines, Inc., then the income of the wine business will be taxed to the corporation.

---

[2] Code Sec. 1(h)(11) applies only to "qualified dividends" of U.S. taxpayers. Very generally, the dividend must be paid by a U.S. corporation and must be paid with respect to stock meeting certain holding periods.

After corporate taxes are paid, the corporation can distribute (or retain) what's left – its after-tax income. Distributions of after-tax income are called dividends (discussed in detail in Chapter 7) and these are taxable at the capital gains rate.

> **EXAMPLE 3.** Napa Wines, Inc., earns $100 in 2019. After paying a corporate tax of 21%, the corporation has $79 in after-tax income. If the corporation distributes all of the $79 to its owner, the owner must include that amount on her tax return as a taxable dividend. Assuming the owner's capital gains rate is 20%, the tax on the dividend is $15.80 ($79 x .2). After paying all taxes due at both levels, the owner has $63.20 left.

Whew! This a lot to follow, but the thread of the tax story should be visible: by using different business entities, a taxpayer can *choose her tax rate*. That's really the essence of *income shifting*, after all: formal legal distinctions can permit taxpayers to shift income advantageously without losing control over the income or changing the economics of their business.

¶202　QUANTIFYING THE VALUE OF *INCOME SHIFTING* AND *TAX DEFERRAL* USING ENTITIES

At this point, you can start to glimpse why business taxation is, potentially at least, such a playground for tax planners. By choosing your business entity, you can also choose the marginal tax rate *and* the timing of taxation. Let's unpack that a little bit.

The tax rules covered in the last section define just two choices for entities: pass-through or corporation. But we can add some sophistication by building in a choice about income timing as well. Pass-through owners have very little control over the timing of income: it flows through each year and is taxed at the owner's personal (marginal) tax rate, or "p."

By contrast, recall that the corporate tax imposes a two-level tax. The first tax (at the corporate tax rate, or "c" is imposed currently. The second tax, imposed at the capital gains rate or "k," can be either current or deferred, depending on the timing of dividends. Corporations have enormous legal flexibility in the timing of dividends: neither the tax law nor corporate law (generally) requires even the most profitable company to pay out dividends. So, unless there are business reasons for paying out dividends, the owners of a corporation can choose their tax timing by choosing their dividend strategy.

14   Core Concepts: A Student's Guide to Corporate and Partnership Tax

Putting all that together, we can now see that we have *three* choices for organizing our Napa wine corporation:

Table 2.1 Tax Rates, Tax Timing and Entity Choice

Entity	Timing	Tax Rate(s)[3]
Partnership or sole proprietorship	Current taxation	p (or 80% of p, if Section 199A fully applies)
Corporation that pays out all earnings as dividends	Current taxation at two levels	c plus k (applicable to after-tax corporate income)
Corporation that retains earnings	Current taxation at the corporate level and deferred taxation at the shareholder level	c plus *tax-deferred* k (applicable to after-tax corporate income)

At this point, you can begin to intuit two important points about business tax planning. One is that *all three business tax rates (p, c, and k) matter*, because different entities face different tax rates and tax timing. We will quantify that point with some examples in a moment, but the basic point is that tax rates often play a big role in entity choice. The second is that *the timing of distributions matters*. A firm that must (for business reasons) pay out its income to owners currently will be taxed very differently than a firm that can choose the timing of distributions.

Don't worry if the intuition isn't solid yet. Let's go back to the Napa sunshine and crunch a few numbers to illustrate what's at stake. To limit the permutations, let's just consider the three options in the table above, and let's use current tax rates. (Later on, we will illustrate how tax rate changes can change the stakes, which is a critical point too, because Congress changes the rates so often.)

To make the math easy, let's assume that the business earns $100 before taxes and that the vineyard owner has complete flexibility either to distribute dividends or retain earnings for the next ten years. What that means in real life is that the Napa wine magnate has enough money outside the business so that she doesn't need to pay dividends to herself to live on; she can instead reinvest the profits in the business if it makes tax sense to do so. Let's also assume that money invested in the business earns a 10% return every year. By the way, the Appendix to this chapter goes into more detail on the underlying math, if you're interested.

---

[3] Throughout this discussion, I assume that all dividends are qualified dividends taxed at k under Code Sec. 1(h)(11).

Table 2.2 Crunching the Numbers on Entity Choice

Entity	Timing	Tax Rate(s)	After-Tax Income after Ten Years
Partnership or sole proprietorship	Current taxation	p = 29.6% (if the vineyard qualifies for Section 199A)	$197.45
		p = 37% (if Section 199A does not apply)	$184.21
Corporation that pays out all earnings as dividends[4]	Current taxation at two levels	c = 21% plus k = 20%	$184.57
Corporation that retains earnings	Current taxation at the corporate level and deferred taxation at the shareholder level	c = 21% plus *tax-deferred* k = 20%	$191.12

The table underscores both key points that we've intuited. First, *entity choice can affect the tax rate on business income.* By assumption, the underlying investment and the pre-tax return are the same in all the scenarios. But the after-tax payoff varies a great deal. Second, *entity choice can permit tax deferral*, which is really another form of tax rate reduction. That is why the two corporate scenarios produce radically different results. Thanks to *tax deferral*, the investor has more to spend if the corporation retains earnings (leaving her $191.12 after taxes) than if it pays out dividends (leaving only $184.57).

Overall, the combination of entity choice and *tax deferral* create a range of tax-driven outcomes, with the investor bringing home anywhere from about $184 to $197. Now, that $13 may not seem like much – it's about the cost of a cheap lunch in New York City. But remember that our simple example starts with an investment of just $100. If you want to see the real-world magnitude of these effects in a multi-trillion-dollar economy, just add a few zeros. The tax savings get really big, really fast.

You've probably noticed that Congress changes the tax rates every few years. Tax rates are a political hot button, and nearly every President and new Congress try to put their stamp on the Code. So it's important to know that these two basic points about entity taxation are always true, no matter what the actual tax rate schedule looks like. Put another way: entity choice can affect tax rates and tax timing, whatever the rate schedule.

Changes in tax rates do affect the magnitude of tax differences, and they can even affect the direction of tax planning. For example, right now, Table 2.2 suggests that there may be a good tax reason to incorporate, especially if a pass-through entity wouldn't qualify for the low rate under Section 199A. In the late 1980s, by contrast, corporations were heavily disfavored by the tax system. The Appendix to this chapter goes into more detail on rate changes.

---

[4] To make the examples comparable, assume that (1) the corporation pays out all earnings as dividends and (2) the shareholder immediately reinvests the (after-tax) amount in the corporation.

We can now see how our initial discussion of *income shifting* and *tax deferral* connects up to the problem of entity choice. Our Napa vineyard owner starts out with just one tax rate, p. But when we understand entity choice, we can (in effect) *shift income* to a menu of options that combines (in different variations) p, c, and k. And some of these options also permit *tax deferral* as well.

One big theme of this book (and of any book on taxation) is that *taxpayer choice leads to tax planning*. It makes sense if you think about it. When the law gives taxpayers a choice, we can expect them to choose the route that permits them to pay the lowest taxes. So, entity choice equals…tax reduction.

¶203 PROBLEM 2.1: CORPORATE VERSUS PASS-THROUGH TAXATION

Barry is a wealthy investor with $1 million to invest. He has identified two appealing projects to invest in. Each of the two investment projects is expected to have the same pre-tax return of 10%. But the managers of Project A plan to incorporate their business, while the managers of Project B plan to operate as a partnership.

Both projects have a long-time horizon. In both cases, management intends to reinvest all business earnings back into the project for ten years, at which point they'll wind up the project. That means that, in Year 10, Barry will get back his original investment of $1 million plus all accumulated earnings. He will keep what's left, after all taxes are paid.

(a) Under current tax rates, which investment should Barry choose? *Hint:* you probably cannot give a definite answer but will need more information. What additional questions would you ask?

(b) Barry spotted a headline on *Forbes.com* (a business website): "Two Taxes Can Be Less than One: The Tax Advantages of Incorporation." Not having any tax knowledge, he is puzzled. Can you explain the point?

ANSWER TO

(a): This problem harks back to the comparisons in Table 2.2. If the project in question will qualify for the full Section 199A deduction, then the table shows that Barry will have the highest after-tax return if he invests in the partnership (Project B). But if the business does not qualify for the Section 199A tax break, Barry may be better off with Project A, the corporation.

To figure out all this, we'd need to ask Barry some basic (and not-so-basic) questions. To begin, we'd want to know Barry's marginal tax rate; it seems likely that he's in the 37% bracket for ordinary income and 20% bracket for capital gains and dividends, but in the real world, we ask rather than assume!

We'd then need more information on the business to determine whether Barry will qualify for the Section 199A deduction. One critical fact will be the nature of the business; some businesses (like law and consulting) cannot qualify.[5] We would also need to know more facts about the project's assets and employees, because of the tests imposed by Section 199A(b)(2).

(b): It isn't intuitive, but the headline is correct: two taxes can be less than one. Table 2.2 makes the point: in any case in which Section 199A does not apply, the hypothetical investor is better off investing in a corporation than in a partnership. Implicit in this result, of course, is the fact that the one tax on pass-through income is imposed at a different rate than the two taxes on corporate income!

¶204   BUSINESS 101: WHAT IS A CORPORATION?

A corporation is a business entity recognized, for many purposes, as a legal "person." Corporations are typically formed under and governed by state corporation law, which sets out the basic rights of shareholders. A corporation is owned by its shareholders (or stockholders; the two terms are interchangeable). Common stockholders typically have four rights.

First, they have the right to vote for the board of directors, which is the governing body of the corporation. Typically, each share carries the same number of votes, with the result that people who own a higher percentage of the stock also have a higher percentage of the vote.

Second, common stockholders have the right to a proportionate share of the corporation's assets upon liquidation, that is, upon the winding up of the corporation and the sale of its properties. The common stock is subordinated to the corporation's debt, meaning that the company must pay off all its creditors (including bank loans, day-to-day bills, wages, and taxes) before it may liquidate and distribute the remainder to stockholders. Once again, the greater the number of common shares owned, the greater the percentage interest upon liquidation.

Third, common stockholders have a right to dividends if and when declared by the board of directors. That may seem to be an odd "right," since it is contingent on action by the board, but keep in mind that shareholders elect the board, and the board is, by law, supposed to protect the interests of shareholders. Dividends are typically cash distributions made pro rata to stockholders; once again, the more shares a stockholder owns, the higher her dividends.

Finally, common stockholders enjoy limited liability, which is a kind of "negative" right. Limited liability means that creditors of the corporate entity can look only to the assets of the corporation for payment. Creditors may not (except in rare cases) legally require shareholders to pay the debts of the corporation.

Not all business entities are corporations. Some take the form of partnerships or other pass-through entities. ¶1105 of Chapter 11 describes the basics of the partnership form.

---

[5] See Code Sec. 199A(d).

EXAMPLE 4. Abbie and Brent have decided to go into business together, running a restaurant to be called Farmstand. They incorporate Farmstand, Inc. by filing legal papers with their home state of Connecticut. Abbie and Brent have agreed that Abbie will own 2/3 of the common stock, and Brent will own 1/3. After several years, Farmstand is doing well, and the company declares a dividend of $100,000. Accordingly, Abbie receives $66,700, and Brent receives $33,300. In Year 10, a restaurant customer slips and falls on a wet floor. He sues Farmstand, Inc., and attempts to sue Abbie and Brent as well. But the suit against Abbie and Brent is dismissed because as stockholders, they are not liable for torts (legal language for wrongs) committed by the corporation. The slip-and-fall victim settles with Farmstand's insurance company. After 20 years, Abbie and Brent are ready to close the restaurant, and they file a document authorizing the liquidation of Farmstand, Inc with the state of Connecticut. Farmstand sells its real estate and equipment and has $1 million left (after paying all corporate-level debt, including taxes). Abbie receives $666,700, and Brent receives $333,300, and their stock is cancelled (because the corporation no longer exists).

APPENDIX 2-1
THE MATH BEHIND THE MADNESS OF ENTITY CHOICE

The discussion of entity choice in this chapter owes much to a classic article written by Al Warren of the Harvard Law School in 1981.[6] Warren models entity choice from an *ex ante* perspective, that is, the perspective of an investor who has $1 to invest and who has not yet committed to any particular entity form. To isolate tax effects, the analysis assumes that the pre-tax return is the same for all investment types, portrayed as follows:

Type of Investment	Taxation of Returns
Non-corporate investment (e.g., equity in a pass-through business)	$W[1 + r(1 - p)]^y$
Corporate equity (dividends)	$W[1 + r(1 - c)(1 - p)]^y$
Corporate equity (retained earnings)	$(1-k)W[1 + r(1 - c)]^y + kW$

W = the amount invested
r = the pre-tax rate of return
y = the number of years before cashing out the investment
p = the personal (individual) income tax rate
c = the corporate income tax rate
k = the capital gains tax rate

---

[6] Alvin C. Warren, Jr., *The Relation and Integration of Individual and Corporate Income Taxes*, 94 Harv. L. Rev. 717 (1981).

Now, a few alterations are needed to reflect big changes in rates since Warren's original 1981 article. The biggest change is that the individual income tax rate is no longer a unitary rate (p) but must be divided into:

p = the usual rate on individual income
p_{199A} = the rate after applying the 20% deduction in Section 199A
p_{div} = k = the rate on qualified dividend income in Section 1(h)(11)

So, under current law, the relevant rates are:

Rate	Top Marginal Tax Rate
p	37%
p_{199A}	29.6%
p_{div} = k	20%
c	21%
k	20%

This is, I emphasize, a simple depiction of the income tax. In any real-world planning situation, you'd likely need to take account of additional provisions. For instance, interest is not always fully deductible, and so the representation of corporate debt may need modification, depending on whether the business interest rules of Section 163(j) apply. This simple model also doesn't capture the taxation of foreign income, which – depending on its type – may be taxed at any U.S. rate from zero to 37%. To add even more complexity, there are considerations that differ from individual to individual: for instance, if I die before I cash out my investment, my capital gains rate (k) is zero, thanks to the step-up in basis at death under Section 1014. I won't delineate all these scenarios at this early stage, but by the end of the course you'll have some insight on these distinctions.

Still, despite these simplifications, Warren's depiction of entity choice is elegant and useful. Using Warren's model, and updating for current law, we can simulate *four* different options: (1) a partnership interest to which Section 199A does not apply, (2) a partnership interest to which Section 199A does apply, (3) corporate stock with annual dividends and reinvestment, and (4) corporate stock with retentions.

APPENDIX 2-1

Investment	Relevant rates	Warren notation (adapted to current law)	After-tax amount, assuming $1m invested at 10% (pre-tax) for ten years	After-tax amount, assuming $1m invested at 10% (pre-tax) for 25 years
Partnership interest (199A does not apply)	$p = 37\%$	$W[1 + r(1 - p)]^y$	$1.842 million	$4.61 million
Partnership interest (199A does apply)	$p_{199A} = 29.6\%$	$W[1 + r(1 - p_{199A})]^y$	$1.97 million	$5.48 million
Corporate stock (annual payout and reinvestment)	$c = 21\%$ $p_{div} = k = 20\%$	$W[1 + r(1 - c)(1 - p_{div})]^y$	$1.846 million	$4.63 million
Corporate stock (retentions)	$c = 21\%$ $k = 20\%$	$(1-k)W[1 + r(1 - c)]^y + kW$	$1.91 million	$5.55 million

There are a few big takeaways here. First, for an individual whose marginal tax rate is relatively low, *e.g.,* thanks to 199A, investing through a pass-through can be more profitable than using a corporation ($1.97 million, using a partnership, is the best outcome in the ten-year scenario). When rates are low enough, one tax can be better than two. Second, the longer the time horizon and the lower the corporate rate relative to the individual rate, the more powerful the effects of *tax deferral*, such that corporate stock with retentions turns out to be the best choice in the 25-year scenario.

The biggest takeaway of all is that rates matter. A lot. With every piece of new tax legislation, Congress may change one or more of the relevant rates, and taxpayers need to be ready to revisit all these numbers in light of the new rates.

CHAPTER 3

Entity Choice and the Limits of *Substance Over Form*

Introduction . . . . ¶300
The "Check-the-Box" Rules . . . . ¶301
Problem 3.1: The Check-the-Box Rules . . . . ¶302
Bollinger and the Limited Reach of *Substance Over Form* in Entity Choice . . . . ¶303
The Use of *Substance Over Form* in Business Taxation . . . . ¶304

¶300 INTRODUCTION

A natural question at this point is whether the *income shifting* and *tax deferral* described in Chapter 2 are, well, legal. After all, one theme of the basic tax course is that Congress and the IRS generally try to rein in taxpayers who try to reduce their taxes using these techniques. From that perspective, entity choice seems a little too good to be true, at least as I've portrayed it so far. Surely the Napa vineyard owner can't really just pick her tax rate and tax timing. Aren't there rules that limit the choice of entity? And what about the *substance over form* doctrine – couldn't the IRS look through the entity to tax the Napa vineyard as what it really is, a sole proprietorship?

These are great questions, but it turns out that the law in this area is incredibly taxpayer-favorable. Entity choice really is – for most businesses – a matter of choice. And because business taxation relies so heavily on formal rules, the *substance over form* doctrine has limited reach when it comes to business taxation.

¶301 THE "CHECK-THE-BOX" RULES

At one time in the deep mists of history, the tax law tried to limit taxpayers' ability to choose between pass-through taxation and corporate taxation. Those rules tried to force taxpayers into the corporate double tax regime as the price of obtaining legal protections, including limited liability and transferable ownership shares. But those rules were fuzzy at the border and susceptible to tax planning. For the last few decades, the IRS has no longer attempted to place meaningful limits on entity choice. Instead, the law has followed the approach now known as "check-the-box."

The check-the-box rules are found in the regulations.[1] The basic idea is that the law carves out a set of entities that must be taxed under the corporate tax rules, and then permits taxpayers to choose their taxation regime in the case of any other entity. The regulations specify that mandatory C corporations include entities incorporated under federal and state corporation law and entities with publicly-traded ownership interests.[2] All other entities, including, most importantly, partnerships and limited liability companies, fall into the check-the-box category, meaning that the taxpayer may elect either the pass-through regime or the corporate tax regime. An election generally cannot be changed for five years, unless the entity's ownership changes significantly.

Now, at first glance, these rules may seem to limit taxpayer choice. After all, if the taxpayer chooses, say, a Delaware corporation for her business, then there is no choice: a Delaware corporation is a mandatory C corporation and thus subject to the double tax. The taxpayer cannot choose pass-through taxation. But most taxpayers can easily sidestep the mandatory C corporation rule by choosing an alternative entity. A limited liability company, for example, typically provides business owners with 99% of the legal attributes of the corporate form, including limited liability and transferable ownership shares.

Putting all this together, there is virtually no constraint on entity choice for the vast majority of private businesses. The owner(s) of a private company can pretty much choose between pass-through and corporate taxation based on which generates the smallest tax bill. It is only when a business "goes public" – that is, when the shareholders intend to sell shares to the public – that the owners are stuck with the C corporation form.

It's critical to keep in mind, however, that the C corporation "double tax" can actually be the most favorable tax regime. It isn't intuitive when you first think about it, but if you've read Chapter 2, you know that two taxes can be less than one. So, the mandatory C corporation rules do not necessarily force taxpayers into an unfavorable tax regime.

¶302 PROBLEM 3.1: THE CHECK-THE-BOX RULES

Yani and Zeke intend to go into business together. They've come up with a great idea for a video game, to be called "Alphabet's End," and they're eager to get started. Yani took tax in law school, and she knows that tax might affect their choice of entity. As they talk to friends and family, the following issues arise:

(a) Yani's law school roommate, now a business lawyer, advises that a corporation is a good idea to limit liability. Zeke does some Googling and finds out that it's easy to form a corporation. For instance, DelawareInc.com offers

---

[1] Reg. §301.7701-2 and -3.
[2] Code Sec. 7704.

a $179 special, and it looks pretty easy to do. What can you tell the parties about how a Delaware corporation would be taxed?
(b) Reading through the DelawareInc.com website, Yani notices that there's something called a "Delaware limited liability company," which offers limited liability, just like a corporation. What can you tell the parties about how a Delaware LLC would be taxed?
(c) Finally, Zeke's brother, a small business owner himself, counsels that a partnership is worth considering because it offers a lot of flexibility to divide up income, losses and risk. Yani notices that DelawareInc.com can also form a "Delaware limited partnership," which also seems to have limited liability in some form. What can you tell the parties about how a Delaware limited partnership would be taxed?
(d) For federal income tax purposes, does it matter whether Yani and Zeke choose Delaware or some other state?

Hint: Consult Reg. §§301.7701-2(a) and (b) and 301.7701-3(a) and (b) as you consider the questions.

Under the "check the box" regulations referenced above, there are just two categories of entities:

- Mandatory C corporations: These include state- and federally-incorporated entities (e.g., a Delaware corporation) and, per Code Sec. 7704, (almost) any entity with publicly-traded ownership interests
- Check-the-box entities: Everything else. These entities can choose to be taxed like partnerships or C corporations. The default is partnership taxation.

So, in answer to the questions above:

ANSWER TO

(a): A Delaware corporation is a mandatory C corporation.
(b): A Delaware LLC is a check-the-box entity unless it has publicly-traded equity, in which case it's a mandatory C corporation.
(c): A partnership is also a check-the-box entity unless it has publicly-traded equity.
(d): For *federal* tax purposes, it doesn't matter whether the parties choose Delaware or some other state.

¶303   *BOLLINGER* AND THE LIMITED REACH OF *SUBSTANCE OVER FORM* IN ENTITY CHOICE

As you may recall from the basic tax course, the *substance over form* doctrine gives the government and courts sweeping powers to recharacterize transactions in accordance with their economic substance. This power is not unlimited, and the government has lost major efforts at times, but the *substance over form* doctrine, very generally, is a powerful tool to limit tax planning.

As the heading of this section has already conveyed, the *substance over form* doctrine plays a limited role in limiting tax decisions about entity choice. This may seem odd because, after all, the distinctions among entities are rife with formalities and formalisms. Think about our hypothetical Napa Vineyard owner. Chapter 2 and the first part of this chapter have shown that the owner might run the very same business using different formal entities. At first glance, it might seem obvious that the government should impose the same tax on the Napa Vineyard business, no matter what formal entity the owner chooses. Isn't the substance the same?

But policy makers have largely opted for form over substance in the realm of entity choice. The form of an entity – as a C corporation or as a pass-through – determines the tax regime that applies. Full stop. Put another way, the IRS and the courts rarely disregard a taxpayer's choice of legal entity, as long as the formalities of the law are followed. The basic doctrine, laid down in a case called *Moline Properties*, is that the tax law generally respects the legal fiction that a corporation exists and is a separate legal person.[3] In particular, the tax law treats a corporation as legally separate from its shareholders so that the actions of the corporation are not attributed to shareholders and vice versa.

So, in our Napa case, the IRS will respect the entity the vintner chooses, provided that she files the appropriate papers with the state and signs the appropriate agreements. By and large, the IRS and the courts will disregard legal entities only in egregious tax shelter cases, and, even then, the courts will often search for an alternative to disregarding legal entities entirely.[4]

Now, it's important not to overread all this. The *substance over form* doctrine does resurface elsewhere in business taxation, as we will see in ¶304, below. It's just that, in the specific area of entity classification, policy makers have decided to let form trump substance.

The *Bollinger* case, decided by the Supreme Court in 1988, provides a good example of the difficulties of applying *substance over form* in the choice–of–entity context.[5] Boiling it down a bit, the question presented in *Bollinger* was whether the IRS could challenge the formal, legal relationship between a corporation and its owners. The answer, said the Supreme Court, was no.

The facts were fairly straightforward. Jesse Bollinger was a real estate developer who formed a corporation called Creekside, Inc. to hold a formal title to real property and to sign loan documents as the borrower. The use of a corporation

---

[3] *Moline Properties, Inc. v. Comm'r*, 319 U.S. 436 (1943).
[4] See, e.g., *ACM Partnership v. Comm'r*, 157 F.3d 231 (3d Cir. 1998) (respecting the existence of the partnership entity but holding that its purchase and sale of Citicorp notes lacked economic substance). Compare *ASA Investerings Partnership v. Comm'r*, 201 F.3d 505 (D.C. Cir. 2000).
[5] *Comm'r v. Bollinger*, 485 U.S. 340 (1988).

for these purposes was apparently an accepted way to circumvent Kentucky's usury laws. (Usury laws cap the rate of interest that individuals can pay on loans. These well-intentioned laws aim to shield borrowers from predatory lending, but they can have the unintended effect of making it impossible for individuals to borrow money when market rates exceed the legal cap.)

Bollinger, like many other business people, had figured out that the usury laws permitted corporate borrowers to pay higher interest rates than individuals. So, he and his partners signed a web of legal agreements that appointed Creekside as their agent so that Creekside could buy and hold property and borrow money to do so. Consistent with the formal terms of these contracts, Creekside did not report taxable income from Bollinger's real estate activities. Instead, Bollinger and his partners continued to report theirs according to the partnership rules.

What was at stake? You may recall that real estate businesses often claim tax benefits like accelerated depreciation and investment tax credits. These "tax goodies" pass through to partners in a partnership, but not to shareholders in a corporation. (That's because, as Chapter 2 explains, corporations are taxed as entities separate from their owners.) So, if the IRS could succeed in taxing Bollinger's real estate business to Creekside, the corporation, it would "lock up" any deductions and tax credits in the corporation, rather than allowing them to be claimed by Bollinger and his partners on their own individual returns.

The Supreme Court opinion rejects the IRS argument and reaffirms that a corporation may act as an agent for its owner. The taxpayers in *Bollinger* probably benefited because they had crossed their tees and dotted their eyes: they had hired lawyers to prepare agency contracts, and apparently, they were buttoned up in identifying Creekside as the agent rather than the owner of the property.

Bollinger showcases the triumph of form over substance in the taxation of business entities. Obviously enough, Creekside Inc. had no mind of its own. It was entirely Jesse Bollinger's creation and would act only in the ways that Bollinger directed. In economic substance, Bollinger and Creekside were the same person. Nevertheless, the Supreme Court held that formalities govern. Jesse Bollinger was legally allowed to (in effect) multiply himself by creating wholly-owned legal entities.

¶304   THE USE OF SUBSTANCE OVER FORM IN BUSINESS TAXATION

Summing up, we've seen in this chapter that the law of business taxation often prizes form over substance. The result is that, in the realm of entity choice, taxpayers have wide flexibility to choose the business entity (and, thereby, the tax regime) that minimizes their taxes. The result is that individuals can multiply the number of taxpayers under their control. In effect, the choice-of-entity rules often permit taxpayers to shift income from individuals to entities so that their income is taxed in the most advantageous way.

To be sure, the law imposes some constraints on entity choice. First, taxpayers do have to form the entity and treat it consistently; that's one lesson of *Bollinger*. Second, as noted in ¶301, above, taxpayers cannot decide year-by-year whether they prefer a corporation or pass-through; they're stuck with their choice for five years under the regulations. Third, selling stock (or other ownership interests) to the public will generally trigger corporate taxation, unless an exception to Code Sec. 7704 applies (see ¶301, above). Still, with the exception of the public trading rule, these rules impose little constraint on the tax planner when it comes to entity choice.

But the tension between substance and form in business taxation is pervasive, and we will see it recur throughout corporate and partnership tax. The check-the-box approach to entity choice represents one end of the legal spectrum: policymakers chose the simplicity and predictability of formal rules. Implicitly, in doing so, they endorsed easy *income shifting* and *tax deferral* via taxpayer choice of entity.

We will see, however, that policy makers do not always choose *form over substance* in business taxation. Sometimes the rules of the Code attempt to recognize the substance, and sometimes the IRS and the courts invoke the doctrine in court. If that sounds frustrating and unpredictable, well, it is! One key skill of the tax lawyer is to understand when the law privileges form and when it attempts to look to the substance. But that skill takes years to develop, and it's a matter of experience more than logic, so don't feel bad if you find it hard to predict when form will govern, and when substance will enter the picture.

PART II
Taxing Corporate Income

CHAPTER 4

Substance Over Form in Corporate Tax: Debt Versus Equity

Introduction	¶400
Debt Versus Equity: The Impact of Taxes	¶401
Indmar and *Substance Over Form*	¶402
Problem 4.1: Debt and Equity	¶403
Business 101: What is Debt?	¶404
Advanced Problem	¶405

¶400 INTRODUCTION

By now, you've probably caught on that this book tends to repeat its plotlines. Once again, we're going to see that the tax law rewards some business decisions and penalizes others. In Chapters 1 and 2, we saw that the Code rewards (some) partnership investments, (some) corporate investments, and some lines of business. This time, we will see that tax considerations can affect corporate decisions about how to finance a new project.

Imagine that a C corporation (in a burst of creativity, let's call it "Bigcorp") has spotted an important new business opportunity. New ventures are never certain, but management's analysis suggests that if Bigcorp invests $100 million, the new line will likely generate net income of about $30 million each year. That's a 30% return – pretty nice! You can see why Bigcorp management is excited about the new project.

One wrinkle is that Bigcorp, like most big (and small) firms, doesn't have $100 million in cash lying around. The company is (let's assume) profitable already, but management has consistently reinvested profits into plant and equipment, new hiring, and other business items. How, then, should Bigcorp go about getting the $100 million it needs to get going on the new venture?

Let's assume that Bigcorp management doesn't want to sell any of its assets to raise the cash. Instead, management wants to go to the capital markets and raise the money from outside investors. "Capital markets," by the way, is an umbrella term that encompasses several ways of raising cash for new projects. There are lots of different ways of doing this, but we can simplify, without sacrificing too much accuracy, by saying that Bigcorp can raise money in two ways: with debt or with equity.

Let's start with debt. Borrowed money, or debt, usually has a set of terms that are familiar to most of us from consumer borrowing (car loans, credit cards, and that sort of thing). In a typical borrowing transaction, the borrower receives $X and agrees to repay $X plus a stated interest rate. There is usually a time limit on the borrowing, and the principal of $X may be due all at once at the end of the term (a so-called "balloon payment") or may be paid in installments at shorter intervals, like a home mortgage (¶404, *infra*, provides a fuller introduction to the business basics of debt). If the borrower fails to repay, the lender (or creditor) has a set of contractual remedies as well as bankruptcy remedies; boiling it down, the lender can force the borrower to sell its assets, if need be, to repay the loan.

Importantly, there is nothing magical about the standard terms of debt I've just described. (This point will motivate the dramatic twist in ¶403, below). Many borrowings have negotiated terms that look very different. From a legal perspective, debt is just a contract, and so the parties have nearly unlimited flexibility to set whatever terms they wish. Still, this kind of "plain vanilla" debt does exist and is a standard starting point for business planning.

Equity, or stock (in the case of a corporate issuer like Bigcorp), typically has different terms. The new stockholder buys stock for $X, and in return, she receives a set of legal rights. Common stock typically possesses voting rights (*i.e.*, the right to vote for the board of directors) and may receive dividends when declared by the board. Critically, stock does not "expire" or need to be repaid at a particular time; nor does common stock have a right to annual dividends. To be sure, stockholders may be unhappy if they expect dividends and the company doesn't pay out. And a failure to pay expected dividends wouldn't look very good to future investors in the corporation. But, as a purely legal matter, the shareholders' only legal remedy is to vote out the board of directors. (Chapter 2, ¶204 provides more detail on the typical terms of common stock.)

Just as in the case of debt, this standard set of terms can be modified in lots of ways. For example, preferred stock (explained in Chapter 6, ¶605) carries a stated dividend. Stock may confer additional voting rights in certain cases (for instance, if a dividend goes unpaid). And stockholders may have rights to have the company buy their stock at set times (or if certain contingencies occur).

Now, back to Bigcorp. Recall that management needs to raise $100 million. Should they borrow the money or issue stock? As a first step, they call their friendly neighborhood investment banker. She tells them that, at current market rates, and given the company's credit rating, Bigcorp could finance its new project with ten-year debt at an interest rate of 10% or common stock with investors expecting a dividend rate of 11%.

If taxes were irrelevant, Bigcorp might be tempted to issue the debt, since the cost is lower. But cost alone isn't the only relevant business factor. Debt and equity "feel" different to management, because they confer different kinds of power on investors. Creditors (*i.e.*, people who lend money) have a very strong power; if Bigcorp for some reason can't pay all of the interest and principal on time, the creditors can force Bigcorp into bankruptcy. Now, corporate managers don't like bankruptcy, because they often lose their jobs. But bankruptcy can also be costly if it forces the too-quick liquidation of a project that could, given time, turn a respectable profit.

Stockholders, by contrast, do not have the right to trigger bankruptcy if their expected return isn't met. Bigcorp stockholders may expect and hope for an 11% dividend, and management's forecasts may show that that is possible, even probable. But the common stockholders cannot force management into bankruptcy court, even if the expected dividend goes unpaid for years at a time. Still, common stockholders, if they band together, could vote in a new board of directors, in which case current management could well lose their jobs.

We still haven't gotten to taxes, yet, but we're nearly there. The big point is that, from a business perspective, management has to compare not only the out-of-pocket cost of debt and equity (here, 10% versus 11%) but also the potential costliness of the remedies granted to debtholders and stockholders. Is an extra 1% a small price to pay for a longer time horizon – or is it highway robbery? Management will have to decide.

Now, enter the tax code. (Cue dark music.)

¶401 DEBT VERSUS EQUITY: THE IMPACT OF TAXES

Corporate debt and corporate stock are taxed very differently, and the classic result is to favor debt over equity. We shall see that current tax law makes this a complex comparison, and sometimes the law now favors equity over debt. But let's start with the classic and clear result and then we can add a few wrinkles.

Put simply (and a little cartoonishly), corporate interest payments are taxed once while corporate dividends are taxed twice. That's because corporations can claim an interest deduction under Section 163(a) when they pay interest, but they cannot deduct dividends. Since interest is deductible by the corporation, a dollar paid as interest is not taxed at the corporate level. By contrast, a dollar paid as a dividend has already been taxed at the corporate tax rate of 21%.

> **EXAMPLE 1.** Suppose that Bigcorp borrows $100 million from the bank at an interest rate of 10%. Every year, then, Bigcorp must pay the bank $10 million in interest. Generally, Bigcorp can deduct the $10 million interest payment, with the result that that $10 million of its income avoids the 21% corporate tax. Put another way, when interest is deductible, borrowers pay interest out of pre-tax income.
>
> Now contrast the case where Bigcorp issues stock for $100 million, with investors expecting an 11% dividend. When Bigcorp pays out the expected $11 million per year, it may *not* deduct the dividend. Put another way, because dividends are not deductible, corporations must pay them out of after-tax income.

Just in case that still isn't clear: suppose that Bigcorp only earns $10 million in pre-tax net income (before the interest deduction) the first year. If Bigcorp has borrowed its money, it can deduct the $10 million interest payment and will report $0 net income to the IRS. By contrast, if Bigcorp earns $10 million pre-tax and is slated to pay dividends, it may not deduct them. Bigcorp must pay the IRS 21% of its income, or $2.1 million, and it will have only $7.9 million left to pay a dividend – which will disappoint its investors, who expected $11 million.

The tax disparity between debt and equity is the logical result of what we have been calling the corporate "double tax" or "two-level tax." If the premise is that the tax system should collect two taxes on corporate equity income, then the Code cannot permit corporations to deduct dividends – because that deduction would zero out the corporate tax paid on that income.

To see the point, imagine a corporation that earns $10 in pre-tax income every year and has just one shareholder. The corporate double tax implies that the corporation should pay tax of 21% on the $10 (sending $2.10 to the IRS). At that point, the corporation has $7.90 left to pay out as a dividend, and that is what is taxable to the shareholder. If dividends were deductible, the double tax falls apart: the corporation could pay a dividend of $10, deduct $10, and owe zero corporate tax. The whole $10 would be taxable only once – to the shareholder.

Putting all this together, you can see how the tax system can weight the scale in favor of debt. Bigcorp management may not like the bankruptcy risk of debt. But once they take taxes into account, debt may look like the better bargain. The interest deduction means that a dollar of interest is way cheaper than a dollar of dividend.

A critical caveat is that two important features of the law can reduce or even reverse the tax bias in favor of corporate debt. First, is the tax rate on shareholders and creditors. For most of the history of the income tax, an individual (or corporation) would pay the same marginal tax rate on dividends and interest. The equal taxation of interest and dividends made the debt-equity comparison easy, because it created an "all else equal" situation; the only difference was that corporate equity income also faced a corporate-level tax. One tax was better than two. Easy!

But today, an individual faces very different rates of tax on dividend income and interest income. The top marginal tax rate on (most) dividends is 20%, while the top rate on interest is 37%.[1] And the corporate tax is at a very low 21%.[2] So it may sound strange, but with rates like this, taxpayers can find that two taxes are *better* than one, as we saw in Chapter 2.

---

[1] See Code Sec. 1(a) through (d) for individual rates and Code Sec. 1(h)(11) for the special rate on qualified dividends (very generally, dividends paid by U.S. corporations to U.S. shareholders).
[2] Code Sec. 11.

¶401

For example, suppose that an individual in the top tax bracket owns corporate debt. If the corporation earns $100 (pre-tax), it will pay no corporate-level tax (because of the interest deduction). The debt holder will pay tax at her 37% rate and have $63 left after taxes. But if the same corporation used its $100 earnings to pay the maximum dividend to a stockholder, she would have a smidgen more to keep after taxes: $63.20 instead of $63. (Here's the math: the corporation would pay $21 in corporate tax, leaving $79 to distribute. After paying 20% tax on the $79 dividend, the shareholder would have $63.20 left.)

Now take it one step further: the small tax bias in favor of equity grows when you take into account the potential value of *tax deferral*, which is possible with stock but not debt. If you look back at Chapter 2, you'll see that current tax rates are especially favorable to corporations that retain earnings – that is, companies that reinvest their earnings in corporate operations instead of paying out dividends. That's because when companies retain earnings, they are helping shareholders reap the benefits of *tax deferral*. So, if we extend the previous example to a ten-year investment, the tax differential grows: the debt holder would have $184 after taxes, while the shareholder would have $191. (These numbers come from Table 2.2 in Chapter 2.)

(A really good question at this point is: why can't corporate debt be structured to reap the same tax deferral? Couldn't a corporation issue debt that doesn't pay annual interest but instead pays a big lump sum in year 10? The short answer is that it used to be possible to do that, but Congress closed that loophole with something called the original issue discount (or "OID" rules).[3] Those rules, which you do not want to read in detail unless you have to, prevent tax deferral by requiring taxpayers to pay current tax on interest income even if payment is deferred.)

The big point here is kind of stunning: *under current rates, the tax system's usual incentives may be reversed. The law may now (slightly) favor corporate equity over corporate debt!* But the situation of the taxpayer matters quite a lot. For a tax-exempt investor, for instance, the traditional debt-equity bias still holds. A tax-exempt investor would prefer to invest via debt, because there is no tax at either the corporate or shareholder level.

The second feature of the tax law that can reduce or reverse the tax bias toward corporate debt is the limitation on corporate interest deductions. Congress has long been aware of the tax bias in favor of debt, and many policy makers have been concerned that the Tax Code was pushing corporate America into taking on excessive levels of debt. In 2017, Congress enacted a new provision (Code Sec. 163(j)) that denies a portion of interest deductions to some highly-leveraged companies.

We won't delve into the details of Section 163(j), which – you'll be shocked to learn – is a complex provision that applies only to some taxpayers in some lines of business at some income levels.

---

[3] For the incurably curious, the OID rules appear in Code Sec. 1272, *et seq.*

¶401

We have waded deep into the weeds of the tax swamp. Stepping back, though, the basic point isn't too difficult. Remember that the classic tax bias in favor of debt comes about because interest is deductible at the corporate level, while dividends are not. It follows, then, that when the Code limits interest deductions, it also reduces (or eliminates) the tax bias in favor of debt.

¶402   INDMAR AND SUBSTANCE OVER FORM

As we have just seen, the tax difference between corporate equity and corporate debt is a structural feature of the corporate double tax. To erase the tax difference, you'd either have to repeal the double tax on corporate equity or impose a double tax on corporate debt. (Some very smart people think those are plausible ideas, but Congress hasn't yet agreed.[4]) Put another way, the debt-equity bias isn't an accidental mistake in the corporate tax: its roots lie in the very structure of the tax itself.

Once upon a time, policy makers might have thought that the debt-equity distinction was defensible. After all, "plain-vanilla" debt is different from "plain-vanilla" equity in obvious ways. Debt pays interest at a set rate, and creditors can trigger bankruptcy if the borrower fails to pay off their debt by a set date. Common stock, by contrast, doesn't guarantee dividends or any other payoff, but it carries voting rights, and its value tracks the fortunes of the company.

Ever since 1918, when the corporate interest deduction was enacted, policy makers have framed the target of the corporate tax as corporate "owners," *i.e.*, shareholders, rather than creditors. And the equity-debt distinction has remained fundamental to the corporate tax ever since.

But this formal distinction is economically arbitrary (as you've already guessed from the adjective "formal"!) From a finance perspective, debt and equity, along with lots of other financial instruments, are simply contracts that offer a series of cash flows with a certain upside and downside risk profile. From that point of view, stockholders aren't "owners" and creditors aren't "outsiders." Stock and debt simply have a certain profile of cash flows plus upside and downside risk, and voting rights and creditors' rights are just risk-reduction features of the contract.

By now, you can see the payoff of this analysis from a mile away: when the law adopts economically arbitrary rules, it creates tax planning opportunities for the well-advised. The debt-equity distinction is Exhibit A, because it permits corporations to choose their preferred tax structure, often with little change in the economics of the deal.

To see how, bear in mind that – until tax rates changed in 2018 – the income tax had a clear-cut bias in favor of debt and against equity. So, from a tax planner's (or manager's) point of view, the best game in the world was to slap the label

---

[4]   U.S. Department of the Treasury, *Integration of the Individual and Corporate Tax Systems: Taxing Business Income Once* (1992); Alvin C. Warren, Jr., *Integration of Individual and Corporate Income Taxes,* AMERICAN LAW INSTITUTE (1993).

"debt" onto an instrument that provides for no dividends, no creditors' rights, no maturity date, and a share of upside and downside risk.

Faced with this kind of tax planning, the courts stepped in. In thousands, of cases, the IRS has invoked the *substance over form* doctrine to deny the interest deduction claimed on "debt" that was really (said the IRS) equity. Over time, the IRS won some and lost some, and the law evolved into a multi-factor test that you can read (do take some Tylenol first) in cases like the recent *Indmar Products v. Commissioner*.[5]

The taxpayer in *Indmar* was a successful, family-owned corporation. Every year, the shareholders made "loans" to their own corporation in exchange for debt instruments bearing 10% interest. That is, the shareholders lent money to their business and the company was (formally) obligated to repay the debt with interest at 10%. The corporation did distribute cash to the shareholders, which it termed interest and principal on the shareholder loans. The company had never paid dividends to its shareholders.

On these facts, you can see why the IRS was suspicious. The corporation's shareholders repeatedly contributed money into their corporation and received money back. Usually, these two-way transactions between shareholder and corporation would be treated as a contribution to capital (when the money goes in) and a dividend (when the money comes out). But the family in *Indmar* chose the more tax-advantageous route of lending.

The tax goal of the *Indmar* strategy was to reduce total taxes by maxing out debt and avoiding distributions on equity. As we have seen, corporations can deduct interest payments but not dividends. At the shareholder level, in this period, both dividends and interest were taxable at the same rate, but returns of "principal" were tax-free as a return of the "lenders'" basis in the loans. Thus, the *Indmar* story illustrates nicely the classic advantage of corporate debt over corporate equity: one level of tax rather than two.

But the *Indmar* case also illustrates how difficult it is to apply the *substance over form* doctrine in debt-equity cases. The law here is a tangled mess, to use a technical term. Well-meaning judges have, over time, enunciated a variety of standards to distinguish between equity and debt, and these typically reflect the "plain vanilla" forms of debt and equity we considered above: debt has a fixed term, while stock doesn't, and debt pays a stated rate of interest, while equity doesn't. And so on.

But these well-intentioned standards are no match for taxpayer ingenuity. No sooner has the law enunciated a test than taxpayers respond by structuring their financial relationships to work around the new test. The test invoked in *Indmar* came from another case, called *Roth Steel*,[6] and required a court to consider eleven factors:

---

[5] 444 F.3d 771 (6th Cir. 2006).
[6] *Roth Steel Tube Co. v. Comm'r*, 800 F.2d 625 (6th Cir. 1986).

(1) the names given to the instruments, if any, evidencing the indebtedness;
(2) the presence or absence of a fixed maturity date and the schedule of payments;
(3) the presence or absence of a fixed rate of interest and interest payments;
(4) the source of repayments;
(5) the adequacy or inadequacy of capitalization;
(6) the identity of interest between the creditor and the stockholder;
(7) the security, if any, for the advances;
(8) the corporation's ability to obtain financing from outside lending institutions;
(9) the extent to which the advances were subordinated to the claims of outside creditors;
(10) the extent to which the advances were used to acquire capital assets; and
(11) the presence or absence of a sinking fund to provide repayments.[7]

(Lest you worry that these factors aren't sufficient to permit a complete analysis, never fear! The *Roth Steel* factors are nonexclusive, so that a court can throw in anything else that seems relevant.)

The eleven factors spring from well-intentioned attempts to distinguish between debt and equity, but they are doomed to fail. Some are just laughable: it cannot be the case that factor (1), the name given to the instruments, should carry any weight at all. Others make more sense on first impression, including factors (2) and (3), which express the traditional approach based on the terms of "plain vanilla" debt and equity. Some seem nearly irrelevant, like factors (7), (10), and (11): many arm's length debt instruments don't have security, aren't used to acquire capital assets, and don't require a sinking fund (which is a pool of money set aside to pay off a specific debt).

Nevertheless, the appeals court in *Indmar* did its best. The Indmar "loans" clearly had some equity-like features: they were demand loans with no fixed maturity date. It seems seriously unlikely that the shareholders of Indmar would ever demand repayment if the corporation hit a rough patch and couldn't pay. But the court held for the taxpayer, emphasizing the debt-like features of the transactions. The Indmar shareholders did call the advances "debt," did (eventually) execute formal notes, and charged a stated rate of interest. The company's financial success made it an attractive borrower, with ample access to third-party loans.

As you can see, debt-equity cases are tricky and fact-intensive, and the result is that the trial court often gets the last word. So *Indmar* is especially notable: the Court of Appeals reversed the Tax Court's holding as "clear error" and ruled in favor of the taxpayer. The appeals court totted up the *Roth Steel* factors and found that eight of the eleven weighed in favor of the taxpayer.

---

[7] Indmar, at 777 (quoting *Roth Steel Tube Co. v. Comm'r,* 800 F.2d. at 630).

The Sixth Circuit's analysis in *Indmar* is a great example of the malleability of debt-equity cases. The eleven factors are so capacious and so underspecified that you can mold the facts to suit either the taxpayer or the IRS, unless the taxpayers involved had no idea what they were doing.

One problem with the *Roth Steel* approach to debt-equity analysis is that some of the eleven factors don't make much sense when the purported lender is also a shareholder. It isn't very likely that the Indmar shareholders, for example, would demand the repayment of the debt to the detriment of the corporation's shareholders, er, because they are the shareholders! An unrelated creditor might, under some circumstances, demand repayment of a debt even if it results in the company going bankrupt. A shareholder-creditor just won't act in the same way. So even though Indmar was highly successful and could have borrowed from a bank, the shareholder-loans just weren't the same as third-party debt.

Put another way, the tax law doesn't – and can't – prescribe a normative capital structure for every corporation. We simply don't know how much debt Indmar would have taken on had it relied only on unrelated lenders. Every company is different, and every management is different, and so it isn't remotely possible for the IRS to judge whether the debt-equity ratio of Company X is right, or whether some "debt" held by shareholders really is equity.

The deeper problem is that the Code's distinction between debt and equity isn't grounded in economic reality. Taxpayers can make hay of any effort by the government to draw the debt-equity line – because there is no line to be found. A basic tenet of finance is that any instrument should be analyzed as a series of cash flows subject to a set of risks. So, a loan to Indmar, for instance, represents a series of cash flows (principal and interest), and the risks include the risk that the company will be mismanaged or lose money in a recession. But "shares" in Indmar may have much the same profile: we can imagine similar cash flows, and the business risks are, of course, the same.

In finance terms, there isn't a ready distinction between "debt" and "equity" even when they're held by unrelated parties. Debt and equity routinely borrow terms from each other. Some bank loans, for example, have what are called "equity kickers," which award the bank a share of the appreciation on the borrower's assets. Some stock has a fixed return and a fixed term: preferred stock often has a "coupon" or stated rate of return, and preferred stock can include provisions that permit (or require) the company to buy back the stock.

Summing up, then, it isn't too strong to say that one pillar of the corporate tax system is grounded in sand, based on a two-pronged argument:

- *Step one*: The corporate tax requires a debt-equity distinction, because only equity is subject to the double tax. If the IRS can't identify *something* as equity, then there is no corporate tax base.

¶402

- *Step two*: The debt-equity distinction isn't grounded in economic reality. From a finance perspective, there is no hard line that separates debt from equity. The value and nature of a financial contract doesn't reflect its nature as debt or equity but, instead, the stated cash flows and relevant risks to investors and the company.

It is no wonder, then, that related parties (as in *Indmar*) can readily defeat the debt-equity distinction, provided they are buttoned-up about the formalities and don't get too greedy. But even companies with arm's length creditors have an incentive to work around the corporate tax using the debt-equity distinction.

In a famous revenue ruling, the IRS attempted to limit a sophisticated effort to issue "debt" with strong equity characteristics.[8] The instruments in question provided an adjustable rate of "interest" and repaid a minimum amount in a fixed period of 20 years. But the instruments were also subordinated to other creditors and convertible into the stock of the issuer. (That is, the holder could turn in her debt instrument in exchange for a fixed number of shares of the company's stock. For that reason, the instrument's value depended, in part, on the value of the company's stock.) Additional terms of the deal created an incentive for holders to convert into stock, and largely for that reason, the IRS ruled that the purported debt was actually equity for tax purposes.

But the IRS ruling represents a limited victory, if that. Convertible debt is still allowable; the ruling just signifies that it can't be too loaded up with incentives to convert. The next tax planner down the road will surely parse the ruling and determine just how much incentive is allowable for the debt to pass tax muster this time.

¶403 PROBLEM 4.1: DEBT AND EQUITY

Jerry and Karen, who are unrelated, each own 50% of the stock in Gourmet Grocers, Inc. ("GG"), a C corporation. When GG was incorporated two years ago, Jerry and Karen each contributed $100,000. Today, GG is doing well, and the two shareholders would like to spend $300,000 to build a second, even larger, store across town. Karen has proposed that each of them should contribute another $150,000 to GG. Jerry objects that he doesn't have that kind of money, and he urges that GG should borrow the money from a bank instead.

The local bank advises Karen and Jerry that a loan of $300,000 would be a stretch for GG. The bank offers to lend only $100,000 for a five-year term at an interest rate of 12%.

"I could lend us more money for a lower interest rate than that," Karen tells Jerry as they walk out of the bank. "And for a longer term too."

Jerry and Karen talk it through, and they make a few decisions. First, Karen is willing to lend $300,000 to GG for ten years at an interest rate of 10%, paid

---

[8] Rev. Rul. 83-98, 1983-2 C.B. 40 (1983).

every year. Second, if GG at any time has insufficient profits to pay the interest or principal on Karen's loan, the company may defer payment indefinitely, with interest accruing on the unpaid amounts. For instance, suppose that in the first year of the loan, GG does not have profits sufficient to pay the $30,000 in interest that is due to Karen. The loan permits GG to elect to add the $30,000 to the amount due to Karen. Going into the second year, then, GG owes Karen $330,000 (rather than the original $300,000), and the interest in year two will be $33,000 (10% of $330,000).

Karen and Jerry come to you for tax advice. Does Karen's loan raise any federal income tax issues?

ANSWER

A judge (or IRS auditor) would evaluate Karen's loan to GG based on some version of the multi-factor test used in *Indmar*. The loan has some of the hallmarks of debt: it is documented as a loan, has a fixed interest rate, calls for annual interest payments, and has a fixed maturity date. But the "loan" also has some features that seem equity-like. For one thing, GG was unable to obtain a bank loan on similar terms, suggesting that Karen may be acting more like a stockholder than a lender in terms of the amount of risk she is taking. For another, the deferred-payment election undermines the claim that the loan has fixed, annual interest payments and a fixed maturity date; Karen will be repaid only if the firm has sufficient profits.

Certainty is difficult to come by in the debt-equity realm, but there are two more secure directions that the parties might take. If the parties want to ensure that the debt qualifies as such for tax purposes, the parties could modify the terms so that there is a final, fixed maturity date and some fixed interest payments regardless of profits. Alternatively, it would be worth exploring whether an equity investment might be more advantageous to the parties for tax and business reasons. As discussed earlier in this chapter, current tax rates mean that Karen will pay tax on interest income at a marginal rate as high as 37%, while dividends face a marginal rate that tops out at 20%. Jerry might object that he doesn't want Karen to have a greater-than-50% voting interest in GG, because that would leave him a minority shareholder. But that issue is easily handled by giving Karen nonvoting preferred or nonvoting common stock.

The larger point is that the parties have considerable room to maneuver here, and that tax planning will likely play a major role in setting the terms of shareholder loans and equity investments.

¶404   BUSINESS 101: WHAT IS DEBT?

Note: The tax law has quite a difficult time distinguishing debt from equity, as we've seen in this chapter. This section doesn't speak to the tax distinction but, instead, focuses on the (non-tax) legal characteristics of debt in a business setting.

Debt arises when a borrower borrows money from a lender. The borrower is the debtor, and the lender is the creditor. (These terms are interchangeable.) When the bank is a lender, we call the debt a bank loan. When the public is the lender, we call the debt "bonds," which are simply debt instruments held by the public. We say that the debtor is the issuer of the bonds, and the creditors are the bondholders.

Debt, along with equity, is one familiar way to finance business projects. To take a simple example, suppose that Apple Computer wants to build a new factory for $100 million. Apple could use its own funds, but perhaps it doesn't have that kind of cash on hand, or perhaps the management has other plans for the cash. To raise the $100 million, Apple could issue stock or could borrow.

Focusing on borrowing, there are (simplifying a bit) two ways Apple could proceed (and probably, in real life, Apple would explore both to see what the best deal would be). First, Apple could borrow $100 million from a bank. The bank loan would have a principal of $100 million, and Apple would have to repay that amount at some fixed date, along with (say) 5% interest, usually paid annually or quarterly.

Second, Apple could issue $100 million of bonds into the bond market. Each bond would represent a fraction of the total debt. So, if for instance, there were 100,000 bonds, each would have a principal amount or face value of $1,000. Bonds also require the borrower to pay interest periodically and to repay the principal on a fixed date.

All of these terms can, of course, be modified and customized. For instance, interest rates can be fixed or "floating," meaning that the interest rate varies, from time to time, based on some market index. One index used worldwide is LIBOR (which stands for the London Interbank Offered Rate). So, if a bank offers to lend to Apple at "LIBOR plus 3%," then the interest rate would be whatever LIBOR is plus three percentage points.

Even fancier arrangements are possible. The interest rate could be tied to the value of a stock market index or a corporation's dividends or the average price of real estate in Paris.

On the principal side, terms also vary. A common structure requires repayment of the principal at the end of the loan. But "installment obligations" require principal to be partially repaid at set intervals. And some debt mixes the two styles, calling for smallish installment payments of principal and then a big "balloon payment" of the remainder at the end of the debt's term.

But whatever the terms may be, the key legal characteristic of debt is that it represents a senior claim on a borrower's assets in bankruptcy. A company goes bankrupt when it can no longer pay off its debts (and cannot negotiate with creditors to get more time). So, if Apple Computer, with $100 million in outstanding bonds due to be paid, found itself with only $80 million in assets, the company would likely go into bankruptcy.

¶404

In its simplest form, bankruptcy is a court proceeding that aims to liquidate the debtor and make an orderly distribution of its assets. Debt has a senior claim in bankruptcy, meaning that debt is paid off before stockholders (or, in the case of partnerships, partners) receive anything. So, in the case of Apple with $80 million in assets and $100 million in debt, the creditors would receive 80 cents on the dollar, and the stockholders would receive nothing at all.

As you can imagine, things can get a lot more complicated than that. Different kinds of debt may carry different levels of seniority. Secured debt, for instance, is a kind of debt that permits the creditor to claim a specific asset (say, a building) in the event of bankruptcy. Secured creditors are allowed to take their (specified) assets without sharing them with other debtors. Unsecured creditors will share equally with creditors of the same class.

You might have heard (or not!) of subordinated debt. Subordination just means that a specific debt has a lesser claim in bankruptcy than some other debt. We might say that the subordinated debt is junior. Because subordinated debt is paid off only after the senior creditors are paid, it is riskier. So-called "junk bonds" are often subordinated debt. But the risk depends, of course, on the creditworthiness of the borrower and the amount of senior debt that is outstanding.

> **EXAMPLE 2.** Farmstand, Inc., has been in business for fifteen years. Its signature restaurant did well for the first decade. The two common stockholders, Abbie and Brent, decided to do a major renovation in Year 10. They borrowed $3 million from Webster Bank at an interest rate of 10% for a term of 5 years. At that time, the restaurant was worth $7 million as a going business, and the assets alone (real estate plus equipment) were worth $5 million.
>
> By Year 15, however, Farmstand is limping along. Abbie and Brent have been unable tto find a buyer for the business, and local brokers estimate that the real estate and equipment are worth only $1 million. Abbie and Brent meet with the bank to see if they can work out an extension of time. But, reading the tea leaves, the bank says no.
>
> Farmstand doesn't go into bankruptcy, because the parties negotiate a settlement. Abbie and Brent agree to sell the real estate and equipment and give the proceeds to the bank. Because Farmstand is a corporation, the bank cannot look to Abbie's and Brent's individual assets for payment. So, the bank ends up with only $1 million repaid on a $3 million loan. And Abbie and Brent walk away with zero.

¶405 ADVANCED PROBLEM

For a more advanced problem, which also contains material from Chapter 5, see Problem C1 in Appendix C.

CHAPTER 5

Tax Deferral and Corporate Formation

Introduction	¶500
Incorporation and *Realization*	¶501
Section 351 and *Tax Deferral*	¶502
Problem 5.1: Section 351	¶503
Substance Over Form in Incorporations: *Intermountain Lumber*	¶504
Business 101: What is Corporate Control?	¶505
Advanced Problem	¶506

¶500 INTRODUCTION

In this part of the book, we will focus on the federal tax rules that apply to corporations. Chapter 2 introduced the idea that a corporation (or, interchangeably, a "C corporation") is the kind of entity subject to the double tax regime. But now it's time to dig into the details – how exactly do the two taxes work?

Let's start with some good news. You already know how one level of the two-level tax works. It turns out that the corporate level tax mostly follows the rules that you learned in your basic tax course. And, by mostly, I mean pretty much 95%. So, a corporation computes its income, takes deductions, calculates taxable income, and claims tax credits pretty much like an individual.

There are some differences between corporations and individuals, of course. One obvious one is that the corporate tax rate is a flat 21%, set by Section 11 of the Internal Revenue Code. Another difference is that there is no rate preference for long-term capital gains realized by corporations. Corporations do, however, face a limitation on the deduction of capital losses in Code Sec. 1211. The limitation works pretty much the same as it does for individuals: corporations may deduct capital losses only against capital gains (and may not deduct capital losses against ordinary income). The main differences are that corporations don't get the $3,000 per year allowance that individuals do, and that the carryover periods are different.[1]

But when it comes to the hard issues that we studied in the basic tax course, there are essentially no differences between individuals and corporations. Corporations can take advantage of the *realization* requirement, they can benefit from *tax deferral*, and so on. Indeed, the basic tax course includes a number of famous

---

[1] *See* Code Secs. 1211 and 1212.

cases with corporations as taxpayers. Think of *Frank Lyon*, the sale-leaseback case,[2] or *Cottage Savings*, the savings and loan mortgage swap case.[3] Both involved basic tax issues (who owns property? what is a *realization* event?) and both cases announced legal doctrines that apply equally to individuals and corporations.

Now for the less-good news. What tax experts call "corporate tax" focuses primarily on two sets of issues that really are unique to corporations. The first set of issues has to do with *realization*: these issues involve the taxation of the entity and its shareholders, and they arise primarily on the formation, combination, and dissolution of corporations. The second set of issues has to do with the second level tax: the tax on shareholders. It turns out that it's not as simple as it might seem to identify distributions and to distinguish distributions from other transactions between a corporation and its shareholders.

To keep our discussion organized, we will follow the sequence used by most casebooks: we will track the tax issues that arise during the lifecycle of a hypothetical corporation from formation to distribution to combination and dissolution.

Before we dive in, here's one more piece of good news. The corporate tax is complicated, and there's no way around that, but the six concepts can help. In every chapter, we will see how even the most technical rules originate with a conceptual problem that you already know about. In this chapter, for example, the key issue is *tax deferral*. So instead of just memorizing rules, you'll be able to understand the rules by connecting them to the underlying conceptual problem that motivates policy makers and taxpayers.

¶501 INCORPORATION AND *REALIZATION*

Let's return to the hypothetical we introduced in Chapter 2 and worked with in Chapter 3. You own a profitable, million-dollar Napa Valley winery. At this stage, you have decided to incorporate the already growing business. A natural first question is to ask your lawyer how to do this. She explains that after you form the corporation, you then sign documents that take you through two steps. Step one is that you transfer title to all of the assets of the winery from you to the corporation. Step two is that, in exchange, you receive all of the stock of the new corporation.

For now, let's keep the hypothetical relatively simple, and we will complicate it as we go to show different wrinkles in the law. Suppose that the winery has just two assets, the land where the grapes grow, and the building where the grapes are processed and stored as wine. Suppose that you receive only common stock in the new corporation, which you will creatively call Napa Valley Wines, Inc.

So far, nothing in all this suggests that taxes are particularly relevant. After all, you've owned the winery for a long time, and nothing has really changed: you still own and run the winery, exactly as you did before incorporation. The only things

---

[2] *Frank Lyon v. U.S.*, 435 U.S. 561, 98 S. Ct. 1291, 55 L. Ed.2d 550 (1978).
[3] *Cottage Savings Ass'n v. Comm'r*, 499 U.S. 554, 111 S. Ct. 1503, 113 L. Ed.2d 589 (1991).

that have changed are the legal formalities. Technically, the corporation owns the winery, and you no longer run the corporation as an individual, but instead as the chairman of the board of Napa Valley Wines, Inc. But your lawyer reassures you that these are just technicalities. As the sole shareholder of the corporation, you retain 100% control over day-to-day operations. If you ever want money for yourself, that's easy to do. You can pay yourself dividends any time you want, and you can dissolve the corporation at any point. So, nothing about the new arrangement has changed your wealth, your income, or your business or personal options.

You can hear the caveat coming. Even though there's been no change in substance, there has been a change in form, and the tax law treats that change in form as a *realization* event. The relevant law here is stated in the Supreme Court case, *Cottage Savings*.[4] I'm sure your memory of that case is crystal clear from your first tax course, but just in case you need a refresher, here are the basics.

In *Cottage Savings*, a savings and loan (S&L) owned a large portfolio of mortgage loans with built-in losses. (Recall that a loan made by a bank is an asset to the bank, because it represents a stream of interest and principal payments that will come to the bank from the borrower.) The S&L wanted to realize those losses for tax purposes: a tax loss is a tax goodie, because it is a deduction that reduces current income (and, under the law at the time, permitted the S&L to receive a refund for past years' taxes).

The barrier to *realization* in that case was that banking regulators would not permit the S&L to sell the loans outright. So, to get around the regulatory constraint, the S&L arranged to swap mortgage loans with another S&L. The case went all the way up to the Supreme Court, where the IRS challenged the taxpayer's position and argued that no *realization* event had occurred. The IRS pointed out that the swap of mortgage pools had not made any change in the economic substance of what the S&L owned. The IRS pressed the Court to apply a substantive test under Section 1001 to determine whether a *realization* event had occurred.

But the Supreme Court ruled for the taxpayer, ruling that a change in "legal entitlements" was sufficient to trigger a *realization* event. On the facts of *Cottage Savings*, the change in legal entitlements was that the individual mortgagors in the swapped pools of loans were different from the original mortgagors.

Now, all of this is highly relevant to the incorporation of a business. Incorporation may change nothing in economic substance, but it does leave both the shareholder and the corporation with "legally distinct entitlements," and so meets the *Cottage Savings* standard for *realization*. Nor is this a recent result. *Cottage Savings*, in fact, drew on a series of cases from the 1920s, which had found that formal changes in corporate stock, notably a change in the state of incorporation, constituted a *realization* event.[5]

---

[4] *Cottage Savings Ass'n v. Comm'r*, 499 U.S. 554 (1991).

[5] *U.S. v. Phellis*, 257 U.S. 156 (1921); *Cullinan v. Walker*, 262 U.S. 134 (1923); *Marr v. U.S.*, 268 U.S. 536 (1925).

Returning to our Napa Valley example, you can now spot the distinct legal entitlements. You, the individual, used to own the assets of the vineyard directly. But in the course of the incorporation, you gave up legal title to those assets and received, in exchange, shares of common stock in Napa Valley Wines, Inc. Setting aside economic substance, which *Cottage Savings* ruled out of bounds, there has clearly been a change in your legal entitlements.

And we're not finished yet. There is another party to the transaction, the corporation. The corporate double tax treats corporations as taxpayers separate from their shareholders. The result is that whenever a corporation is a party to a transaction, the tax consequences exist at two levels: the shareholder level and the corporate level.

In our Napa Valley case, the corporation too has experienced a change in its legal entitlements. When Napa Valley Wines, Inc. was created, its only asset was its capacity to issue shares of stock. But in the course of the incorporation, Napa Valley gave up shares of its stock and received in exchange the assets of the vineyard. So, at least potentially, the corporation could have a *realization* event as well.

You probably will remember from your basic tax course that a *realization* event implies that each party should recognize gain or loss. Under Code Sec. 1001, we measure gain or loss by the difference between the taxpayer's basis in the assets surrendered and the amount realized, or, here, the fair market value of the asset received in exchange.

EXAMPLE 1. Suppose that the owner of the Napa Valley vineyard has a basis of $70 in the vineyard. At the time of incorporation, the vineyard is worth $100.

If the incorporation is treated as a *realization* event, the owner would realize a gain of $30 on the transfer. The character of the gain and loss would be determined under Code Secs.s 1221(a)(2) and 1231, because the vineyard is real property used in the trade or business. If the owner has no other Section 1231 items on her tax return, then the gain will be long-term capital gain.

The corporation's tax treatment is also pretty clear. It exchanged stock worth $100 for a vineyard worth $100, and so under general tax principles (found in Code Sec. 1012), the corporation has a cost basis of $100 in the vineyard.

If you're very sharp-eyed, you might spot one remaining issue. The corporation exchanged its own stock for a vineyard worth $100. But what is a corporation's basis in its own stock? That's a puzzler, because the corporation didn't invest any money to create its stock. So, does the corporation have a zero basis in its stock and $100 of gain? That seems weird, because the corporation didn't really earn $100 of income in any substantive sense.

¶501

Luckily, Congress acted to keep us from having to deal with this conceptual headache. Code Sec. 1032 provides that a corporation recognizes no gain or loss on the issuance of its own stock in exchange for property. (That rule lets us off the hook here, but don't over-read it. A corporation can still be a taxable party to an incorporation if it transfers property other than stock.[6]

¶502 SECTION 351 AND *TAX DEFERRAL*

Now, if you think about it for a few minutes, you can see why this application of the *realization* doctrine would make business owners very unhappy. Think about the Napa Valley operation. From the owner's perspective, incorporating the business isn't at all like selling it. She will still own the business, as before, and she will still control the business, as before. All that is changing is, literally, a pile of legal papers that define a new entity and set of organizational formalities.

Congress has recognized that treating incorporation as a *realization* event is problematic. Not only would it raise taxes on seemingly innocuous transactions, but it could discourage business owners from taking productive actions, which often include formalizing their operations. In response to these problems, Congress enacted Code Sec. 351, which provides what is called "nonrecognition" treatment to certain incorporations. Nonrecognition is a technical term that means that gain and loss will not be taken into account for tax purposes, provided that the transaction meets the requirements of Section 351. Technically speaking, the transaction is still a *realization* event under Section 1001, but Section 351 provides a special override, called nonrecognition.

When Section 351 applies, the shareholder does not recognize gain or loss, but that gain or loss is not forgiven. Instead, it is deferred, using a mechanism that you have seen before, carryover basis. (If you'd like to refresh your memory, have a look at Code Sec. 1015, which provides *tax deferral* for gifts using the carryover basis rule.) Carryover basis, in Section 351 transactions, ensures that any gain or loss is preserved for future *realization* events.

> **EXAMPLE 2.** Let's build on the facts of Example 1. Recall that the owner of the Napa Valley vineyard has a basis of $70 in the vineyard, and she has owned both for years. At the time of incorporation, the vineyard is worth $100. In Example 1, we saw that the *realization* doctrine would trigger $30 of gain. How would Code Sec. 351 change that result?
>
> Section 351 provides nonrecognition treatment to the shareholder. So, the vineyard owner no longer has to report gain on her tax return. Instead, the owner carries over the basis in the vineyard ($70) into her stock. When the legal formalities are complete, the owner is now the sole shareholder of Napa Valley Wines, Inc., and she has a basis of $70 in her stock.

---

[6] *See* Chapter 6, *infra*.

The result of all of these machinations is that the Code has awarded *tax deferral* to the business owner. To see why, consider the fair market value of Napa Valley Wines, Inc. The corporation owns the vineyard, and we know that the vineyard is worth $100. So, it follows that if the shareholder sold her stock to someone else, they would pay $100. When and if that sale takes place, the shareholder, who has a basis of $70 in her stock, would realize and recognize gain of $30.

The prospect of *tax deferral* should awaken your tax planning instincts. You know from the basic course in taxation that *tax deferral* is usually beneficial to the taxpayer, since paying tax on, say, $30 of gain later is better than paying that tax today. The shareholder benefits from the time value of money in the meantime.

You might conclude that Code Sec. 351 is an outright gift from the Congress to the taxpayer. But three wrinkles in the law make the gift a little less rich than it first appears. First, only some transactions qualify for Section 351 treatment. If you consult Section 351(a), you'll see the major requirements are that the shareholder must transfer property; the shareholder must receive stock and only stock in exchange; and that the shareholder must be in control of the corporation afterwards. In the next chapter, we will take a closer look at some of these technical requirements, but, for the moment, just note that not every incorporation transaction will qualify for nonrecognition.

A second wrinkle is that some shareholders may not want nonrecognition treatment. Suppose, for example, that the Napa Valley vineyard owner had a basis of $110 in the vineyard (which is worth $100). If she sold the vineyard outright, she would realize a loss of $10. Under Code Secs. 1221(a)(2) and 1231, that ordinary loss would be a valuable "tax goodie," deductible against other income. The key here is that Section 351, at least formally, is mandatory and not elective: *tax deferral* is mandatory, and deferring losses is no fun at all. In the next chapter, we will see that there are certain tax planning moves that a taxpayer can use to defeat Section 351, but those moves are not always available and may come at an unacceptable economic cost.

A third, and crucially important feature of Section 351 is that it awards *tax deferral* at the shareholder level but, in effect, charges a price: it duplicates the tax-deferred gain at the corporate level.

EXAMPLE 3. Return to the facts of Example 2, which showed that Code Sec. 351 provides nonrecognition treatment to the shareholder. The vineyard owner reports no gain on the exchange and takes a basis of $70 in her stock. To complete our tax analysis, we have to take a look at the consequences to the corporation. We've already learned that Section 1032 excuses the corporation from realizing any gain or loss on the issuance of its stock. But we haven't yet answered an important question: what will be the corporation's basis in the vineyard it now owns?

The answer lies in Code Sec. 362, which provides (generally) that the corporation carries over the shareholder's basis. In our example, that means that Napa Valley Wine, Inc. now owns a vineyard worth $100 but has a basis of only $70. The result is that the corporation will have $30 of gain if it ever sells the vineyard.

One way to think about this is that Section 351 contains an unstated but major quid pro quo. The tax man offers *tax deferral* to the shareholder but at the cost of subjecting any built-in gain to the corporate double tax system. To see why, imagine that, immediately after the incorporation, the corporation sells the vineyard for $100. The corporation will report $30 of gain on its tax return and will pay tax at the 21% corporate rate. When the corporation distributes its earnings to the shareholder, that amount will be taxed as a dividend. By contrast, in an incorporation treated as a *realization* event (have a look at Example 1), the corporation takes a fair market value in the vineyard. With a basis of $100, the corporation would owe no further tax if it sold the vineyard.

At this point, you may reasonably feel confused, or at least a little shaky in your grasp of these concepts. That feeling is so understandable that it could be a model for this entire subject! But you will find that your grasp of all of this becomes much firmer as you go through the following problems. Let's turn now to take a closer look at the technical requirements of Section 351 and at tax planning problems and opportunities.

¶503   PROBLEM 5.1: SECTION 351

As you work through the following problem, stick close to the text of Code Sec. 351 and the coordinating basis rules in Sections 358 and 362. These are highly technical rules, and nearly every word has a specific and important meaning.

Donna has formed Donna, Inc., a C corporation, and plans to start an organic apple orchard. Donna is (initially) the sole shareholder. Consider the federal income tax consequences of the following events:

(1)   Donna receives 200 shares in Donna, Inc. in exchange for the contribution of Greenacre (basis = $20, FMV = $100), which is undeveloped farmland, to Donna, Inc.

(2)   The facts are the same as in (1) except that, at the same time, Evan contributes $100 in cash to Donna, Inc. and receives (from Donna, Inc.) 100 shares of newly-issued common stock?

ANSWER TO (1)

Beginning with (1), the starting point for the analysis is Code Sec. 351(a), which — as you already know — extends nonrecognition treatment to some, but not all, incorporations. The key requirements are that:

- A person transfers property (here, Donna transfers Greenacre)
- To a corporation solely in exchange for its stock (here, Donna receives common stock in Donna, Inc.)
- Immediately afterward, the transferor is in control of the corporation (here, Donna owns 100% of the stock, which meets the control test of Section 368(c)).

Now that we know the transaction meets all of the requirements of Section 351, we should examine the tax consequences to both taxpayers – Donna and the corporation. Donna realizes, but does not recognize, gain of $80 on Greenacre, thanks to Section 351(a). Donna's basis in the Donna, Inc. stock is $20, thanks to Section 358(a), and the corporation's basis in Greenacre is also $20, thanks to Section 362(a).

You can double-check whether these results make sense by keeping in mind the overarching goal of Section 351: to award tax deferral but not tax forgiveness, and to subject the built-in gain at the time of incorporation to the corporate double tax. Donna now owns stock with a basis of $20 and a fair market value of $100. That's right, because if she sells her stock later on, she will report gain of $80. The corporation owns Greenacre with a basis of $20, so that the $80 of built-in gain is now "inside" the corporation. If Donna, Inc. later sells Greenacre for $100 or more, the $80 of gain will be subject to the two-level corporate tax.

ANSWER TO (2)

Moving on to (2), does Evan's entry into the deal affect Donna's tax situation? Once again, we go back to the eligibility conditions set out in Section 351(a).

- Both Donna and Evan are people transferring property (in Evan's case, the property is cash)
- Both transfer their property to the corporation solely in exchange for stock but
- Neither Evan nor Donna, on his or her own, is in "control" of the corporation using the 80% test of Section 368(c).

The potential snag, then, comes up in the control test. But here's where careful reading of the Code is critical. Go back to Section 351(a):

> No gain or loss shall be recognized if property *is transferred to a corporation by one or more persons* solely in exchange for stock in such corporation and *immediately after the exchange such person or persons are in control* (as defined in Section 368(c)) of the corporation.

¶503

I've emphasized the relevant language so that we can parse it. Section 351 applies if, after the exchange, "such person or persons" are in control. Now, when you first read that language, you might suppose that it means that only a transferor who has 80% control will qualify. But the language, "such person or persons are in control," means that we aggregate all the stock received by Donna and Evan in testing for control. Under that aggregate test, both Donna and Evan meet the terms of Section 351, since as a group, the two of them own 100% of the stock.

So, who *would* fail Section 351 due to the control test? Suppose that Donna had incorporated Donna, Inc. many years ago. Evan then comes along as a new investor and puts in property worth $100 in exchange for 50% of the stock. In that case, Evan would not qualify for Section 351 nonrecognition treatment, because he would be the only transferor at that time and would receive less stock than required for control under Section 368(c).

The control group test is, like many Code rules, a trap for the unwary – and an opportunity for the wary. An unsophisticated Donna and Evan might not realize that, for Section 351 to apply to them both, they need to transfer their property at (about) the same time. If too much time separates their transfers, the second transferor will not be part of the control group. The result would be full realization of all built-in gain and loss under Section 1001 for the second transferor.

But the control group test can also be a tax blessing for the well-advised. By forming or avoiding control groups, the parties may be able to award tax deferral under Section 351 to parties who want it, while permitting current realization for those who prefer it. The next section illustrates how tax planners might sidestep Section 351 – and how the *substance over form* doctrine can limit planning options.

¶504   SUBSTANCE OVER FORM IN INCORPORATIONS: INTERMOUNTAIN LUMBER

Intermountain Lumber is a classic corporate tax case with a twist.[7] Usually, the taxpayer seeks to apply Section 351 to obtain the benefit of *tax deferral*. But in this case, the taxpayer sought to defeat Section 351 by arguing that the control requirement was not met. Why? Because the particular facts in this case meant that if Section 351 did not apply the taxpayer could obtain a stepped-up basis without bearing the tax cost of recognizing gain.

Once you understand the facts, this convoluted point will be clearer. It all began with a fairly familiar small business scenario. Mr. Shook owned a sawmill, and Mr. Wilson was one of his big customers. Simplifying a bit, Shook decided to invest more money in his business and to take on a partner, Wilson. Shook and Wilson decided to incorporate the sawmill business. Wilson agreed to co-sign a loan for the corporation, and in return, Shook agreed to sell Wilson a 50% interest in the business.

---

[7] *Intermountain Lumber Co. & Subsidiaries v. Comm'r*, 65 T.C. 1025 (1976).

All that is pretty straightforward and not exactly newsworthy. "Business Owner Takes on Partner" is not exactly a shocking headline. But the issue arose because of the two steps that Shook and Wilson took to implement their agreement. In step one, Shook transferred the sawmill to the new corporation and received all of the stock in return. In step two, Shook and Wilson agreed to permit Wilson to pay over time to acquire 50% of the stock. The two agreements were signed at the same time, but the eventual tax issue would be whether the two steps should be treated as separate transactions or as one integrated plan.

The IRS did not question the transaction initially. The case arose only later, after a third party, Intermountain Lumber, had purchased Shook and Wilson's sawmill business. The new owner realized that it could benefit from claiming a higher basis in the sawmill. (Remember that higher asset basis is useful in two ways: it supports higher depreciation deductions and lowers the gain on the sale.) To support its basis claim, Intermountain looked back at the incorporation and took the position that it had not met the requirements of Section 351, because Shook did not obtain the required "control" of the corporation. A failed Section 351 deal, remember, is a *realization* event: it means full gain (or loss) recognition to the incorporator and a fair market value (rather than carryover) basis to the corporation.

You might think that Intermountain Lumber was misguided in claiming a *realization* event. In general, a taxpayer shouldn't realize $100 of gain in order to gain $100 dollars of additional basis. That's because of the logic of *tax deferral*: paying tax on $100 now to acquire deductions of $100 later is generally not a sound financial move. But the wrinkle in this case was timing: the incorporation had taken place before Intermountain had entered the picture. So, possibly the statute of limitations on collection of the tax had already expired. And even if not, the taxpayer on the hook for the additional tax was Mr. Shook and not Intermountain. (Cold! But that's just business.)

Intermountain Lumber can be a confusing case, because it seems, at first glance, that Shook and Wilson are just like Donna and Evan in Problem 5.1, above. After all, didn't Shook and Wilson band together to incorporate the sawmill, with Shook contributing the sawmill and Wilson contributing cash? But there is a key distinction here between *Intermountain* and the Donna-Evan hypo. Wilson did not contribute property to the corporation: instead, he purchased his stock directly from Shook. Put another way, Wilson was not a "transferor" within the meaning of Section 351(a). Thus, the transaction would qualify for Section 351 treatment only if Shook, standing alone, had "control" immediately after the exchange.

The IRS took the position that Shook did have control, because he transferred the sawmill to the corporation and received 100% of the stock in exchange. If you view the transaction that way, then the terms of Section 351 were met, and it follows that the sawmill had a carryover basis to the corporation under Section 362. Intermountain, for its part, wanted to integrate the two steps of the transaction. Intermountain argued that Shook and Wilson intended for the sale of 50% of the stock to be an integral part of the transaction. Taking that view, Shook had only 50% of the stock immediately after the transfer. Since 50% falls short of the 80% threshold required by Section 368(c), the transaction failed to qualify under Section 351.

In the end, the taxpayer won: the court ruled that, in substance, Shook owned only 50% of the corporate stock.

Taking a broader view, *Intermountain Lumber* provides both a tool for taxpayers and a warning. The case provides one roadmap for taxpayers who want to sidestep the nonrecognition regime of Section 351: a simultaneous contractual agreement to sell stock received in the incorporation to a party that did not contribute property to the corporation will defeat "control" and, thus, trigger *realization*.

At the same time, however, *Intermountain Lumber* sends a warning to future taxpayers by applying the *substance over form* doctrine to the determination of control. The result is that tax planners cannot rely on purely formal transfers or separate contractual steps to establish (or defeat) control. The courts may well look past the formalities to take notice of the parties' intentions and to aggregate seemingly separate contracts into one larger transaction. Planners beware!

¶505 BUSINESS 101: WHAT IS CORPORATE CONTROL?

You already know what a corporation is, and basically how common stock works. (See Business 101: What is a Corporation? in Chapter 2). Common stockholders typically possess voting rights, and those voting rights are the key to corporate control.

Let's dig into what voting rights mean – and don't mean. Common stockholders do not directly vote on every corporate decision. That would obviously be silly: shareholders could not possibly be informed enough to consult on every business judgment, and the cost of consultation could be prohibitive. Instead, shareholder voting rights permit shareholders to elect the group of people that runs the corporation, called the Board of Directors.

Now, typically, the Board of Directors itself doesn't get down into the weeds of every business decision. They don't particularly want to advise on whether to save ten cents per ream of copy paper by switching from Brand X to Brand Y. But the Board is charged with several important tasks. One is to advise on the overall strategic direction of the business. For example, a media company might need to decide whether to set up a pay wall to charge for its content or whether it should offer content for free. The Board would vote on such decisions. A second function of the Board is to appoint and monitor corporate management. "Management" refers to the high-level corporate employees who implement the day-to-day business of the corporation. Just to give you a little bit more terminology, the chairman of the corporation is the Chairman of the Board, while the CEO is the Chief Executive Officer, and she is part of management.

Putting all of this together, we can begin to see how corporate control works. When one shareholder or a group of like-minded shareholders controls sufficient votes, they can elect the number of directors needed to gain control over corporate decisions and corporate management. You might notice that I express corporate control rights in very general terms. In some cases, and in some corporations, the majority of votes will entitle the holders to elect a majority of the Board, and a majority of the Board is sufficient to make corporate decisions and replace corporate management. But in other cases, or in other corporations, a super majority of votes or directors might be needed. Going forward, I will ignore those special cases and assume that 51% constitutes voting control, but you should keep in mind the possibility of real-world wrinkles.

Note, too, that corporate voting is not democratic. One person might own many votes, and it is her voting power, and not her personhood, that matters. So, if you own 90 shares out of 100, you control the company, even if 10 other people each own one share and are really unhappy with your business decisions.

EXAMPLE 4. *A corporate takeover.* BigMedia, Inc., is a venerable television broadcasting operation. Its profits are sound but not stellar. Marcella, the CEO of NewMedia, Inc., has analyzed BigMedia and is convinced that its business model is stale. With new management and new priorities, she thinks, BigMedia could be much more profitable.

Marcella has made her pitch to BigMedia's current board, and they weren't interested. So, to make these changes, Marcella will need to gain control of BigMedia and install a new Board and new management. To do that, she doesn't need to own 100% of the stock, but she does need 51% of the votes.

There are two ways Marcella can get the votes that she needs. One route is to go into the stock market and buy common stock. For that, obviously, she will need money and time, because it will take time for 51% of the of the stock to change hands. A second route is two lobby other shareholders to adopt her position. If she can persuade powerful stockholders, who own large blocks of stock, to go with her, then together they can take control of the Board. The downside to that strategy is that it requires coalition building and maintenance. And, of course, the current board and management will be doing some lobbying of their own. They know that if Marcella wins control, they will all lose their jobs. (Being a Board member isn't technically employment; it's more of an independent contractor gig. But it can be lucrative, to the tune of several hundred thousand dollars a year for each member of a big corporate board.)

Once Marcella has 51% of the vote, she can generally elect a majority of the Board, and that majority will vote to replace current management with management prepared to implement Marcella's ideas.

One more wrinkle is worth noticing. So far, I've sketched out the formal rules on corporate control, which are written down in corporate charters and state corporate law. But often, corporate control is a less formal matter that is determined by the distribution of shareholdings. For example, suppose that the stock of Corporation X is very widely held, so that no current shareholder owns more than 5%, and only a couple of shareholders own that much stock. In that kind of setting, most shareholders won't pay much attention to corporate matters; they own too little of the company to spend much time on its affairs. When the majority of votes are held by passive shareholders like this, someone might gain effective control of the corporation by buying much less than 51% of the stock. Depending on the issues at stake, the amount of publicity, and the approval or opposition of current management, a 30% block of stock in this setting could give a shareholder a major voice on the Board and even *de facto* control.

¶506 ADVANCED PROBLEM

For a more advanced problem, which also contains material from Chapter 4, *see* Problem C1 in Appendix C.

CHAPTER 6

Limitations on *Tax Deferral:* Boot and Services in Corporate Formation

Introduction	¶600
Tax Deferral and Boot	¶601
Nonqualified Preferred Stock	¶602
Compensation for Services	¶603
Problem 6.1: Section 351 and Boot	¶604
Business 101: What is Preferred Stock?	¶605

¶600 INTRODUCTION

In a sense, Section 351 makes the formation of a corporation a non-event for tax purposes. As Chapter 5 discusses, a typical corporate formation is not a *realization* event, and the taxpayer enjoys *tax deferral* on any built-in gains or losses on the assets that have been incorporated. But the protective umbrella of Section 351 doesn't cover all possible transactions. In this chapter, we will see that the rules deny *tax deferral* in particular cases.

¶601 TAX DEFERRAL AND BOOT

One of the oddest tax terms, but one of the most useful, is "boot." (Throw that term around in the right circles, and you'll be pegged as a tax insider.) The phrase probably comes from the idiom "to boot," as in "She gave me an ice cream cone and a free cookie to boot." In a Section 351 transaction, "boot" arises when a party to a nonrecognition transaction receives not only stock but also other consideration.

> **EXAMPLE 1.** Cara and Darrell are starting a business together, and they've decided to incorporate. They want to run the show 50-50 in all things, and they have decided that each person should put in $100 worth of cash or property. Cara puts in $100, and Darrell contributes Greenacre, with a value of $105. If the parties stopped there, Darrell would have put more into the business than Cara, for the same 50% stake. But the property (let's assume) isn't easily divisible – Darrell can't just hack off $5 worth and keep that.

Luckily, there's an easy way to even things up. If Darrell takes $5 in cash back from the corporation, he will have contributed $100 ($105 - $5 cash back). You might think that Cara is now being treated unfairly, but actually, it works just right. Cara and Darrell each have 50% ownership of the corporation. The corporation's total assets are $200 (property worth $105 plus cash of $95 left after paying Darrell his $5). Thus, Cara and Darrell each own stock worth $100, meeting their original goals.

You'll note that the payment of boot in this example has nothing to do with taxes. The cash payment just evens out the "lumpy" contribution that Darrell made. And that's a very typical scenario. Land, buildings, machines, and other items of property aren't as readily divisible or as easily saleable as cash or liquid securities. And so, to even out the stakes in accordance with the business plan, one or more shareholders may receive cash or other boot in the formation.

The Code could ignore boot entirely. After all, you could still argue that Cara and Darrell have made a "mere change in form," combining their cash and property in exchange for a controlling stake in the enterprise. But, instead, the Code seizes on the receipt of cash as a trigger for *realization*. Under Code Sec. 351(b), Darrell (the stockholder who gets the boot) will recognize gain, but not loss, up to the amount of the boot he receives. Sections 358 and 362 adjust the shareholder's basis in her stock and the corporation's basis in its property to take account of the *realization* event.

> **EXAMPLE 2.** Continuing Example 1, we now need to add some tax-relevant facts. Suppose that Darrell has a basis of $75 in Greenacre. That means that he has $30 ($105-75) of built-in gain. Put another way, if he had sold Greenacre instead of contributing it to the corporation, he would have *realized* $30 of gain.
>
> Section 351(b) provides that Darrell will recognize $5 of gain (equal to the $5 in cash boot he receives). You can infer that, afterwards, Darrell should have $25 of built-in gain remaining. The shareholder basis rules in Section 358 do just that. Via a complex up-and-down adjustment in Section 358(a), Darrell ends up with a basis in his stock equal to $75 (initial basis of $75 less cash of $5 plus gain of $5). At the corporate level, Section 362(a) is relatively straightforward: the corporation's basis in Greenacre is $80 (original basis of $75 plus Darrell's gain of $5).
>
> You can apply the basis rules mechanically and get the right answer, but it's helpful to be able to see *why* this is the right answer. Darrell's stock, we know, has a fair market value of $100 (see the initial set of facts above). To preserve his remaining built-in gain of $25, he should have a basis of $75 – and that's what Section 358(a) prescribes. At the corporate level, the Section 362 rules award a basis of $80 in Greenacre. Remember that Greenacre itself is worth $105 – and so the basis rules also preserve $25 of built-in gain in Greenacre at the corporate level.

What's the logic of the up-and-down computation in Section 358? It may seem nonsensical to adjust shareholder basis *down* by the amount of cash and *up* by the amount of gain, since the two are the same. But there is method in the seeming insanity. The downward adjustment, in effect, allocates basis to the cash, dollar-for-dollar. That's a necessary first step, because cash always has a basis equal to its value (there's no such thing as "appreciated cash," at least when it's U.S. currency). So to ensure that Darrell has a basis of $5 in his $5 in cash, we have to subtract $5 from the "pot" of basis that he goes in with, or $75.

The second step, the upward adjustment, gives Darrell "credit" for the gain he realizes and recognizes. Remember that basis represents an investment of tax-paid (or after-tax) money in something. By paying tax on the $5 of gain in the deal, Darrell has "earned" $5 more in basis to put into the "pot" of basis he brought to the deal. In Darrell's case, the up and down offset each other. But that isn't always true.

> **EXAMPLE 3.** Suppose that Darrell had an initial basis of $103 in Greenacre, so that he came to the deal with built-in gain of just $2, but still received $5 in boot. Section 351(b) would trigger *realization of just $2 of gain*. (Have a look at the language of Section 351(b)(1): "gain (if any)...shall be recognized".) To see why, keep in mind that the backdrop to Section 351 is the *realization* requirement. If Darrell had not qualified for Section 351 at all, he would have *realized* only $2 of gain. Nothing in the logic of Section 351 itself requires Darrell to be taxed on more gain than he had: that would be a kind of arbitrary overtaxation. Instead, the Code triggers just $2 of gain.
>
> Looking ahead, now that Darrell has *realized* all of his built-in gain, he should have a fair market value basis in his stock, and the corporation too should have a fair market value basis in Greenacre. And the basis rules accomplish just that.
>
> Section 358 gives Darrell a basis of $100 in his stock ($103 initial basis less $5 cash plus $2 gain). And Section 362 gives the corporation a basis of $105 in Greenacre ($103 initial basis plus $2 gain).

This is a fair amount of detail, and the numbers can get even more complex when there are multiple parties and different kinds of boot. But the basic philosophy of the boot rules should make some sense. The presence of cash in the deal alleviates the *valuation* problems that make *realization* tricky in a corporate formation. Cash has the lovely property that it is worth its face amount, and so we know that Darrell has received at least $5 in value. To that extent, then, the tax law can tag Darrell with gain and be confident that they haven't overtaxed him.

To be sure, the Section 351(b) rules implicitly require at least a rough valuation of Greenacre: Darrell can't know whether he has built-in gain at all unless he knows that Greenacre is worth more than his basis in it. But if, in a typical transaction, boot received is small in amount, and assets have been held for long

¶601

periods with substantial appreciation over time, then precise valuations won't be needed. Darrell can just report his $5 in gain and move ahead.

¶602 NONQUALIFIED PREFERRED STOCK

The Code's treatment of boot in corporate formations signals an important tax principle: even when the law otherwise permits *tax deferral*, the presence of cash in the deal will force *realization* to that degree. Thus, $10 of boot triggers up to $10 in gain recognition but leaves the remainder of the *tax deferral* intact.

As you can easily imagine, tax planners are well aware of this principle, and they've made it a priority to create legal workarounds. Of course, the easiest workaround is not to include any boot in the deal! When shareholders receive only stock in a corporate formation, and when they are in control afterward, the whole transaction is tax-deferred. But sometimes the parties need, or want, to include boot in the deal. So the Holy Grail for tax planners would be to create a payout that would "feel" cash-like to the shareholders but would not trigger *realization* under Section 351.

Enter preferred stock. (The business basics of preferred stock are covered below, in ¶605, infra.) Preferred stock is an odd animal even in its simplest form. It's counted as "stock" for Section 351 purposes, and yet it typically has many debt-like features, including a stated, fixed "principal" amount (called a par value) and a stated, fixed return (dividend rate).

> **EXAMPLE 4.** Company X issues preferred stock, with a par value of $100 and a fixed, annual dividend of 5% ($5 per share). The terms of the stock provide that the preferred is senior to the common stock in both dividends and liquidation proceeds. That is, if the annual dividend is unpaid, then Company X may not pay any dividends on any other class of stock (including common stock) until all dividends (including back dividends, or "arrearages") are paid on the preferred stock. And, if Company X liquidates, the preferred shareholders must receive $100 per share before the common is paid anything. Because market interest rates are 5% at the time of issuance, buyers pay Company X $100 per share of preferred.

Preferred stock, even in this plain vanilla form, lies somewhere on the financial spectrum between common stock and debt. The annual dividend promises a fair amount of liquidity, and the return is fixed and limited, so the preferred holders will not share in the upside or downside risk that the common stock bears. Preferred stock isn't quite debt, though, because it doesn't convey creditors' rights on the holders: if Company X doesn't pay its annual dividend, the preferred stockholders cannot force the company into bankruptcy.

Back in the 1980s, tax planners started to push the limits on preferred stock, loading up on "cash-like" features that were attractive to stockholders who wanted liquidity but taking the position that the interests remained "stock" for purposes of Section 351. The right to sell one's stock back to the issuing corporation for a fixed price, for instance, would ensure that stockholders could cash out at a set price, regardless of market price fluctuations. This kind of planning served a double purpose: it guaranteed liquidity to any shareholder who wanted it, while also permitting every shareholder to claim nonrecognition treatment.

In response, Congress enacted Section 351(g), which treats as "boot" any so-called nonqualified preferred stock in a transaction that otherwise meets the requirements of Section 351(a). If you have a look at Section 351(g), you'll see that Congress enumerated several features that are not terribly common (haha!) in plain-vanilla preferred stock that add significant liquidity and marketability. For example, stock is non-qualified preferred if the holder of the stock has the right to require the issuer to buy it back. And that should make sense: if I can require the issuer to buy my stock back for, say, $100 per share at any time, that's pretty cash-like. Most debt doesn't even have that feature.

> **EXAMPLE 5.** Bette contributes appreciated property to Hollywood Corp. in exchange for common stock worth $100 and non-qualified preferred stock worth $20. Under Section 351(g), Bette is taxed as if she received $100 in stock and $20 in cash "boot." Applying Section 351(b), Bette recognizes gain up to $20. (And, applying Section 358(a), she adjusts her basis downward by the fair market value of the nonqualified preferred stock and upward by the amount of gain recognized.)

The nonqualified preferred rules make sense as a response to tax planning, but they aren't costless in the tax system. The boot rules in Section 351(b) can pose a *valuation* problem if the boot in question is anything other than cash or marketable securities. And Section 351(g) potentially compounds that *valuation* issue by requiring taxpayers to determine the fair market value of stock in new companies, closely-held companies, and other hard-to-value situations.

¶603   COMPENSATION FOR SERVICES

You may recall from the basic tax course that there is a difference in the application of the *realization* requirement to income from labor and income from capital. Taxpayers who earn income from capital often can take advantage of tax deferral, as in the case of Section 1015 gifts, or even tax forgiveness, as in the case of Section 1014 inherited property. In contrast, taxpayers who earn wages and salaries typically must report the fair market value of their compensation as soon as they receive it. For instance, if I go to work for a big corporation, and they pay me some of my compensation in the form of company stock, I may very well have to immediately report ordinary income equal to the fair market value of that stock as soon as I receive it. (There are special rules that can grant *tax deferral* to the recipients of stock and stock options, but these are special exceptions and not the general rule.[1])

Section 351 reflects the same dichotomy between income from capital and income from labor. As we've already seen, taxpayers who contribute property can benefit from *tax deferral* provided they receive stock in the corporation. Taxpayers who contribute services, by contrast, cannot receive *tax deferral* in a corporate formation, even if they receive only stock and no cash at all.

> **EXAMPLE 6.** Harold and Doria have decided to incorporate a new business. Doria contributes cash of $100, and Harold agrees to work for the company for a low salary for at least two years. In exchange, Harold and Doria each receive 50% of the common stock.

You might understandably suppose that this is an incredibly common and plain-vanilla scenario. That's because it is. Very often, the founders of the firm bring different assets to the table. Some people have capital, some people have know-how and labor power. Nevertheless, Section 351 will not apply to the taxpayer who contributes services in exchange for his stock.

> **EXAMPLE 7.** Continuing Example 6, Section 351(a) cannot apply to Harold, because he contributed services and not "property." The result is that Harold must report ordinary income equal to the fair market value of the stock. And that value may be very hard to determine. We know that the new company has $100 in cash, thanks to Doria, but surely the promise of Harold's labor, and the prospect of future business revenues, are worth something too. In theory, the value of the stock equals the present value of all expected future cash flows that Harold will receive, extending into the infinite future. Needless to say, the problem here is not trivial.

The exclusion of contributed services from Section 351(a) ensures consistency across taxpayers. We've seen that compensation in the form of stock is generally taxable at fair market value. The "property" requirement in Section 351 ensures that taxpayers cannot use a corporate formation as a clever workaround to snare some unwarranted *tax deferral*.

But, as you can imagine, taxpayers have not accepted the differential treatment of property and services without a fight. One famous case is *James v. Commissioner*.[2] William James had agreed to form a corporation with C.N. and Lula Talbot. James was a builder, and the Talbots owned land, so it was a match made in real estate heaven. Until the IRS got involved.

James and the Talbots decided to build a rental apartment building. The Talbots agreed to contribute their property to a new corporation in exchange

---

[1] For the general rules, *see* Code Sec. 83.
[2] 53 T.C. 63 (1969).

for half of the stock. James agreed to oversee the business end of the development in exchange for the other half of the stock. He did quite a bit of legwork, negotiating with architects and lenders to put the deal together. Scrutinizing the transaction, the IRS concluded that James had received his half of the stock in exchange for services. The results were striking (and disastrous) for all concerned. James had to report the fair market value of the stock as ordinary income before he ever received a dime. And the Talbots suffered too, because the deal no longer qualified for Section 351 at all. Sure, they contributed property, but they received *only 50% of the stock*, not enough to meet the 80% "control" test.

But wait! Wasn't James part of the control group, since he and the Talbots acted together? Nope. If you go back and read Section 351(a) very closely, you'll see that only people who transfer property are counted in the "such person or persons" who must have control immediately after the transaction. Big lesson here: the services exclusion can mess up *tax deferral* for all the parties to the deal, not just the services provider himself.

James's lawyers tried valiantly to sneak his contributions into the "property" category. They argued that he contributed contracts including a loan commitment and agreements with architects and construction vendors. But the Tax Court looked to the substance of what James had done: he had used his know-how, connections, and hard work to put the deal together. The contracts weren't something James owned; instead, they were for the benefit of the new corporation. Personal services like this, the court concluded, just aren't property.

People in the Talbots' situation might be tempted to try a workaround. A literal reading of the Code suggests one: James would be treated as a transferor, and all his stock would be counted for control purposes, if he transferred any property at all. So maybe he could contribute a dollar along with his services. That idea wouldn't grant any *tax deferral* to James himself, since he'd still be receiving 99.9% of his stock for services. But it would preserve nonrecognition for the Talbots, since now James would be part of the control group, and together they'd have 100% of the stock.

The vulnerability of this plan is, of course, the *substance over form* doctrine. The transfer of $1 to preserve a tax goodie for someone else isn't, in substance, a meaningful transfer of property. The regulations under Section 351 reflect this approach: they provide that stock is not treated as issued for property if the contributed property is "relatively small" in comparison to the value of the stock received for services. So $1 wouldn't pass muster; James would have to come up with a chunk of money or actual property to be included in the control group.

¶603

¶604 PROBLEM 6.1: SECTION 351 AND BOOT

Luna and Harry plan to incorporate LunaCorp. Luna will contribute appreciated real estate (basis = 85, FMV = 100), and Harry will contribute $90 in cash. Luna and Harry will each receive 50% of the stock. In addition, to even out their financial contributions, Luna will receive $10 in cash "boot."
(1) Would Section 351 apply? Do you need more facts to answer with confidence?
(2) How would Luna and Harry be taxed?
(3) Can you think of any circumstance in which Luna or Harry would prefer to avoid Section 351?

ANSWER

The first step is to determine whether Section 351 applies. Looking at Section 351(a), we see that two shareholders have contributed property, and together they have received all of the stock of LunaCorp. It's a fair guess that the deal will qualify under Section 351, but to be 100% buttoned-up about it, we should find out more about the stock that Luna and Harry each receive to be sure it isn't nonqualified preferred subject to the Section 351(g) rules.

Assuming that Section 351 applies to both Luna and to Harry, we can begin with the tax treatment of Harry, which is straightforward. He contributed $90 of cash in exchange for stock, and so, under Section 358(a), he has a basis of $90 in his stock. Keep in mind that the fair market value of Harry's (and Luna's) stock is $90; the corporation initially received $90 from Harry and $100 in property from Luna, but it then paid out $10 in boot. So, the company now has total assets of $180.

Luna receives boot of $10, and so the rules of Section 351(b) come into play. She goes into the deal with built-in gain of $15 (the difference between the $100 fair market value of her real estate and its $85 basis). She must recognize $10 of gain, and her basis in the stock is $85. (Thus, she has remaining $5 of built-in gain in her stock, which is worth $90.) The corporation's basis in the real estate, per Section 362(a), is $95 (original basis of $85 plus Luna's gain of $10. (Thus, the corporation too has built-in gain of $5 – since the real estate has a fair market value of $100.)

Harry is, in effect, buying stock for cash, and so he's indifferent to whether Section 351 applies; he has no gain or loss either way. By contrast, a transferor of property, like Luna, might want to avoid Section 351 if she has a built-in loss in her real estate. Section 351 is asymmetrical: boot triggers gain but not loss. So, avoiding Section 351 would allow (indeed, require) Luna to treat the exchange as a realization event, permitting her to deduct the entire loss.

A taxpayer in Luna's situation might also prefer to avoid Section 351 if, for some reason, her marginal tax rate right now is much lower than it will be in the future. Tax planners usually assume that *tax deferral* is valuable to the taxpayer, because it permits the taxpayer to capture the time value of money on the unpaid tax. But if rates today are very low compared to the future, the lower tax rate may outweigh the disadvantage of realizing gain now.

¶605 BUSINESS 101: WHAT IS PREFERRED STOCK?

Corporations always issue common stock, but they may also issue preferred stock. Preferred stock typically has a "par value," analogous to the principal amount of a debt, and a "dividend rate," analogous to the interest payable on a debt. Thus, for example, I might buy preferred stock issued by General Motors, paying $1,000 (the par value) which preferred stock has a 7% dividend rate. Preferred stock may be callable by the company (meaning that the company can buy back the stock at a set price). It may or may not have voting rights (but typically does not).

You can think of preferred stock as a hybrid between debt and equity. Like debt, it promises holders a fixed set of payments. And, like debt, the fixed payments mean that preferred stockholders do not directly benefit if the corporation earns huge profits. (We say that the preferred stock does not fully participate in the upside of the business.) But like equity, preferred stock does not grant creditors' rights to holders. That is, if the company fails to pay dividends, the preferred stockholders cannot send the company into bankruptcy.

Still, preferred stock is senior to common stock in the event of bankruptcy. Typically, preferred stock is "preferred" in two ways: dividends and liquidation. The dividend preference means that the company must pay all outstanding dividends on preferred stock before it can pay any dividends on common stock. The liquidation preference means that when the corporation liquidates (winds up its business), it must repay the entire par value of the preferred stock before distributing anything to common stockholders.

> **EXAMPLE 8.** ABC Corp. has two classes of stock: common and nonvoting preferred. The preferred stock has a par value of $1,000 per share and a dividend rate of 5%. The dividend preference is cumulative, meaning that if ABC goes a year without paying preferred dividends, it still must eventually pay the unpaid amounts: the dividends "accumulate" over time. The preferred stock ordinarily does not confer rights to vote for the Board of Directors; however, if ABC goes two years without paying a preferred dividend, then the preferred stockholders as a class may elect 1/3 of the board.
>
> In Year One, ABC owes a total of $50,000 in preferred dividends (*i.e.*, there is $1 million par value of preferred stock outstanding, and it carries a 5% dividend rate). ABC has $70,000 of distributable earnings in that year, and the Board of Directors wants to pay the maximum dividend on the common stock. According to the terms of the

preferred stock, ABC must pay the entire $50,000 owed to the preferred stockholders before it can pay any dividends on the common. Thus, the maximum amount available for common dividends is $20,000.

In Year Ten, ABC winds up its business. It still has $1 million of preferred stock outstanding. After paying all debts and selling all assets, ABC has $1.2 million in assets. ABC must pay all $1 million owed to the holders of preferred stock. Thus, there is just $200,000 to be paid to the common stockholders upon liquidation.

If, in Year Ten, ABC had just $700,000 in assets, the entire amount would go to the preferred stockholders, and zero would go to the common stockholders.

If, in Year Ten, ABC had $5 million in assets, it would pay $1 million to the preferred stockholders and $4 million to the common stockholders.

CHAPTER 7

Realization: Corporate Distributions and Redemptions

Introduction	¶700
Realization and the Distribution Rules	¶701
Problem 7.1: Distributions and Dividends	¶702
Income Shifting and the Dividend Rules	¶703
Substance Over Form and Redemptions	¶704
Problem 7.2: Redemptions	¶705
Business 101: What is a Dividend? What is a Stock Buyback?	¶706
Advanced Problem	¶707

¶700 INTRODUCTION

The problem of *realization* causes repeated trouble for the corporate tax. At the corporate level, the *realization* requirement applies in the now-familiar ways that you've learned in the basic tax course. A C corporation realizes income when it sells property, collects rents, and so on. At the shareholder level, though, the problem of *realization* takes on a new form. The law must now define when shareholders have received a "dividend."

Now, you might think that it's pretty obvious when a dividend has been paid and received. After all, corporations announce their dividends proudly and publicly. So, if X Corporation decides to pay a dividend to its shareholders, it will issue a press release saying that a dividend of (say) 50 cents per share of common stock will be paid to all shareholders who hold stock on November 1.

All that is true, as far as it goes. A conventional cash dividend is definitely taxable to shareholders and constitutes a *realization* event. Done! But if you think about it, it's highly likely that taxpayers in this context will bring the same kinds of tax planning resources we've already seen time and again. This time, the goal of tax planning will be to avoid a *realization* event: If a clever tax planner can extract cash from the corporation without triggering a *realization* event, then the shareholder can continue to benefit from *tax deferral*.

> **EXAMPLE 1.** Carrie owns 20% of the stock of PrairieCorp. PrairieCorp. has amassed a large fund of cash from operations and could pay a large dividend. Carrie (and several other major shareholders) wouldn't mind having cash to spend and invest, but they'd prefer to continue deferring the shareholder-level tax if possible.

The key to tax planning in this context is to see that there are many different ways that a corporation might confer an economic benefit on its shareholders, and only some of these will be immediately recognizable as "dividends." Just off the cuff, you can probably think of a few possibilities. For instance, a corporation might loan money to its shareholders. Yes, the loans would eventually have to be repaid, but in the meantime the shareholder can use the cash, and, as we know from the basic tax course, the receipt of loan proceeds is not taxable. Presto! The shareholder has received cash and is not taxable on the cash as a dividend.

Another strategy might be for the corporation to pay for items that benefit shareholders. Maybe the corporation could pay a shareholder's rent, or provide one with a corporate car, or make investments that would personally benefit a shareholder. Here again, the corporation has used its assets to help out shareholders financially, but there is no public announcement, and no cash distribution.

We will see that the law has evolved to anticipate these kinds of tax strategies and more. The ingenuity of taxpayers is limitless, and the law has responded with burgeoning rules that attempt to counter the most common kind of tax planning. Still, we will see that a well-advised taxpayer can often, quite legally, navigate around these rules.

¶701   *REALIZATION* AND THE DISTRIBUTION RULES

Let's begin with the logic underlying the law, and then we'll dig into the details. The core task of the corporate distribution rules is to determine when to apply the second level of tax in the corporate double-tax system. More precisely, the second level tax is supposed to apply *when a corporation distributes its income to shareholders*. It follows, then, that the distribution rules must determine when a corporate distribution constitutes the distribution of "income" and when a corporate distribution should be taxed in some other way, or not at all.

The important point here is that Congress intends for the double tax to apply to corporate income, and not to distributions that are not income. How could a distribution not be income? Well it could be a return of basis, for example. We know from the basic course in taxation that basis measures what the taxpayer put into an investment. If I contribute $100 to a corporation and only ever get $100 back, it's apparent that I haven't made any money (and the corporation hasn't either). So, I shouldn't be taxable on the return of the $100.

For this reason, Code Sec. 301 distinguishes between a "distribution" and a "dividend." A distribution, generally speaking, occurs whenever a corporation transfers property to its shareholders. If I'm a shareholder in Apple, and the company sends me a check for $10, that's technically a "distribution." It may or may not also be a dividend, but to know whether it's a dividend we need some additional information. Specifically, we'll need to know whether the distribution was made out of income already realized at the corporate level.

This idea underlies the ordering rules that appear in Section 301(c). Paraphrasing, the law says that any distribution is, first, a "dividend" to the extent of a corporation's earnings and profits. (We will look at earnings and profits shortly, but it is basically a measure of income realized at the corporate level.) If a distribution exceeds earnings and profits, it is then treated as a return of basis to that extent. Any remaining distribution is treated as gain on the stock.

EXAMPLE 2. James is the sole shareholder of Trek Corp. James has a basis in his stock of $60, and the corporation has earnings and profits of $100. If Trek Corp. distributes $105 to James, the first $100 is a dividend, and the remaining $5 is a return of basis under Section 301(c). Accordingly, James realizes dividend income of $100. He does not pay tax on the $5 return of basis but, instead, reduces the basis in his stock to $55.

The central point to grasp at this stage is that corporate "distributions" are not always "dividends." Put another way, a corporation can dip into different pots of money to make distributions to shareholders. One source is corporate earnings, of course. But corporations may also return contributed capital to shareholders or, in some cases, make distributions based on income not yet realized at the corporate level.

That last scenario may be a little hard to grasp, but try an example. Suppose that a corporation has an asset with a very large but unrealized gain. The corporation doesn't want to sell the asset, because that would be a *realization* event. Instead, the corporation borrows against the asset and distributes the money to shareholders. (Remember that borrowing is not a *realization* event.) Because the corporation hasn't realized the gain, there is no corresponding amount of corporate income ("earnings and profits," to use the technical term). Thus, the distribution will be treated as a return of capital to shareholders and, after basis is exhausted, as a capital gain.

The easiest way to proceed (really!) is by example.

¶702 PROBLEM 7.1 DISTRIBUTIONS AND DIVIDENDS

Ursula is the sole shareholder of LeGuinCo., a C corporation ("LGC"). As of January 1, 2018, LGC had accumulated earnings and profits ("E&P") of $1 million. Ursula's marginal tax rate on ordinary income is 37%, and her marginal tax rate on long-term capital gains is 20%. Ursula has held her stock for 3 years as of January 1, 2018. Ursula's stock basis is $500,000.

How would the following transactions be taxed?

(a) In 2018, LGC has current E&P (computed as of December 31, 2018) of $200,000. On December 31, 2018, LGC distributes to Ursula $350,000 in cash.

(b) Same facts as in (a) except that LGC distributes Greenacre to Ursula (basis = $100,000, FMV = $350,000).
(c) Same facts as in (a) except that LGC distributes cash of $1,250,000 to Ursula.

ANSWER

To solve this problem, we have to take a tour through the various rules that work together to define when the distribution is a dividend. Section 316(a) defines a dividend as a distribution made out of earnings and profits. Earnings and profits, in turn, is defined in Section 312. Setting aside the complexities of Section 312, the basic idea is that earnings and profits represents a pool of after-tax corporate earnings out of which dividends might be paid. It isn't an actual pool of cash. There is no particular reason to suppose that a corporation would keep its earnings on hand in liquid form. Instead, earnings and profits is an account, a running tally of corporate income, less corporate taxes paid, and less distributions of dividends.

Applying these rules to part (a) of the problem, we now know that the key fact is that the corporation has current year E&P of $200,000 and accumulated E&P of $1 million. The key authorities here are Section 316 and the regulations that implement it. According to the regulations, we must perform a two-step analysis.[1] We first look to current-year E&P. Here, current E&P is $200,000, so we know that $200,000 of the $350,000 distribution is a dividend. The regulations under Section 316 tell us that we then look to accumulated E&P. In this case, accumulated E&P is $1 million, so that there is more than enough for the remainder of the distribution ($150,000) to be a dividend. So, we conclude that the entire $350,000 distribution is a dividend. Finally, we go back to Section 301(c), which tells us that the dividend is included in the income of the shareholder.

Part (b) of the problem involves a distribution of property in kind. Section 301(b)(1) tells us that the amount of the distribution is the fair market value of the property, or $350,000. The dividend analysis is the same as in part (a) of the problem: There is more than enough E&P for the entire distribution to be deemed a dividend and included in the shareholder's income.

Part (b) poses two additional issues. One is that since the shareholder receives Greenacre rather than cash, we need to know what her basis in the property is. Section 301(d) gives us the answer: She takes a fair market value basis of $350,000.

The second issue is whether the corporation itself incurs any tax on the distribution of Greenacre to its shareholder. On the one hand, a distribution doesn't

---

[1] Reg. §1.316-2(a) provides, in part, that "every distribution made by a corporation is made out of earnings and profits to the extent thereof and from the most recently accumulated earnings and profits. In determining the source of a distribution, consideration should be given first, to the earnings and profits of the taxable year; second, to the earnings and profits accumulated since February 28, 1913, only in the case where, and to the extent that, the distributions made during the taxable year are not regarded as out of the earnings and profits of that year."

¶702

feel like a sale or exchange under Section 1001, so it doesn't "feel" taxable. On the other hand, Greenacre does have a basis of only $100,000, meaning that in the hands of the corporation it has built-in gain of $250,000. That built-in gain disappears when Section 301(d) awards the shareholder a fair-market-value basis. There is a long history here, but for our purposes it is enough to say that Section 311(b) requires the corporation to treat the distribution of appreciated property as a *realization* event. In this case, then, LGC must report gain of $250,000, as if it had sold Greenacre. (The character of the gain will be determined under Section 1221, based on the corporation's use of Greenacre.)

Finally, part (c) of the problem illustrates what happens if a distribution exceeds E&P. The distribution of $1,250,000 exceeds the sum of current E&P ($200,000) plus accumulated E&P ($1,000,000). The result, per Section 301(c), is that the shareholder reports a dividend of $1,200,000, and reduces her basis in her stock by the remaining $50,000 of the distribution. Going forward, then, Ursula has a basis of $450,000 in her LGC stock.

¶703   *INCOME SHIFTING* AND THE DIVIDEND RULES

The dividend rules in Sections 301, 312, and 316 are highly formal. The rules don't attempt to measure anyone's Haig-Simons income, and they don't require taxpayers or the IRS to attempt the *valuation* of corporate stock. Instead, they create a set of predictable and administrable rules based on relatively easily audited corporate accounts. The advantage of this approach is that it's relatively simple, as things in the tax world go. But I'm sure that you can predict the downside: The use of highly formal rules can permit taxpayers to shift income and defer taxes.

We've already seen the potential for the corporate tax regime to create new options for *tax deferral*. The shareholder-level tax applies only when corporations choose to distribute income. And, per usual, we can expect that businesses and shareholders will exercise that choice in a way that minimizes their taxes. Indeed, we saw in Chapter 4 how the relationships among various tax rates can reward or penalize companies that pay dividends.

The next point is that the dividend rules also permit *income shifting* among taxpayers. Because dividend income is not linked to economic income, taxpayers may be able to choose not only *when* dividend income arises but also *which taxpayers* must report it.

> **EXAMPLE 3.** Aaron founds a C Corporation with a contribution of $10. Accordingly, Aaron has a basis in his stock of $10. In Year 1, the corporation earns $100; it does not earn any additional income in the future and is not expected to do so. Accordingly, the value of the corporation is $110, equal to Aaron's original $10 contribution plus the $100 in earnings. (Let's ignore the $21 in corporate tax that would be payable, just to make the math super easy.) Aaron's stock has appreciated by $100, but since he hasn't sold his stock, there's no *realization* event, and he owes no taxes in Year 1.

In Year 2, Aaron sells his stock to Betsy for $110. He now realizes a gain of $100 (remember, his basis is $10), and it's a capital gain under Section 1221, since (let's assume) he's an investor and not a dealer in stock. Note what has already happened: Aaron not only deferred his income (compared to Haig-Simons) by a year, but he also converted the character of the income into capital gain (rather than ordinary dividend income).

You might say, "So what?" After all, as of this writing (2020), the marginal tax rate on dividends is often the same as the rate on capital gains, thanks to Section 1(h)(11). But not all dividends are eligible for that lower rate. And, keep in mind that capital gains are usually better than ordinary income, because capital gains can offset capital losses.[2]

And, in any event, we aren't done. At the end of Year 2, Betsy now owns the stock. In Year 3, the corporation makes a distribution of $100, and since Betsy owns the stock, she receives the money. Note that Betsy *hasn't made a profit* on the stock, and her Haig-Simons income, accordingly, would be zero.

Put another way, the dividend itself doesn't make Betsy any better off economically. She paid $110 for the stock originally. She receives a dividend of $100 in cash, but the value of her stock will fall by the same amount. So, at the end of Year 3, Betsy has $100 in cash and stock worth $10—still a total of $110.

But the tax law puts on blinders to the economics of the deal. Instead, the distribution is a *realization* event, and, under the rules of Section 301, the whole distribution is a dividend, since the corporation has E&P of $100. So, Betsy has $100 of taxable dividend income, even though her economic income is zero.

At this stage, you might think that the whole situation is a mess (and you're right). But you might also think that the rules harm the taxpayer. After all, poor Betsy has to pay tax on the dividend even though she isn't any better off. But the advantage here is likely all to the taxpayer and against the IRS. The key is to realize that a savvy Aaron and Betsy will know the tax rules, and they will pair up in ways that minimize their taxes.

For instance, suppose that Aaron has lots of capital losses, so he can really use a capital gain to offset them. And suppose that Betsy has a low or even zero tax rate on dividends. Now, the game benefits the taxpayer: Aaron can legally report capital gains, while Betsy isn't too bothered by the artificial income produced by the dividend. Even if there's a small tax cost to Betsy, she and Aaron can adjust the stock price so that they both come out ahead after taking taxes into account.

---

[2] *See* Code Sec. 1211.

Year	Economic income	Distributions and sales	Aaron's income	Betsy's income
1 Aaron acquires stock for $10 and corporation earns $100	+$100	-	-	-
2 Aaron sells to Betsy for $110	0	Sale for $110	+$100 Capital gain	-
3 Corporation pays dividend of $100	0	Dividend of $100		+$100 Dividend
4 Betsy sells to C for $10		Sale for $10		-$100 Capital loss

And we aren't done with Betsy just yet. At this point, she has a basis of $110 in her stock, but the stock is only worth $10. When she sells the stock in Year 4, she will have a capital loss of $100. Once again, you might think, "Poor Betsy!" because she has $100 of dividend income and then a potentially unusable capital loss the next year. But the well-advised Betsys of the world will take all this into account.

When the dust clears, the tax system as a whole has—in a sense—gotten its share. Arithmetically, one capital gain of $100 reported by Aaron is offset by one capital loss reported later on by Betsy, leaving the appropriate $100 of dividend income reported by Betsy in the system. But along the way, the Code's formalistic dividend rules have created a situation that—for the well-advised—permits taxpayers to choose tax timing and the identity of the taxpayer who reports different types of income.

The easiest way to see the potential for tax planning here is to imagine it as a game. (A very nerdy game, but hey, this is tax.) The rules of the game are this: Find two taxpayers such that Taxpayer 1 prefers a capital gain, while Taxpayer 2 prefers the combination of dividend income and a capital loss. Go!

One possibility—maybe you'll think of others—arises when Taxpayer 2 is itself a corporation. Intercorporate dividends (*i.e.*, a dividend paid by one corporation to its corporate shareholders) are entitled to something called the dividends-received deduction, which lowers the tax rate.[3] Thus, a corporation is an excellent candidate for the role of Taxpayer 2 in the game: The dividend is taxed at a low rate, while the capital loss will offset otherwise-taxable capital gains. (Of course, a key planning point would be to ensure that the corporation has enough capital gains to make the capital loss valuable.)

The Code now limits this strategy, to a degree, by imposing a minimum stockholding period of 45 days for corporations wishing to claim the dividends-received deduction.[4] That rule prevents the easiest version of the game, in which a corporation snaps up the stock right before the dividend and sells right afterward.

---

[3] *See* Code Sec. 243.

[4] *See* Code Sec. 246(c).

Lightning transactions like that permit the corporate stockholder to make a pure "tax play" without much if any economic risk. The holding-period rule imposes an economic cost on the game—the corporate stockholder has to take some risk of price fluctuations in the stock during the 45 days. But the basic game remains on the shelf for savvy taxpayers to play.

¶704 SUBSTANCE OVER FORM AND REDEMPTIONS

Distribution rules have faced additional challenges from savvy tax planners. One headache has been the tax treatment of redemptions. A redemption is a transaction in which a corporation purchases its stock from its stockholders. You might hear the transaction called a "stock repurchase" or a "stock buyback," but the basic deal is the same.

Now, at first glance, a redemption is a straightforward sale of stock for cash. Clearly, it's a *realization* event. Section 1001 would seem to apply, and the usual tax consequences would follow: The taxpayer would recognize gain or loss based on her basis and the amount realized. And for most taxpayers, the gain (or loss) would be capital in character under Section 1221.

But a simple example will show you why a redemption might sometimes be a distribution in disguise.

> **EXAMPLE 4.** Josh is the sole shareholder of X Corporation. The corporation has plenty of E&P, and Josh would very much like to extract $10,000 in cash from the business, but he would prefer capital gain to dividend income. (Remember that dividends are ordinary in character and, therefore, less valuable than capital gains, because they cannot be used to offset capital losses.)
>
> Giving it a few minutes' thought, Josh realizes that he has a ready alternative to dividends that will meet his objectives. Since he's the sole stockholder, he could just sell some of his stock back to the corporation for $10,000 in cash. Presto! The corporation would have less cash; Josh would have more cash; and Josh would remain the sole shareholder in X Corporation.
>
> If the redemption of Josh's stock were taxed as a sale, it would indeed offer two tax advantages. First, Josh would have capital gain rather than ordinary dividend income. Second, under Section 1001, he would recover basis in his stock, reducing the amount of gain. For example, if he has a basis of $2,000 in the stock sold, his gain would be only $8,000 (compared to income of $10,000 if the payment were made as a dividend).

The problem for the corporate tax, then, is that redemptions can—especially in closely-held companies—be a tax-preferred substitute for dividends. The tax incentive to distribute via redemptions was especially strong under mid-twentieth-century tax rates. For years, the top marginal tax rate on dividends was

70% while, simultaneously, the top rate on long-term capital gains was 20%. A fifty-percentage-point gap in taxes fuels quite a lot of tax planning. The stakes are a bit lower today, but as Example 4 in Chapter 5 shows, there are still some tax savings to be had if a redemption can be substituted for a sale.

You can see that redemptions pose a *form-over-substance* problem. Before we had Section 302, taxpayers like Josh in Example 4 could reach the same financial result via different forms—with different tax consequences. Choose a dividend, and Josh is taxed one way; choose a redemption, and he's taxed in another.

The drafters of the Code might have taken a variety of approaches to the problem of redemptions. For instance, they might have adopted a bright-line rule treating all redemptions as distributions. But they didn't. Instead, they drafted a set of rules that take a *substance-over-form* approach. To be sure, Section 302 contains rules—it isn't the loose, judge-made standard you're familiar with. But Section 302 aims to distinguish between redemptions that function as sales and redemptions that function as distributions. So, the aim is, broadly, to look through to the substance of a redemption, past its form. (We will see this move made again and again in business taxation: Congress will add specific rules that aim to backstop the more general *substance-over-form* standard.)

Section 302 draws the dividing line based on the change in the taxpayer's percentage ownership in the corporation. A sole shareholder, like Josh, will find that (nearly) any redemption is treated as a distribution, because no redemption reduces his percentage ownership in the company. By contrast, a shareholder who significantly reduces her stake in the corporation may receive sale treatment.

The rules of Section 302 are complex and can be tricky. Reading closely is key, and the attribution rules of Section 318 introduce even more fun by treating members of a family (among other related parties) as owning one another's stock for purposes of determining percentage ownership. But the next section presents a problem set that illustrates the basic contours of the Section 302 regime.

¶705   PROBLEM 7.2: REDEMPTIONS

Hagrid and Ron formed Hippogriff Corp. ("HC") several years ago. The business has done well financially, but Ron has decided to move on in his career and go to law school. To pay his law school tuition, Ron needs to convert some of his HC stock to cash. Please consult Section 302 to analyze the tax consequences of the following transactions to Ron if (beforehand) Ron and Hagrid each own 50 shares of the single class of HC common stock. Assume that Ron and Hagrid begin with a basis of $4 per share of stock (or $200 in total basis for each).

(1)   Hagrid buys 10 shares from Ron for $1,000 (or $100 per share)

ANSWER TO (1)

This transaction is a sale, not a redemption, because no assets leave HC. Thus, Ron realizes and recognizes gain of $960 ($1,000 amount realized less basis of $40) under Section 1001. On these facts, the gain should be capital under Section 1221.

(2) HC buys 10 shares from Ron for $1,000.

ANSWER TO (2)

This time, it's a redemption, because HC is the buyer. Under Section 302(a), the redemption will be treated as an exchange (as in Part (1) of the problem) if any of the exceptions in Section 302(b) apply. Otherwise, the transaction is a distribution, as Section 302(d) tells us.

The easiest (and best) place to begin a Section 302 analysis is with the safe harbor in Section 302(b)(2). If Ron can meet that test, his redemption will be taxed as a sale. Reading the statute, we see that the redemption has to meet two tests:

- Ron must own less than 50% of the stock after the redemption
- He does meet this test. After the redemption, Ron owns 44% of the stock (40 of 90 shares outstanding). You might be a little confused about the 90 in the denominator there: Doesn't HC have 100 shares? The key is to realize that the redemption reduces the outstanding stock: The 10 shares HC buys are no longer out there.
- In addition, Ron's percentage ownership after the redemption must be less than 80% of his ownership beforehand.

You can think of this as a simple equation:

$$\frac{\% \text{ after}}{\% \text{ before}}$$

Plugging in the numbers, the ratio for Ron is 44%/50%, which is 88%. So, the redemption fails the Section 302(b)(2) test. Having failed the Section 302(b)(2) safe harbor, Ron must then look to the rest of Section 302(b) for relief. He can't meet Section 302(b)(3), because he isn't terminating his interest in HC. And we will just assume that Section 302(b)(4) and (b)(5) aren't relevant.

That leaves Section 302(b)(1) and the mysterious standard, "not essentially equivalent to a dividend." This is an old rule derived from even older case law. It's a catchall that is (very generally speaking) intended to allow an "out" for transactions that really don't feel like dividends but technically can't get to that result otherwise. Here, you could argue the point either way, with no completely

¶705

certain answer. On the one hand, Ron is reducing his ownership by only a small amount, and he's still a substantial shareholder. On the other hand, Ron no longer can block Hagrid's decisions with a 50-50 vote. He has given up control to Hagrid, and that could be a bigger deal than the raw numbers indicate.

Section 302(b)(1) is often frustrating in just this way. For that reason, taxpayers seeking certainty would be well-advised to meet the Section 302(b)(2) safe harbor if they can. For now, let's assume that Ron can't meet any of the Section 302 exceptions. The result is that the entire $1,000 is taxed as a distribution under the normal rules of Section 301. Assuming HC has plenty of E&P, Ron reports a dividend of $1,000.

One puzzle is what happens to the basis in the shares of stock Ron sells back to HC. After all, he simply doesn't have them anymore. The answer is that he adds the basis in those shares ($40 in the example) to his remaining stock. That's only fair—after all, Ron wasn't able to recover any basis in this redemption. The basis-preservation rule allows him to keep the basis and use it in the future. Small consolation, but something!

(3) How (if at all) would your answer to (2) change if HC redeems 20 shares (rather than 10) for $2,000?

ANSWER TO (3)

Now Ron meets the Section 302(b)(2) tests. After the redemption, he owns 30 of 80 shares or 37.5%. He's well under 50% ownership, and his Section 302(b)(2) fraction is 75% (37.5%/50%), which is (you'll be shocked to learn) less than 80%.

So, Ron is taxed as if the redemption is a sale. He reports a capital gain of $1920 ($2,000 less basis of $80).

(4) Consult Section 318 to figure out whether the answer to (2) and (3) would change if the other 50% of HC is owned by Ron's mother (Molly), rather than Hagrid.

ANSWER TO (4)

Some tax lawyers believe that Section 318 was a terrible late-night joke by the drafters of the Code that somehow got enacted into law. Section 318 imposes attribution rules that can be insanely complicated, and it draws a huge number of really arbitrary lines.

But there is some method behind the seeming joke. The idea is, once again, a kind of *substance-over-form* gambit. Taxpayers often don't live in isolation, after all. They have spouses, children, and parents. If a taxpayer could "sell" stock to another member of her family, she might look as if she had reduced her percentage ownership in the family business without, in substance, doing so.

¶705

So, Section 318 creates rules that attribute the stock owned by one member of a family to other members of the family. (Section 318 also applies to entities, including corporations, partnerships, and trusts under common ownership.) Put another way, Section 318 treats a family as a single taxpayer for purposes of Section 302 (and a couple of other corporate provisions).

Thus, if Ron's mother, Molly, owns the other 50% of HC, the Section 302 calculation for Ron changes quite a bit. Section 318(a)(1)(A) tells us that a taxpayer is treated as if he owns stock owned by his parents. Thus, Ron is treated as owning Molly's stock when we calculate the Section 302(b) change in ownership.

Applying these rules, Ron can't get sale treatment on these facts. Before the redemption, he is deemed to own 100% of the HC stock (*i.e.,* his stock plus Molly's). After the redemption, he still owns 100% of the stock, because he is still treated as owning Molly's stock. Accordingly, Ron fails Section 302(b)(2) left and right. He owns more than 50% of the stock and he hasn't reduced his percentage ownership at all.

He also can't argue that he qualified under Section 302(b)(1), because he hasn't changed his percentage ownership or control position at all.

Accordingly, Ron reports a $2,000 distribution, which will be a dividend if HC has sufficient E&P.

¶706 BUSINESS 101: WHAT IS A DIVIDEND? WHAT IS A STOCK BUYBACK?

We've seen that the term dividend has a very specific meaning in tax. But dividend is also a term that you'll hear in business and in corporate law, and its meaning changes a bit depending on context.

In the business world, a dividend usually means a cash dividend paid to a stockholder. If you listen to the business news, you'll often hear that some public company or another has declared a dividend, and the announcer will say that the dividend is some amount per share like $0.50. So, if Apple, for example, declared a $0.50 dividend, and you own one hundred shares, Apple would send you a check for $50. Just as classroom examples predict, the price of stock declines following the payment of a dividend to reflect the outflow of cash from the corporation.

Closely-held corporations can also pay dividends, but they have a different business "feel." That's because, in a closely-held company, most or all of the shareholders are also insiders and are involved with management decisions. So, when a closely-held company distributes a dividend, it's usually not news to the shareholders. They have probably consulted among themselves to decide how much the company can afford to distribute and when.

Why do companies pay dividends? The starting point is to remember that a corporation isn't really a "thing" and certainly is not a person. It's just the legal name that we give to a set of standard contracts that enable people to come together to engage in business. Stockholders are people who bring money, or capital, to the business. Like any other investor, a stockholder expects to earn a return on her money. And we can actually be more precise than that: If shareholders are rational, then they should only buy stock in Company A if the expected return is greater than the return on stock in Company B. Otherwise, they should buy the B stock.

Continuing on with this perspective, dividends are just the name we give to the payment of cash by a corporation to its stockholders. There are lots of reasons why stockholders might want cash. Most ordinary people need cash most of the time, after all! But in the context of big business, we assume that stockholders are wealthy and hold diversified investments, so that they could raise cash in other ways if it makes sense to do so.

Once we make all these assumptions, you can see that a rational stockholder would want a company to keep its cash as long as the company can produce a return that is greater than the return on any alternative investment. Concretely, if Company A is producing 10% annually, while Company B is only producing 7%, then a stockholder would want Company A to retain and reinvest its earnings (as long as the reinvested money can earn the same 10%). A stockholder in Company B, by contrast, would want the corporation to pay dividends (and maybe go out of business altogether).

This is a simple theory, and a stylized one, but it's still useful to see why management might pay dividends (or not), reflecting stockholders' best interests.

¶707 ADVANCED PROBLEMS

For more advanced problems, *see* Problems C2, C3, and C4 in Appendix C. (Problem C3 also contains material discussed in Chapter 8).

CHAPTER 8

Substance Over Form: Disguised Dividends and Stock Dividends

Introduction	¶800
Disguised Dividends	¶801
Stock Dividends and *Eisner v. Macomber*	¶802
Stock Dividends and Code Sec. 305	¶803
Problem 8.1: Disguised Dividends and Stock Dividends	¶804
Advanced Problem	¶805

¶800 INTRODUCTION

People don't like taxes. (A blinding insight, I know. Do take a moment to recover from the shock.) And so, given the choice, taxpayers will avoid or defer the tax on dividends. In this chapter, we explore two sets of rules – one made by judges, and one by the Congress – that take a *substance over form* approach to detect and tax hidden dividends.

¶801 DISGUISED DIVIDENDS

The easiest way to avoid the dividend tax is to avoid paying a dividend. That sounds like a (really lame) joke, but it's actually a fundamental point about corporate tax planning. As you know, shareholders do not pay taxes on retained earnings until dividends are paid, and this *tax deferral* can be valuable, as Chapter 2 shows, depending on the relationships among tax rates.

But shareholders may chafe at the absence of distributions. Small business owners, in particular, may need distributions in order to pay their bills; when their business is also their sole investment, they may not have a meaningful choice about deferring dividends.

For that reason, the disguised dividend has been a favorite gambit of closely-held businesses ever since the advent of the shareholder-level tax. By disguising a dividend as something else, shareholders hope to avoid the distributions tax. But the IRS quickly grew wise to these wiles, and a body of case law has developed to help the IRS and the courts ferret out dividends-in-disguise.

You may have already encountered a disguised dividend in your basic course on taxation. One common case is *Exacto Spring Corporation v. Commissioner*,[1] in which the IRS alleged that salary paid to the CEO was actually a disguised dividend. You can now revisit the facts with a firmer grip on the corporate tax angle. William Heitz was both the chief executive and majority shareholder of the Exacto Spring Corporation. He earned a high salary (more than $1 million per year), but the corporation had paid out very little in dividends, despite being highly profitable.

The IRS argued that Heitz – who had *de facto* control of the corporation – had inflated his salary in order to avoid the corporate double tax on dividends. As you know, salary is deductible, while dividends are not, and under the rate schedule at the time, dividends were taxed at the same rate as salary. So Heitz could effectively avoid the corporate-level tax on any profits sent out as "compensation" rather than as a "dividend."

The facts of *Exacto Spring* posed a *valuation* problem for the court. The company argued that Heitz was worth his $1 million salary, and the company had simply retained its earnings all this time. That sounds like a reasonable business decision, at least on its face, and the court faced a nearly impossible task in determining whether Heitz was overpaid, because both Heitz and his product were unique. There simply was no comparable employee in a comparable company.

The Seventh Circuit opinion by Judge Posner is a fun read. It begins by eviscerating the multi-factor test, derived from the case law, that attempts to determine whether someone is overpaid. Posner criticized the test as unreliable in concept and misapplied in practice. The multi-factor approach, he wrote, "does not provide adequate guidance to a rational decision."

Posner instead endorsed the "independent investor" test, which he described as providing an indirect market test. Under the independent investor test, a judge (or the IRS) asks what rate of return a shareholder would expect, *ex ante*, to receive on an investment in the particular corporation, taking into account the riskiness of the venture and so on. If the investor ultimately receives at least that return, then the tax law treats any compensation paid as reasonable. The logic is that compensation is economically reasonable if shareholders as a group have received an adequate return on their capital. Under this test, compensation would be excessive only if compensation is so high that investors have been denied their expected return.

Judge Posner's criticism of the conventional seven-factor test has considerable merit. In many cases, judges have very limited ability to determine whether a given executive is overpaid, and the multi-factor test requires them to do just that. The catch is that the independent investor test doesn't avoid the *valuation* problem – it just shifts it to a new arena. The problem, keep in mind, is to come

---

[1] 196 F.3d 833 (7th Cir. 1999). This case is also discussed in Alstott, Taxation in Six Concepts (CCH 2018) at ¶803.

up with a method of measuring the relative value of labor and capital contributed by an individual to a corporation. (Heitz, for instance, contributed his labor as CEO and his capital as a shareholder.) The conventional test attacks the problem by valuing the labor component. The independent investor test flips the inquiry: it attempts to value the return on capital and then assumes that the rest can be attributed to labor.

The catch is that setting a value on the return to capital is not, in principle, any easier than determining reasonable compensation. The facts in *Exacto Spring* are atypical here, because the IRS's own expert found that the investors expected a 13% return. Given that finding, the way was open for Judge Posner to apply the independent investor test and resolve the case. But once the independent investor test is adopted, the IRS and taxpayers will face the task of determining what rate of return investors in a specific corporation would have demanded, years ago, in order to make their investment. The expected rate of return is not an item stated in corporate documents: corporate equity by its nature does not guarantee any particular return.

And expected rates of return vary from company to company based on the risk and return profile of the particular business and industry. So, the independent investor test, in practice, may ultimately prove as messy and variable as the despised seven-factor test. The unavoidable problem is that the law demands *valuation* in the context of closely-held businesses, where valuing either labor or capital is likely to be difficult.

Exacto Spring illustrates one common fact pattern – a dividend (arguably) disguised as compensation. But shareholders have found other ways to cloak dividends in more tax-favorable garb. For instance, in *Baumer v. United States*, the IRS alleged that a father had steered a favorable business opportunity away from his wholly-owned corporation and to his son.[2] The benefit of the resulting deal, the IRS argued, was in effect a dividend to Baumer, followed by a gift to his son.

Simplifying a bit, in *Baumer*, the corporation granted an option to the son to purchase real property on favorable terms. The corporation charged a nominal fee of $10 for the option, but the son, er, failed to pay even that. (Killer fact!) Later on, a buyer offered to purchase the property at a good price. The son exercised his option and made a tidy profit.

Baumer argued that the whole scenario was just a canny business deal with his son as full co-partner. The IRS recharacterized the facts as a sweetheart deal engineered to transfer corporate funds directly to Baumer's son. Since Baumer (and not his son) was the owner of the corporation, the IRS contended, the deal was in substance a disguised dividend to Baumer, followed by a gift to his son.

Baumer also posed a *valuation* issue for the court, because the corporation hadn't transferred cash to the son. Instead, it transferred an option. In principle, the deemed dividend to Baumer should have been the value of the option at the

---

[2] 580 F.2d 863 (5th Cir. 1978).

¶801

time it was granted to the son. But at that time, the value wasn't readily determinable. The strike price (exercise price) of the option was the fair market value of the land at the time. But the son received the option for free, meaning that he would capture any future appreciation in the property's value.

Now, valuing an option is a tricky business, because the value of an option is a complex function of probabilistic changes in asset prices and interest rates, among other variables. (Indeed, option valuation is so difficult that the 1997 Nobel-equivalent prize in economics went to two professors who developed a formula for doing it.) In *Baumer*, the appeals court recognized the *valuation* problem and resolved it by holding the transaction open (for valuation and tax liability purposes) until the date that the son exercised the option.

¶802   STOCK DIVIDENDS AND *EISNER V. MACOMBER*

We usually think of, and portray, *substance over form* as a judge-made doctrine. But the idea of taxing in accordance with economic substance can be (and often is) built into statutory rules. In Chapter 7, we saw that Code Sec. 302 recharacterizes some redemptions as distributions. While the rules of Section 302 are (mostly) bright-line, they do serve the purpose of distinguishing redemptions that function as sales from distributions in disguise.

But taxpayer ingenuity is limitless, and so the Code has still more rules that aim to identify disguised distributions.

Section 305 of the Code addresses what we call colloquially a "stock dividend." A stock dividend occurs when a corporation distributes additional stock to its existing stockholders. The stockholders may receive shares of the same kind of stock they already own, or they may receive shares of a different class of stock, including newly created classes of stock. The key is that a stock dividend is made in kind, in the form of the corporation's own stock, and is distributed (not sold) to the existing stockholders.

(An important aside on terminology: the uninitiated may refer to *all* dividends as "stock dividends," using the term to mean "a dividend paid on corporate stock." But in the language of tax, a "stock dividend" refers only to the in-kind distribution of stock. A stock dividend, then, is a specific subset of the larger class of dividends, which in turn is a subset of the larger class of distributions.)

Now, you've probably already encountered a stock dividend, although you may not remember. In most basic tax courses, students read the famous case, *Eisner v. Macomber*,[3] to illustrate the *realization* requirement. When we teach the case in basic tax, we frame the legal issue in *Macomber* as whether a stock dividend paid to a shareholder creates a taxable event or not. But now that you know some corporate tax, we can deepen our understanding of *Macomber* as a case that addresses stock dividends.

---

[3]   252 U.S. 189 (1920). This case is also discussed in Alstott, Taxation in Six Concepts (CCH 2018) at ¶ 603.

The basic facts are easy. Mrs. Macomber was a common stockholder in Standard Oil, who received a stock dividend of additional shares of common stock. (This is, unsurprisingly, called a common-on-common stock dividend.) The tax controversy arose because, in 1916, Congress enacted a Code section that provided that shareholders would be taxed on stock dividends. More precisely, the Code provisions specified that the market value of a stock dividend would be considered a distribution. A distribution, under the rules you now know, is taxable as a dividend to the extent of corporate E&P.

In the basic tax course, we discuss *Macomber* as a case about timing: when will Mrs. Macomber *realize* her stock's appreciation for tax purposes? Mrs. Macomber took the position that a stock dividend did not constitute a *realization* event, implying that she should be taxed only upon a cash dividend or sale of the stock.

From the perspective of the corporate tax, we can frame the issue differently. The asset in question here is corporate stock, and the legal issue is the timing of the collection of the second level tax on corporate earnings. Put another way, the corporate earnings here (the profits of Standard Oil) have already been realized at the corporate level, but the corporation has retained its earnings. The issue before the court, then, is what kind of events constitute a "distribution" that triggers the shareholder level tax on those retained earnings.

The subject of *Macomber* is a Code section taxing stock dividends. The statute expressed Congress's position that any distribution by a corporation, whether in cash or in the form of stock, was sufficient to tax the shareholder on a portion of corporate earnings. Congress was concerned that stockholders could evade the second level of tax on corporate income by forgoing cash dividends. In order to collect the second level tax, Congress decided to tag the payment of stock dividends as a "distribution," and to measure the amount of the distribution by the value of the additional stock received.

You might reasonably object that the congressional rule seems like an arbitrary approach to *valuation*. After all, the payment of a stock dividend is a purely formal event. It doesn't make the shareholder any richer. And the value of the stock dividend may bear no relationship to the gains (or losses) experienced by individual shareholders. A simplified version of *Macomber* will illustrate the point.

EXAMPLE 1. Suppose that Mrs. M. is the sole shareholder of Standard Oil. She owns one share, which she initially bought for $1. In Year 1, the stock appreciates to $200. In Year 2, when the stock price is still $200, the corporation pays a stock dividend of one share per share owned.

The stock dividend, standing alone, should not change the total value of the company. Before the stock dividend, Mrs. M. had one share of stock worth $200. After the stock dividend, she has two shares, each worth $100. The *per share* price has declined. But the total value of her Standard Oil holdings is the same.

The Code section at issue in *Macomber* would have taxed her on the value of the new stock distributed to her, or $100. But the $100 value is not linked in any clear way to Mrs. M's economic position. She has made (on a mark-to-market basis) $199, not $100.

And, weirdly, the amount of Mrs. M.'s income under the congressional approach depends on the ratio of the stock dividend to the existing stock outstanding. Suppose that Mrs. M. had received a two-for-one stock dividend, *i.e.*, two new shares for each one share she started with. She would then end up with three shares. The total value of her stock would still be $200, and her gain is still $199. But now, each share would be worth $66.67. And so, the stock dividend of two shares would constitute a distribution of $133.33!

The arbitrariness of the *valuation* approach here might seem to be a decisive argument against the congressional approach and in favor of Mrs. Macomber. But think about the distribution rules we learned in Chapter 7. Section 301 itself reflects an arbitrary measure of shareholder income – measured against the baseline of a mark-to-market approach. Exhibit A is the *income shifting* mandated by the character and timing rules that govern dividends. (See ¶702 of Chapter 7.) The Code routinely over- and undertaxes shareholders (measured against a mark-to-market baseline) because cash distributions out of E&P represent a formalistic and arbitrary approach to *valuation*.

Despite all this, the Court in *Macomber* struck down the stock dividend statute as unconstitutional. The Court reasoned that the Sixteenth Amendment authorized income taxation, but that a tax on stock dividends lay outside the scope of any proper income tax.

Summing up: when we read *Macomber* from a corporate tax perspective, we can understand the Court's holding as saying something about the events that fall within the "distribution" rules in Section 301. Read in this light, *Macomber* holds that a distribution of common-on-common is not such an event. That narrow rule is still good law today, and it's reflected in Section 305. But Congress has, over time, restricted *Macomber* to that narrow holding: we will see that other kinds of stock dividends now are taxable as distributions.

¶803   STOCK DIVIDENDS AND CODE SEC. 305

Today, Section 305 prescribes the treatment of stock dividends, and on a first look, it's kind of a mess. The general rule, found in Section 305(a), codifies the *Macomber* result: the default is that stock dividends are not taxable. That makes sense. But Sections 305(b) and (c) then carve out what seem to be a hodgepodge of exceptions involving different configurations of common and preferred stock. It isn't immediately clear what work the exceptions are doing or how they can even be valid, given the holding in *Macomber*.

But on a closer look, there is a method to the seeming madness. The task of Section 305 is to distinguish between taxable and non-taxable stock dividends. And the drafters of the statute had to do that in the shadow of *Macomber*. And so, you can begin to see that the exceptions in Sections 305(b) and (c) must identify stock dividends that – in some way – represent a clearer *realization* of dividend income than a straight common-on-common distribution.

In fact, the rules reflect a very basic idea: taxpayers should be taxed when stock dividends are, in *substance*, a substitute for a cash distribution. This principle explains Section 305(b)(1), which taxes a stock dividend if the shareholder had (and declined) the option to receive cash.

> **EXAMPLE 2.** C Corporation has one class of common stock. It notifies shareholders that they may elect to receive either (a) a cash dividend of $1 per share or (b) one additional share of common stock. Theresa elects to receive the stock. She nevertheless will be treated as having received a distribution equal to the fair market value of the common stock, and that distribution will be taxable under the rules of Section 301. (That is how Section 305(b) operates: a taxable stock dividend is treated as a distribution of property, governed by the rules of Section 301.)

This result should make sense under a principle called "constructive receipt." The idea is that a taxpayer shouldn't be able to fend off taxable income by choosing to receive it later. So, if, for instance, my employer writes me a check for my salary on December 31, I am taxable when I receive the check, even if I choose to cash it in January (the next taxable year).

Theresa in the example is in a similar situation: she could have received cash but chose to receive additional stock.

We can now see how Section 305(b)(1) can be reconciled with *Macomber*. In *Macomber*, the shareholder didn't receive cash and had no option to receive cash from the corporation. She could have sold her stock, yes, but that would have changed her percentage ownership in the corporation. So, Section 305(b)(1) operates in a different space: where the taxpayer could receive a cash distribution but chooses not to.

Once you understand Section 305(b)(1), it's a short hop to Section 305(b)(2), which taxes a stock dividend if some shareholders receive stock while others receive property (remember that "property" is defined in Section 317(a) as anything *other than* stock in the distributing corporation). Section 305(b)(2) is really a backstop to the choice rule, because it describes essentially the same kind of situation: some shareholders get cash (say) while others get stock.

You might object that there's no choice in this case, and that seems like a big deal initially. But keep in mind the *alter ego* problem: shareholders control the corporation. And so, it's unlikely that the corporation will force a cash payout or a stock dividend on unwilling shareholders. (That's like saying that I forced myself to choose candy over broccoli. Really, I had no choice!) Typically, these

¶803

scenarios involve different classes of stock, with shareholders choosing which class to own based on whether they want cash payouts or not.

EXAMPLE 3. C Corporation has issued two classes of common stock, Class A and Class B. Halle owns all 100 shares of Class A and prefers cash dividends. Igor owns all 100 shares of Class B and prefers that the corporation retain earnings so that he can defer taxes. C Corporation's articles of incorporation provide that it may pay a dividend on the Class A stock and not on the Class B stock. In the event of liquidation, holders of the Class A and Class B stock will share liquidation proceeds based entirely on the number of shares owned (of any class of common stock). For instance, if at liquidation, one person owns three shares of Class B, while another owns one share of Class A, the former receives three times the liquidation payout as the latter.

In 2019, C Corporation pays a dividend of $100 per share on the Class A common and a two-for-one stock dividend on the Class B common. Accordingly, Halle receives a check for $10,000 ($100 x 100 shares), and Igor receives 200 additional shares of Class B common stock for a total of 300 shares.

In this situation, Halle is clearly taxable on her cash dividend under Section 301; nothing in Section 305 changes that. The issue here involves Igor. At first glance, he seems to fall squarely within *Macomber:* he has received a common-on-common stock dividend and had no option to receive cash.

But when you think about what just happened, you realize that Igor isn't in a Macomber situation at all. In *Macomber,* all common stockholders received a stock dividend and only a stock dividend. The result was twofold: (a) no stockholder received cash, and (b) no stockholder increased their percentage interest in the corporation.

But here, one stockholder (Halle) did get cash, while the other (Igor) increased his percentage ownership in the corporation. Before the stock dividend, Halle and Igor were equal claimants on the company: each held 100 shares of common stock and would receive half of the liquidation proceeds if the company dissolved. But after the stock dividend, Igor had three times the claim on the company that Halle had: he owned a total of 300 shares to her 100. And so, if the company liquidated, he would receive three-fourths of the total payout (300/400).

Section 305(b)(2), then, is a backstop to Section 305(b)(1). It captures cases in which there is no *formal* choice between cash and a stock dividend, but the corporate structure creates the *substance* of choice: in the example, Halle and Igor had deliberately opted into different kinds of common stock that would carry different dividend policies.

CHAPTER 8 | Substance Over Form: Disguised Dividends and Stock Dividends

The rest of the exceptions in Section 305 are variations on the same theme. We won't go through them in detail – hey, we have to leave something for the professor to do in class! But when you work through them, you'll see that each exception follows the same pattern: the Code's drafters were trying to anticipate clever taxpayers who would create classes of stock that would direct cash to some shareholders while awarding others a greater stake in the company.

¶804 PROBLEM 8.1: DISGUISED DIVIDENDS AND STOCK DIVIDENDS

(1) Marianne is the sole shareholder of Sensibility, Inc., a C corporation. The business has done well, and Marianne is financially comfortable. Marianne's sister, Elinor, has been less fortunate, and Marianne would like to help her out. Marianne arranges for Sensibility, Inc., to lease a car for Elinor's use at a cost of $1,000 per month. Please comment on the federal income tax consequences, if any, of these arrangements.

ANSWER TO (1)

You might think that Elinor should have income of $1,000 per month, since she's the one getting the free car (and apparently a rather nice one!). But the key issue is *why* Sensibility, Inc. is providing her with the car.

The answer is not (on the facts given) that Elinor is working for the company; if that were true, then some or all of the $1,000 might be taxable as wages to Elinor and would be deductible by the corporation. Nor, on the facts given, is Elinor a customer, who receives the car because Marianne wants to cement a business relationship. In that case, the corporation could deduct the lease payments as a business expense, and Elinor would have to include those amounts in income.

Instead, Sensibility is providing Elinor with the car at Marianne's direction, and Marianne's motive is personal. When a corporation spends money to further the personal objectives of its shareholder, the result is a deemed distribution. Here, Marianne should be deemed to receive a distribution from Sensibility, Inc. equal to the $1,000 monthly lease payments. The distribution will be taxed under the usual rules of Section 301; assuming that Sensibility has sufficient earnings and profits, the entire amount will be a dividend.

But wait! Isn't Elinor now taxed a second time? That seems pretty harsh. But, in fact, Elinor won't have to pay any tax at all. Marianne (per the facts) seems to be motivated by "detached and disinterested generosity" toward her sister, and so the $1,000 per month should be excludable to Elinor as a gift under Section 102.[4]

---

[4] The "detached and disinterested" standard comes from *Comm'r v. Duberstein*, 363 U.S. 278 (1960), which is also discussed in Chapter 3 of Alstott, TAXATION IN SIX CONCEPTS (Wolters Kluwer 2018).

(2) Jude owns 100 shares of the single class of common stock in Obscure Corporation, a C corporation. How would the following transactions be treated for federal income tax purposes?
   (a) Obscure Corporation distributes to Jude (and the other common shareholders) one share of common stock for each current share owned. Thus, Jude receives an additional 100 shares of Obscure Corporation common stock.

ANSWER TO (2)(a)

This case echoes *Eisner v. Macomber*. Jude and the other shareholders receive only common stock, and so no one's percentage ownership in the company increases. The stock dividend is not taxable under Section 305(a).

   (b) Obscure Corporation offers its common shareholders a dividend reinvestment plan. Shareholders may choose to reinvest their quarterly dividend in Obscure stock without paying any brokerage fees (as stockholders would have to do if they purchased more stock in the stock market). Jude goes online and enrolls in the dividend reinvestment plan. Accordingly, his next quarterly dividend of $100 ($1 per share) is reinvested in $100 worth of Obscure Corporation common stock.

ANSWER TO (2)(b)

The element of choice here should tip you off that Section 305(b)(1) has come into play. In joining the dividend reinvestment plan, Jude has, in substance, elected to receive additional common stock in lieu of a cash dividend. (By the way, a dividend reinvestment plan is a real thing.) The result under Section 305(b)(1) is that Jude is taxed on the $100 dividend, even though he received no cash.

And those pressure points, those gaps in the law, motivate how taxpayers strategize – and how Congress and the IRS respond.

¶805 ADVANCED PROBLEM

For a more advanced problem, which also contains material from Chapter 7, *see* Problem C3 in Appendix C.

CHAPTER 9

Realization and *Tax Deferral* in Corporate Acquisitions

Introduction.. ¶900
The Basics of Taxable Acquisitions: Just Two Structures .... ¶901
Realization and Taxable Acquisitions .... ¶902
Tax Deferral and Reorganizations.. ¶903
Problem 9.1: Taxable Acquisitions and Reorganizations........................... ¶904
Business 101: What is a Corporate Acquisition................................. ¶905
Advanced Problem .... ¶906

¶900 INTRODUCTION

Corporate acquisitions are the stuff of headlines. Disney buys Fox! AT&T buys Time Warner! And so, as you might expect, tax planning for acquisitions is itself a big business. A larger or smaller tax bill could change the form, the pricing, or even the feasibility of a corporate takeover.

Still, the tax basics of corporate acquisitions will feel very familiar to you, because the basic problem is one of *realization*. Some takeovers, called taxable acquisitions, require the *realization* of gain or loss. Others, called tax-free reorganizations (a term that we will see is a misnomer), award *tax deferral* and use a carryover basis regime similar to the Section 351 rules on corporate formation.

This chapter introduces the basics of taxable and tax-free acquisitions. Chapter 10 will delve into greater detail on the important topic of tax-free reorganizations, which combine complicated statutory requirements with a penumbra of judicial doctrines grounded in *substance over form*.

You probably feel that you know quite a bit about *realization*, and you do. For that reason, taxable acquisitions are going to be a breeze. The one new wrinkle is that *realization* can occur at two levels, thanks to the two-level corporate tax. That is, a given deal could trigger the reporting of gain or loss by shareholders, the corporation, or both.

One critical caveat: form often governs in the taxation of corporate acquisitions, so the formalities matter. Depending on the form chosen, the very same economic deal can be taxed very differently. Put another way, tax planning in this arena is dangerous stuff: even a small change in form can trigger a big change in tax liability.

¶901 THE BASICS OF TAXABLE ACQUISITIONS: JUST TWO STRUCTURES

From a tax perspective, a corporate acquisition is a *realization* event. The owners of the target business sell it to new owners for money, stock, or other consideration. In *Cottage Savings*[1] terms, the sellers have exchanged one set of legal entitlements for another: the owners of the target used to own a business, and now they own money (or stock, or other consideration).

Simplifying a bit, the tax law recognizes two structures: a stock sale and an asset sale. A stock sale typically involves the *realization* of one level of tax, while an asset sale usually (but not always) involves two levels of realized tax.

Now, you might take pause at my claim that there are only two kinds of structures for corporate acquisitions. If you read any business site, you'll see reference to a wide variety of possibilities: mergers, tender offers, subsidiary mergers, stock-for-stock deals, and so on. But this is the rare occasion where the tax law takes a relatively simple approach, squeezing most of these variations into just two boxes: stock sale or asset sale.

To explain how the tax law fits all corporate acquisitions into these two categories, we need some terminology to describe acquisitions. Four business terms will help us describe the key features of corporate acquisitions. First, there is the *target corporation* (or just the *target*). The target is the corporation that is the object of the acquisition. The buyer (which may itself be a corporation or an individual) wants to acquire the business owned and operated by the corporate target.

Second, there are the *selling shareholders*. Any corporation, as you know, has shareholders (or stockholders). As a group, the stockholders own the corporation in the sense that they elect the board of directors and own the residual claim on corporate profits. So, one way to sell a corporation is to sell all of its stock (or at least a controlling stake of stock). In that scenario, the shareholders are the sellers. The buyer will often pay them cash for their stock, but deals can also be done for any kind of consideration, as long as the parties agree.

Third, there can be a *selling corporation* – that is, a target corporation that sells its own assets to the buyer. Legally, any corporation can sell its own assets, including the entirety of its business. This kind of acquisition can be challenging for lawyers to document because it requires writing contracts that list every asset of the company, including intangibles like goodwill. But it can be – and is – done, often for business reasons.[2]

Fourth, when a selling corporation has sold all its assets, it may well go out of business. When the corporation takes formal steps to dissolve, we call it a *liquidation*. Typically, the target corporation in an asset sale liquidates after selling all

---

[1] *Cottage Savings Ass'n v. Comm'r*, 499 U.S. 554 (1991).
[2] See *Business 101: What is a Corporate Acquisition?* in ¶905, below.

of its assets, and that makes sense: there's nothing left except cash (the proceeds of the acquisition), and the shareholders want to take their money and dissolve the remaining corporate shell. And so, the corporation files papers with its state of incorporation and makes a final liquidating distribution to shareholders. The shareholders receive the proceeds of the acquisition, and their shares disappear (legally speaking), because there is no longer a corporation.

In some asset sales, the target corporation may stay in existence instead of liquidating. That scenario is most common when the target has sold some but not all its assets. For instance, a corporation with two lines of business might have sold off just one line. And so, it might retain the sales proceeds and reinvest them in the remaining business (or pay a dividend to shareholders).

We now see how the tax law can shoehorn pretty much any taxable acquisition into just two models: the stock sale and the asset sale. In a stock sale, the key features are that (a) the selling shareholders give up their stock and receive money or other consideration, and (b) the buyer now owns the stock of the target corporation, which remains in existence. In an asset sale, by contrast, (a) the selling shareholders do not transfer stock to the buyer, and (b) the buyer will not operate the target in its historic form. (Having bought the business, the buyer will either own the business directly or contribute it to a new corporation that the buyer controls.)

The IRS classifies all taxable acquisitions based on which of the two models they most resemble. For example, a taxable acquisition that takes the form of a state-law merger will be classified, for tax purposes, as either a stock sale or an asset sale, based on the terms of the deal. If the target corporation survives the merger (*i.e.*, the buying corporation disappears in the merger while the target continues to exist), then the tax law views the deal as a stock sale by the target shareholders. That's because the effect of the merger is to shift ownership of the target, which continues to exist. If the target corporation disappears in the merger (*i.e.*, the buyer survives the merger while the target goes out of business), then the merger is treated as an asset sale. The effect is the same as if the target sold all of its assets to the buyer and then liquidated.

It's important to keep in mind that this rare simplicity applies in the realm of taxable acquisitions. Reorganizations, as we will see, come in a larger variety of structures and impose a bewildering array of tax requirements. But let's enjoy the simplicity while it lasts!

¶902 *REALIZATION* AND TAXABLE ACQUISITIONS

We can now work through the taxation of (taxable) stock sales and asset sales. The headline on this one is easy: stock sales incur one level of tax, while asset sales usually incur two.

Start with the easy one: stock sales. You already know how stock sales are taxed, and you've known it since the early days of the basic tax course. The selling shareholders realize gain or loss measured by the difference between each taxpayer's basis in her stock and the amount realized. That's it! The buyer takes a cost basis in the stock, under familiar principles codified in Code Sec. 1012.

Importantly, nothing changes for the target corporation when its stock is sold. The basis of all its assets remains the same and the corporate identity is intact. And so, all of its tax attributes, including net operating loss carryovers and capital loss carryovers, remain unchanged as well. This creates an interesting wrinkle for the buyer in a stock acquisition. Because the buyer will fully inherit the tax position of the target, the buyer needs to conduct due diligence to be sure that there are no tax surprises in the offing, like exhausted depreciation allowances or big gains.

> **EXAMPLE 1.** *A stock sale.* Suppose that S owns all of the stock of T Corporation, a C corporation.[3] S has a basis of $30 in her stock. Buyer, an individual, offers to buy all the stock of T for $100 in cash. S accepts the offer, with three consequences. First, S realizes gain of $70, which will be capital in character under Section 1221 (except in the unlikely event, on these facts, that S is a dealer in stocks). Second, Buyer takes a basis of $100 in the stock under Section 1012. And third, T Corporation does not realize any gain or loss, and it retains its historic basis in its assets. (Tax lawyers sometimes describe this last point as "no step up in inside basis.")

A taxable asset sale is really only a little more complicated. The target corporation sells its assets to the buyer, who pays cash or other consideration. The sale is a *realization* event for the target corporation, so it realizes gain or loss on each of its assets, measured by the difference between basis and amount realized. The buyer then takes the assets with a cost (FMV) basis under Section 1012.

If the target corporation doesn't liquidate, then that's it. One *realization* event at the corporate level. The target shareholders won't realize any income unless and until the corporation makes a distribution of the proceeds. An ordinary distribution (with the target corporation remaining in business) will then be taxable as a dividend to the extent of E&P under Section 301, as we learned in Chapter 7.

Commonly, though, the target corporation liquidates. Formally, the target distributes all of its remaining assets to its shareholders and then goes out of business. In a typical asset sale, the only remaining asset is the cash (or other consideration) paid by the buyer, and the shareholders usually are eager to get their hands on it and reinvest (or spend) it.

Now, you might think that a distribution in liquidation would be taxed like any other distribution – under the rules of Section 301. But no. Section 331 of the Code treats a corporate liquidation as a sale of an individual shareholder's stock in exchange for the final, liquidating distribution.[4] (The terminology can

---

[3] We need to be sure that the target is a C corporation. If it is, instead, an entity taxed under Subchapter K (the partnership tax rules), a sale will have different consequences to some degree.

[4] We will see, below, that the consequences to a corporate shareholder may be different.

be confusing, because the Code calls the transaction a "distribution in complete liquidation" and then recites that it is treated as a sale of the stock.) Thus, when the target liquidates, the second level of tax is due: the target shareholders realize gain or loss equal to the difference between their stock basis and their amount realized.

> **EXAMPLE 2.** *An asset sale.* Suppose, just as in Example 1, that S owns all the stock of T Corporation, a C corporation. S has a basis of $30 in her stock, and T has a basis of $40 in its assets. Buyer, an individual, offers to buy all the assets of T for $100 in cash. T accepts the offer, with three consequences. First, T realizes gain of $60 ($100 amount realized less inside basis of $40). The character of the gain will be determined asset-by-asset. Second, Buyer takes a basis of $100 in the assets under Section 1012. And third, if T Corporation liquidates, S will realize gain equal to the amount realized less her basis of $30. Ignoring the corporate-level tax due on T's gain of $60, we can treat S's amount realized as the full $100 and see that she will have gain of $70.

By now, you may have spotted one of the major tax issues in an asset sale: how should the amount realized be allocated among the assets of the target corporation? In the example, the buyer pays $100 overall but is purchasing hundreds, maybe thousands, of separate assets, often including plant and equipment and intangibles. The allocation can be a matter of keen concern for both seller and buyer. The seller needs to allocate the amount realized among the assets sold in order to determine the character of gain and loss on each asset. The buyer also needs to allocate the purchase price among the assets in order to determine its basis in each. The solution is Section 1060 of the Code, which prescribes an allocation method based on the relative fair market values of different asset classes.

Summing up to this point, a very basic rule of thumb is that stock sales generate one level of tax, while asset sales usually generate two. For that reason, stock sales often are preferable from a tax perspective. But depending on the parties' tax rates and on nontax considerations, asset sales can be viable as well.

From a tax perspective, we can frame the issue in terms of whether the second level of tax in an asset sale is "worth it." The key tax difference between a stock sale and an asset sale is that the inside basis of the target's assets is adjusted to fair market value in an asset sale. If the target's assets have increased in value above their historic basis, the buyer would love to claim that stepped-up basis and thereby increase its depreciation deductions. But the seller wouldn't be eager to pay a second level of tax just to accommodate the buyer.

And so, the issue comes down to money: will the buyer pay extra to the seller to compensate for the second level of tax in an asset sale? Generally, the answer is no, and once we spell it out, you'll readily see why. The tax goodie for the buyer is an additional dollar of basis; that basis will translate into a dollar of extra deductions over time. But that extra dollar of basis requires the seller to realize an extra dollar of taxable gain. If the parties are in the same 21% tax bracket, they typically will not agree on an asset sale, because it won't be worth it. It wouldn't

¶902

make economic sense to pay 21 cents now in order to gain 21 cents (the value of the depreciation deduction) over time.

But buyers and sellers often are in different tax brackets, and there may be special tax circumstances, including loss carryovers or foreign parties, that can make it worthwhile for the seller to accept an asset sale.

For instance, if the target corporation is itself wholly owned by a corporation, then the liquidation step is tax-free under Section 332. Thus, the buyer can get the benefit of a stepped-up basis while the seller incurs only one level of tax. This might seem like an incredible corporate freebie, but it should make sense once you think about it. The selling corporation is itself subject to the corporate double tax. So, the proceeds of the asset sale will be taxed a second time, eventually, when they are distributed to the (individual) shareholders of the corporate seller. Put another way, Section 332 (tax-free corporate-to-corporate liquidations) parallels the 100% dividends-received deduction of Section 243. In both cases, the Code gives a pass when money is transferred from one corporation to a related one, postponing the second level of tax to the ultimate distribution from corporation to individual shareholder.

¶903   TAX DEFERRAL AND REORGANIZATIONS

We've focused on taxable acquisitions up to this point, but we haven't yet looked at the alternative – or considered how taxpayers can choose between taxable and tax-free forms. At first glance, you might wonder why anyone would ever do a taxable deal at all – isn't tax free always better? The answer is that a "tax free" reorganization offers *tax deferral* that is often attractive to the sellers, but the requirements of the reorganization rules may be impossible (or too costly) to meet. And buyers may prefer a taxable deal, because they can benefit from a stepped-up (fair market value) basis in stock and assets.

First, a word on terminology. The term "tax-free reorganization" is doubly confusing. For one thing, reorganizations (or "reorgs") in the tax sense have nothing (necessarily) to do with bankruptcy reorganizations. (For nonlawyers: a bankruptcy "reorganization" is what happens when a company files for bankruptcy under a law called Chapter 11, which authorizes a court to discharge debt and order the reorganization of the business along sounder financial lines.) There is one kind of tax reorg that can be undertaken in bankruptcy,[5] but otherwise, reorgs involve entirely solvent businesses.

For another thing, "tax free" is an imprecise term. A reorganization involves an acquisition[6] that is, in principle, a *realization* event but qualifies for specific

---

[5] See Code Sec. 368(a)(1)(G).

[6] The Code also permits some so-called non-acquisitive reorgs, but we will not discuss them; they're typically covered in very advanced courses.

nonrecognition treatment under Section 368 and related provisions. So, the reorg is "tax free" in the sense that the Code excuses the parties from full *realization* of all gain or loss. But the Code doesn't forgive the tax due. It creates a carryover basis regime that provides *tax deferral*, not tax forgiveness — just like Section 351. And if parties receive cash or other "boot," they may be required to recognize all or part of their gain.

Whew! That's a lot to digest all at once. Let's go through a few examples and you'll quickly catch on. Reorgs should remind you – a lot – of Section 351 and having that model in mind will help you put the pieces together.

In the remainder of this section, we will introduce the rules that award nonrecognition and impose carryover basis. These are complicated rules (you're shocked, shocked to hear that), but we can summarize the major points. In Chapter 10, we will add another layer of complexity: the reorg rules are contained not only in the relevant Code provisions but also in a body of case law that imposes additional requirements based on *substance over form* principles.

¶903.01   WHAT QUALIFIES AS A REORG?

Section 368 of the Code defines several types of reorgs. For corporate acquisitions, the most important are probably the so-called "A," "B," and "C" reorgs, which correspond to Section 368(a)(1)(A), (B), and (C).[7] Each type of transaction has different requirements, and these are highly technical. As an opening bid, we can summarize them this way:

- An "A" reorg is a statutory merger or consolidation, meaning that it must be executed pursuant to a merger (or consolidation) statute. Very generally, these rules require that all the assets (and liabilities) of one corporation be transferred to another, with the transferor then ceasing its legal existence.[8]
- A "B" reorg is a stock-for-stock acquisition. To qualify, the corporate buyer must acquire a controlling stake in the target, solely in exchange for the buyer's voting stock.[9]
- A "C" reorg is also a stock-for-assets acquisition. The corporate buyer must acquire substantially all of the assets of the corporate target, solely in exchange for the buyer's voting stock.

---

[7] More complicated acquisitions may also incorporate a "D" reorg, defined in Code Sec. 368(a)(1)(D), but for (relative!) simplicity, we will stick with the three more straightforward acquisitive reorgs.

[8] See Reg. §1.368-2.

[9] "Control" is defined in Code Sec. 368(c) and has a very precise meaning: the ownership of stock possessing at least 80 percent of the total combined voting power of all classes of stock entitled to vote and at least 80 percent of the total number of shares of all other classes of stock of the corporation.

I can't emphasize often enough (can you tell?) that the reorg rules are highly technical and full of potential missteps. For instance, the "A" reorg definition is not nearly as permissive as it seems on its face. Read literally, the "A" reorg would seem to apply to a cash merger, but as Chapter 11 shows, a large body of case law limits the consideration that can be paid in an "A" reorg and requires that a large chunk of it take the form of stock in the acquirer. To take another example, the term "substantially all" in the "C" reorg definition is a highly demanding test and not at all intuitive. So is the term "voting stock" in "B" and "C" reorgs. And so is the term "control" in a "B" reorg. Predictably, any real-world reorg will be heavily lawyered.

Still, even this much detail shows you why some deals may not be able to qualify as tax-free reorgs. Most importantly, any reorg requires the buyer to pay all (or a large part) of the consideration in the form of its stock. This will be a sticking point, and possibly a flat "no," for many acquirers and selling shareholders. Some selling shareholders want to cash out and aren't interested in acquiring a large chunk of stock in a third party. Some acquirers want to keep full control of their own companies and won't want to bring in new shareholders. And even if an acquisition can get over this hurdle, there are many more to be negotiated.

And, of course, some buyers and sellers may actively *not* want reorg status. While *tax deferral* is (usually) a good thing, there are several situations in which the parties might prefer a taxable deal with a *realization* event. To take one example, selling shareholders holding onto a built-in loss generally will prefer to realize that loss now rather than defer it. And you can imagine other circumstances as well: perhaps a seller knows that her tax rate will be much higher in the future, so it's worth it to trigger *realization* now. Or perhaps a seller has loss carryovers that will shelter any gain, while the buyer prefers a stepped-up basis in the target's assets. The headline is that all this will be carefully negotiated at the outset of the deal, based on the specifics of the buyer's, seller's, and target's tax situations.

¶903.02   HOW DOES A REORG AWARD *TAX DEFERRAL?*

Let's use an "A" reorg (a statutory merger) to illustrate how nonrecognition and *tax deferral* operate in reorgs. (The details will differ for "B" and "C" reorgs because of differences in form, but the big picture is still fairly accurate.)

> **EXAMPLE 3.** *An "A" reorg.* Suppose that S owns all of the stock of T Corporation, a C corporation.[10] S has a basis of $30 in her stock. T has a basis of $40 in its assets. Buyer Corporation, a C corporation, offers to acquire T in exchange for Buyer Corporation common stock with a fair market value of $100.

---

[10] The reorganization rules generally apply only to a target that is a C corporation.

S accepts the offer and the parties agree that T Corporation will merge into Buyer Corporation, with Buyer Corporation surviving. Assuming that the deal meets all the other requirements for an "A" reorg, there are three tax consequences:

- First, the selling shareholder, S, realizes but does not recognize her gain of $70, thanks to Section 354. She will take a carryover basis of $30 in the Buyer stock she receives. Going forward, she has $70 of built-in gain (measured by the difference between the $100 fair market value of the stock and its $30 basis).

- Second, the target, T Corporation, also realizes but does not recognize its gain of $60, thanks to Section 361.

- Third, Buyer Corporation, which survives the merger, takes a carryover basis of $40 in the assets of T Corporation, thanks to Section 362. Thus, Buyer inherits a built-in gain of $60.

These rules, taken together, preserve the double tax in the corporate system and award two levels of *tax deferral*. At the shareholder level, S has a built-in gain of $70, which she will recognize at some later point when she sells her Buyer stock. At the corporate level, Buyer Corporation takes a carryover basis of $40 in the target's assets, preserving a built-in gain of $60.

¶904 PROBLEM 9.1: TAXABLE ACQUISITIONS AND REORGANIZATIONS

Sven, an individual, owns all the stock of Corporation. He paid $100 for the stock ten years ago. Corporation has assets with a basis of $95. Brendan, an individual, has offered to buy Corporation's business, and the parties have agreed on a price of $175.

How will the three parties (Sven, Brendan, and Corporation) be taxed if:

(1) Brendan pays Sven $175 in cash for the stock.

ANSWER TO (1)

From the facts given, we know that Sven has a basis of $100 in his stock. This is a cash transaction, so we know that Sven will realize and recognize $75 of capital gain. (Under Section 1221, stock held by an investor is always a capital asset, and there are no facts indicating that Brendan is a dealer rather than an investor in the Corporation stock.) Corporation has no realization event and thus retains its historic basis of $95 in its assets; that is, there is no step-up in basis. Brendan will have a basis of $175 in his Corporation stock.

(2) Brendan pays Corporation $175 in cash for all its assets. Corporation then liquidates, distributing the cash to Sven.

ANSWER TO (2)

Now there is a realization event at the Corporation level, so let's begin there. Corporation realizes and recognizes gain of $80 ($175 - $95). (The character of the gain will depend on whether the assets sold are capital assets under Section 1221.) Ignoring the corporate-level tax due on that gain, Corporation then distributes the $175 in cash to Sven. Under Section 331, the liquidation is a realization event for Sven, so he realizes and recognizes capital gain of $75. Brendan has paid $175 in cash for Corporation's assets, and so he now has a stepped-up basis of $175 in those assets.

(3) Now suppose that the buyer is Brendan, Inc., a C corporation. Instead of paying cash, Brendan, Inc. offers to pay Sven with $175 worth of Brendan, Inc. stock. The parties agree and the acquisition takes the form of a merger. Corporation merges into Brendan, Inc., with Brendan, Inc. surviving. Corporation goes out of existence and Sven receives the $175 worth of Brendan, Inc. stock.

ANSWER TO (3)

Assuming that this transaction otherwise meets the requirements of Section 368(a)(1)(A), it will be a tax-free reorganization. Accordingly, Sven does not recognize gain; instead, he takes a carryover basis of $100 in the Brendan, Inc. stock. Brendan, Inc., now owns all the assets of Corporation with a carryover basis of $95.

(4) Of these three transactions, which has the best tax consequences for Sven? For the buyer?

ANSWER TO (4)

This is a difficult question to answer without more facts. If all the parties have equal tax rates, then the answers are relatively clear: the tax-free reorg in (3) is best for Sven, because he pays no current tax and so reaps the benefits of *tax deferral*. The asset purchase in (2) is best for Brendan, if we add the assumption that Corporation's assets include depreciable property, since Brendan would prefer higher depreciation deductions.

(5) How would your answer to (4) change if Corporation's stock were currently owned by two shareholders: Xena, a taxable shareholder with a $0 basis in her stock, and Yale University, a tax-exempt shareholder.

ANSWER TO (5)

The point of the question is to think through the selling shareholders' interests when they have diverse tax situations. Here, Xena will likely prefer a tax-free reorg, since her low stock basis means that a taxable deal would trigger $175 of gain. By contrast, Yale is a tax-indifferent party and will weigh the choice among transactions solely on a pre-tax basis; relevant non-tax factors will include the value and marketability of the Brendan, Inc. stock and transaction costs if Yale plans to sell the stock.

¶905   BUSINESS 101: WHAT IS A CORPORATE ACQUISITION?

In common usage, an acquisition (or takeover) occurs when one group of investors sells a business to another group. In 2018, for example, Disney agreed to pay $71 billion to acquire many of the businesses owned by 21st Century Fox, including their broadcast television channels and Fox News. In casual discussions (including many news stories), the terms "takeover" and "merger" are used synonymously with "acquisition." But as we will see, "merger" has a more precise, technical meaning as well.

When we analyze an acquisition for tax purposes, we must be precise about terminology and acquisition structure. A corporate acquisition involves a target that is a C corporation. The buying and selling shareholders may (or may not) also be C corporations.

When the target is a C corporation, there are several ways it can be acquired. Here, we will consider three of the primary forms. First, the buyer can buy a controlling share of the stock of the target. Depending on state law and the corporate charter, as little as 51% of the stock can give the buyer control over the Board of Directors. Control of the Board, in turn, gives the buyer control over corporate decisions, including the power to hire and fire management and make major decisions about business plans.

In a stock acquisition of this kind, the buyer purchases the stock from selling shareholders. Stock purchases can be made on the open market, without direct negotiation with the company or shareholders; these are typically cash purchases made without publicity. A buyer seeking a large stake can also make a "tender offer," which is a public offer to purchase shares for a set price.

From a legal perspective, a stock acquisition is fairly straightforward, because the only asset that changes hands is stock. A downside, however, is that because the target corporation remains in existence, so do all of its historic liabilities. A target that has known (or potential) liabilities, like a major pending lawsuit or environmental liabilities, may not be a good candidate for a stock acquisition for this reason. And so, a buyer needs to do serious due diligence. Unless the parties agree on some kind of indemnity, the buyer is on the hook for any and all debts, tort claims, and past taxes that the target may owe.

The second type of acquisition is an asset purchase. The target corporation sells its assets to the buyer, and consideration is paid to the target itself. If the target retains business assets, it can continue operating and choose to retain the consideration or pay it out to shareholders as a dividend. If the target sells all its assets, it typically will liquidate (formally cease conducting business) and distribute the consideration received to shareholders, who surrender their stock.

In an asset acquisition, the buyer typically seeks to purchase the entire business, including not only hard assets (like plant and equipment) but also business intangibles like trademarks, customer lists, and going-concern value (goodwill). And so, asset acquisitions involve complex contracts and negotiations over precisely what is and isn't included in the sale. (By contrast, a stock purchase necessarily buys the whole corporate package.) But a big upside of an asset acquisition is that the buyer doesn't (generally) have to assume liabilities of the target: the parties can pick and choose which liabilities, if any, will be transferred.

A third kind of acquisition is a merger. In a merger, two companies combine pursuant to the terms of state law. The target corporation may merge into the buyer (or a subsidiary of the buyer), with the buyer (or sub) surviving: in that case, the target transfers its assets to the buyer and ceases to exist as a separate corporation. This kind of merger operates very much like an asset transfer in substance, although the legal mechanics are different.

A merger can also run the other direction: the buyer (or a subsidiary) can merge into the target, with the target surviving as a legal entity and retaining its historic assets. In that kind of transaction, the selling shareholders receive cash (or other consideration) for their stock, and controlling shares are issued to the buyer as part of the merger. This kind of merger operates, in substance, very much like a stock acquisition, although once again the legal mechanics are different.

Acquisitions can be friendly or hostile, depending on the relationship between the target's shareholders and the buyer. A friendly acquisition typically involves negotiations with the target's Board (or directly with shareholders) and reflects agreement on terms. A hostile acquisition proceeds without the consent of the target's Board, and sometimes against its express wishes. In that scenario, the acquirer makes a public offer to buy target stock, in effect bypassing the Board and going directly to the open market and to shareholders.

> **EXAMPLE 4.** Farmstand, Inc., was incorporated in 2010. It runs a chain of profitable farm-to-table restaurants. Abbie and Brent, Farmstand's two shareholders, respectively own 2/3 and 1/3 of the common stock.
>
> McDonald's, Inc., a major restaurant chain, has approached Abbie and Brent with an offer to acquire Farmstand. McDonald's has offered to pay $3 million for 100% of the stock.
>
> Abbie favors the sale because she is ready to retire, but Brent objects to selling their business to a fast-food chain. McDonald's, for its part, is not interested in owning only 2/3 of the stock.

¶905

Abbie's lawyer advises changing the structure to a stock purchase followed by a merger. Under this plan, McDonald's buys Abbie's stock for $2 million. McDonald's then holds 2/3 of shareholder votes and can, under state law, vote to approve a merger of Farmstand with a subsidiary of McDonald's, with Farmstand surviving. The result is that Farmstand survives the merger as a wholly-owned corporate sub of McDonald's, and Abbie exits the scene for $2 million in cash. Put another way, the merger enables Abbie and McDonald's to accomplish a 100% acquisition without Brent's consent. Brent will receive $1 million in consideration in the merger and will no longer own stock in Farmstand. (From a tax perspective, this is a *realization* event for both Abbie and Brent.)

¶906 ADVANCED PROBLEM

For a more advanced problem, *see* Problems C5 and C6 in Appendix C. (Problem C6 also contains material discussed in Chapter 10.)

CHAPTER 10

Substance Over Form and Corporate Reorganizations

Introduction . . . . ¶1000
Reorgs and the Problem of *Realization* in *Marr* . . . . ¶1001
Continuity of Proprietary Interest . . . . ¶1002
How Much Continuity . . . . ¶1003
Problem 10.1: Continuity of Interest and Corporate Reorganizations . . . . ¶1004
Advanced Problem . . . . ¶1005

¶1000 INTRODUCTION

In Chapter 8, we took an initial look at the tax-free reorganization rules. If I've done my job as author, then you learned three important things about reorgs:

1. Reorgs aren't tax free; they're tax deferred.
2. The Code lays out formal rules that reorgs must meet.
3. A reorg must also meet additional requirements, set out in the case law.

In this chapter, we will take a closer look at point 3: we will take a look at some of the greatest hits from the case law to show how they attempt to identify transactions that are reorgs in substance as well as in form.

The best place to start is with the "A" reorg, found in Section 368(a)(1)(A). If you took that provision at face value, you would believe that any "statutory merger or consolidation" is an "A" reorg. But you would be wrong. So wrong. The basic story is one we've seen before in the basic tax course. Way back in the early days of the income tax, the Congress enacted simple, open-textured rules. As taxpayers grew more and more sophisticated, they began to engineer transactions that met the Code's requirements in form but not in substance. The IRS and the courts then added additional rules to try to confine reorgs to something like their intended scope.

The doctrines we will study in this chapter are, in that sense, broadly in the category of *substance over form*. They add a penumbra of judge-made law to the literal words of the Code, and they exist in order to limit tax planning. But most tax lawyers would distinguish between the general *substance over form* doctrine, which applies to all taxpayers at all times, and the specific judicial doctrines that add a gloss to the reorg rules. Put another way, the reorg rules have, over time, spawned something like a specialized set of *substance over form* rules, which now are understood to apply only to reorgs. If your mind isn't yet boggled, I'll just add that in addition to all this, the general *substance over form* doctrine also applies, adding yet another layer of law to the layer cake which now looks like this:

> General substance over form
> (Gregory v. Helvering)*

> Judicial requirements for reorgs (continuity of interest, continuity of business enterprise, business purpose)

> Code provisions (Sections 368, 354, 356, 358, 361, 362)

*293 U.S. 465 (1935)

I hasten to add that this chapter will only introduce you to the middle layer of law. We will focus on the continuity of interest doctrine, but we won't cover it in depth. For that, you need a good treatise and a stack of cases – sorry to sound like a teacher, but there's no substitute for reading the actual cases. In addition, we will not delve into the other extra-statutory doctrines that govern reorgs: business purpose and continuity of business enterprise. These have their own regulations and their own line of cases. Still, even a brief introduction to continuity will illustrate the headline point that you cannot look to the Code (and Regulations) alone to determine whether a given deal is a reorg.

¶1001 REORGS AND THE PROBLEM OF *REALIZATION* IN *MARR*

I wish I could tell you that the judicial doctrines that apply to reorgs are crystal clear and closely tied to a set of policy objectives. But no. The doctrines originated as judges tried to divine the essence of a reorg. Over time, though, as doctrine built upon doctrine, the judicial decisions themselves grew formalistic and arbitrary. The result is that reorgs, which originally encompassed something like "small changes in form to a continuing business controlled by the same stockholders" have become capacious enough to encompass deals that are, in substance, outright sales from one owner to another.

The best way to understand all this is to follow the arc of a set of cases that, for good or ill, shaped the reorg rules. The earliest cases established the baseline proposition that even a small change in business form can trigger a *realization* event.

In *Marr v. U.S.*, the taxpayers were shareholders in General Motors of New Jersey.[1] In 1916, they exchanged common and preferred stock in GM of New Jersey for stock in a successor corporation, GM of Delaware. This transaction is, understandably enough, called a reincorporation. The old company was incorporated in New Jersey, and the management decided that it liked Delaware better. So they filed legal papers to stop being a New Jersey corporation and start being a Delaware one.

The change required a few formal steps. The parties had to merge the old New Jersey corporation into a new Delaware corporation, with the Delaware corporation surviving. But the substance was a reincorporation: the "new" company had the same assets and shareholders as the old one, although the terms of the new stock were slightly different than the terms of the old.

The issue in the case is whether the taxpayer *realized* gain when he gave up his GM (New Jersey) stock in exchange for GM (Delaware) stock in 1916. Marr's basis was about $75,000, while the fair market value of the stock was around $400,000. In swooped the IRS, demanding payment of tax on what it claimed was $325,000 in gain. Marr objected that he hadn't sold his stock; he should, he claimed, continue on with no *realization* event and a basis of $75,000. As authority, Marr invoked *Eisner v. Macomber*,[2] which you might remember from your basic tax class. *Macomber* held that a stock dividend is not a *realization* event. Marr argued that his exchange, like the stock dividend in *Macomber*, was not a sale of stock but a continuing interest in the same corporation.

The Supreme Court ruled for the IRS, holding that stock in GM (Delaware) was "essentially different" from stock in GM (New Jersey). That seems like a stretch, because the two corporations had, um, exactly the same assets and business. But the court found sufficient difference in Marr's holdings to apply the *realization* doctrine. New Jersey corporate law, the court noted, was different from Delaware corporate law; indeed, that's why the company reincorporated. And so Marr had different legal rights as a shareholder in the new corporation. And, the court noted, Marr held a slightly different interest in the new company: the preferred stock he received had a different dividend rate, and the preferred stock as a class had a higher liquidation value.

In *Marr*, the Supreme Court refined and limited its holding in *Macomber*. In doing so, however, the Court potentially opened the door for the IRS to collect tax on small, formal changes in business organizations, like reincorporations. Acting in 1918 and again in the early 1920s, the Congress enacted the reorg rules to protect some "mere changes in form" from *realization*. But, as we shall

---

[1] 268 U.S. 536 (1925).
[2] 252 U.S. 189 (1920).

see, there was considerable uncertainty in the scope of the reorg rules. It took the IRS, the courts, and Congress some time to draw the line between reorgs and taxable transactions.

Marr is also worth keeping in mind because it establishes the baseline rule of *realization*. Every reorg takes place in the shadow of a *realization* event. If the parties fail to meet even one requirement for reorg treatment, they will trigger the same consequences as if they had undertaken a fully taxable acquisition.

¶1002 CONTINUITY OF PROPRIETARY INTEREST

The text of the reorg definitions in Section 368 has evolved over time, but the language can sometimes appear broad enough to encompass a wide variety of transactions. Section 368(a)(1)(A), for instance, seems to treat "any statutory merger or consolidation" as a reorg. But if we read that language literally, we would be reading the *realization* requirement out of the Code. No one (at least no one with a lawyer) would sell a company by selling its stock for cash. Instead, they would merge their corporation into the buyer, collect their cash, and contend that the deal was an "A" reorg.

During the first few decades of the income tax, it fell to the courts to defend the *realization* requirement by clarifying the substance to the reorg definition. One of the major lines of doctrine has come to be called the "continuity of proprietary interest." It's also called "continuity of interest" (the term I prefer) or the awkward acronym COPI. Very generally, continuity of interest requires that the selling shareholders in a reorg must preserve a significant ownership interest in the successor corporation. In other words, the selling shareholders cannot simply sell their stock for cash and go off and reinvest. They must receive non-cash consideration that represents a continuing interest in the business.

Stated this way, continuity of interest is pretty vague. It isn't at all obvious what constitutes a significant ownership interest or a continuing interest in a business. The courts clarified the matter as courts do: slowly, and one case at a time.

Reading all of the case law on continuity of interest would be deadly. But we can get a window into the process via a famous 1940 case called *LeTulle v. Scofield*.[3] (A brief but useful aside on tax procedure: Scofield was the IRS Commissioner at the time. Older income tax cases name the Commissioner in their title, while later ones just refer to him or her as the Commissioner. So in *Gregory v. Helvering*, the Commissioner is Helvering. In *Eisner v. Macomber*, the Commissioner is Eisner. And so it follows that when you refer to a case by its short name, you use the taxpayer's name – there are, after all, hundreds of *Helvering* and *Eisner* cases!)

Simplifying a little, LeTulle was an individual who owned real property through a corporate entity called the Gulf Coast Irrigation Company. An unrelated corporation, the Gulf Coast Water Company, offered to buy the property

---

[3] 308 U.S. 415 (1940).

owned by the Irrigation Company. LeTulle agreed, and so the Irrigation Company sold its land to the Water Company in exchange for $50,000 in cash and $750,000 worth of Water Company bonds. The bonds had a maturity of between two and thirteen years after the sale.

LeTulle treated the transaction as a reorg under Section 368, which, at the time, provided that a reorganization includes "the acquisition by one corporation of [...] substantially all the properties of another corporation." The deal met the terms of the statute, LeTulle argued: the Irrigation Company sold its assets to the Water Company and then dissolved, transferring to LeTulle the cash and bonds received.

The IRS admitted that the deal literally met the terms of the statute, but it contended that it lacked continuity of proprietary interest. An earlier Supreme Court case, *Pinellas Ice & Cold Storage Co. v. Commissioner,* had invalidated a purported reorg in which the seller received cash and short-term notes of the buyer.[4] The Court there looked to *substance over form*: "In substance the petitioner sold for the equivalent of cash; the gain must be recognized."

The facts of *LeTulle* seemed stronger for the taxpayer's claim: LeTulle received some cash, yes, but the bulk of the consideration consisted of longer-term notes. The taxpayer could argue with a straight face that he had a continuing interest in the business of the buyer (the Water Company). After all, the Water Company would only pay off its bonds if it remained solvent for the next 13 years.

The case law in the lower courts since *Pinellas Ice* also seemed to support the taxpayer's claim. The courts had begun to rule that "receipt of long-term bonds, as distinguished from short-term notes, constitutes the retention of an interest in the purchasing corporation." The result, under the law at the time, was that reorg status hinged on the line between long- and short-term bonds.

But in *LeTulle*, the Supreme Court refused to draw that line and instead set a new standard. Bonds, the court ruled, can never suffice for continuity of interest, no matter how long their term:

> We are of opinion that the term of the obligations is not material. Where the consideration is wholly in the transferee's bonds, or part cash and part such bonds, we think it cannot be said that the transferor retains any proprietary interest in the enterprise. On the contrary, he becomes a creditor of the transferee...[5]

After *LeTulle*, then, only stock can satisfy the continuity of interest requirement. The selling shareholders (or the selling corporation) must receive at least some stock in the corporate buyer, and the stock interest must be substantial enough so that the taxpayer (the seller) retains a continuing proprietary interest in the buyer.

---

[4] 287 U.S. 462 (1933).
[5] 308 U.S. 420-21.

Although the text of the reorg rules has changed since 1940, *Le Tulle* remains good law. Every reorg must meet the continuity of interest test. And to do so, the seller must receive stock in the buyer corporation. The regulations now spell out some aspects of continuity of interest but note that stock consideration is key and that all facts must be considered.[6]

Le Tulle illustrates a tension in the continuity of interest cases. By requiring stock consideration and by ruling bonds out of bounds, the Court seems to strike a blow for *substance over form* and for clarity. No longer would lower courts spar over the dividing line between long- and short-term bonds.

But the *Le Tulle* holding is less satisfying when you realize that "stock" can take many forms. For example, common stock in a company with only common stock is a very different financial contract than common stock in an identical company that has layers of debt and preferred stock that must be paid before the common stockholder receives anything. To take another example: very junior debt may not be economically distinguishable from very senior preferred stock, but the latter qualifies for continuity purposes, while the former does not.

And so, unfortunately, *Le Tulle's* seemingly solid standard actually maps onto one of the least defensible distinctions in the corporate tax: the debt versus equity distinction. As Chapter 4 discusses, the distinction between debt and equity is both legally fundamental to the corporate tax and economically indefensible. So if the Supreme Court in *Le Tulle* thought that it was avoiding fussy line-drawing problems, it was dead wrong.

Le Tulle also leaves open another tricky distinction: how much stock must the selling shareholder receive? Clearly, all cash will not suffice, and all stock will. But in between, there are infinite possibilities, and *Le Tulle* doesn't tell us just how much continuity is enough. That problem would be left to future decisionmakers.

¶1003 HOW MUCH CONTINUITY?

Today, the text of Section 368 leaves open the continuity problem only for "A" reorgs and not for "B" and "C" reorgs. That's because Sections 368(a)(1)(B) and (C) specifically require that the consideration paid must consist solely of buyer voting stock, and so continuity is automatically satisfied.

Over time, the case law, IRS ruling guidelines, and regulations have reached a consensus that continuity of interest is met if something like 40-50% of the consideration paid to the sellers consists of buyer stock.[7] But the regulations warn that "all facts and circumstances" must be taken into account to determine whether "in substance" continuity is preserved.[8] That sentence stands as a warning to tax planners who might be tempted to craft "stock" that, in substance, insulates the selling shareholders against the risks of the business.

---

[6] Reg. §1.368-1(e).

[7] *See* Reg. §1.368-1(e)(2)(v), Ex. 1 (40% stock and 60% cash).

[8] *See* Reg. §1.368-1(e).

Still, continuity of interest continues to dog the tax law, particularly in non-standard transactions. A good illustration is *Paulsen v. Commissioner*, a 1985 case that involved two savings and loan associations' ("S&L's") debt.[9] Simplifying a bit, Paulsen was a shareholder in Commerce, an S&L organized as a corporation. Commerce merged into Citizens Federal, an institution organized as a mutual savings and loan. A mutual S&L has no stock. Instead, every depositor and every borrower has specified governance rights and a right to dividends, based on the dollar amount of their deposits or borrowings. And so the Board is chosen, not by shareholders, but by the collective vote of depositors and borrowers.

In the merger, Paulsen gave up his Commerce stock and, in return, became the owner of deposit accounts in Citizens Federal. The deposit accounts had a cash face amount but were restricted so that they could not be withdrawn before a year had elapsed. Paulsen considered the merger a reorganization, but the IRS deemed the transaction to be a *realization* event. The case went all the way up to the Supreme Court, which ultimately ruled for the IRS.

Paulsen argued that the Citizens Federal deposits should be considered stock, because they were the only form of equity that Citizens Federal could issue. As a mutual S&L, Citizens Federal could not issue traditional stock; deposits were its only means of giving the Commerce shareholders a continuing interest in the joint enterprise.

But the Court said no. It held that the Commerce-Citizens Federal merger had failed the continuity of interest test, because the former Commerce shareholders, including Paulsen, had received only the equivalent of short-term interests in Citizens Federal. Paulsen's deposits, after all, could be withdrawn as cash a year after the merger. The Court recognized that the Citizens Federal deposits (unlike deposits in a stock S&L) also conferred voting and dividend rights, but it considered the value of those rights to be small compared to the cash value of the deposits.

¶1004 PROBLEM 10.1: CONTINUITY OF INTEREST AND CORPORATE REORGANIZATIONS

Stella is the founder and sole shareholder of Stellcorp, a C corporation. She has a basis of $100 in the stock. Terence has offered to pay Stella $500 for her stock. Stella is tempted to take the deal, but she would prefer to defer taxes until later if possible. Stella and Terence have agreed, in principle, on several possible deal structures. Can you advise Stella on the federal income tax consequences of each?

(1) Terence will pay Stella $500 in cash for her Stellcorp stock. Stella will reinvest her money in a diversified portfolio of stocks.

---

[9] 469 U.S. 131 (1985).

ANSWER TO (1)

This deal would be a taxable sale of Stella's stock. She would realize and recognize $400 in capital gain (her stock is a capital asset under Section 1221). Thus, Stella could only reinvest whatever she has left of the $500 *after* paying taxes on the $400 gain.

(2) Terence is the sole stockholder of Terry Corp., a C corporation. TerryCorp. agrees to buy Stella's Stellcorp stock for $200 in cash and $300 worth of TerryCorp. common stock.

ANSWER TO (2)

This deal cannot qualify as a reorg, despite the use of TerryCorp. stock. It is not a merger and so does not qualify under Section 368(a)(1)(A). It does involve a stock-for-stock deal; the consideration includes cash, and so it cannot qualify under Section 368(a)(1)(B), which applies only if the stock is acquired "solely for voting stock" in the acquirer. None of the other reorg provisions in Section 368 will apply, and so the deal will be taxed as per (1). Stella will realize all $400 of her gain, even though she has received TerryCorp stock (in part) rather than 100% cash.

You might have gone off track here by focusing on the fact that 60% of the consideration is stock, and so the general continuity of interest requirement seems to be met. That would be a very good point if this were otherwise an "A" reorg! But don't forget that the judicial requirements on continuity of proprietary interest operate *in addition to* the statutory criteria. Here, the "B" reorg doesn't meet the Code's requirements, and so it cannot possibly be a reorg, despite the significant transfer of TerryCorp stock.

(3) Stellacorp will merge into TerryCorp., with TerryCorp. surviving. Stella will receive TerryCorp. common stock worth $500.

ANSWER TO (3)

This deal is likely an "A" reorg. Assuming that the merger takes place under state law, the deal certainly meets the continuity of interest requirement, since 100% of the consideration consists of stock in the acquirer.

Stepping back a bit, this is a better tax deal for Stella, because she achieves continued tax deferral. She will pay tax on any gain only when she sells the Terrycorp. stock. But note that it is a *different* business deal than (1). Instead of reinvesting in a diversified portfolio, she will be stuck with a large investment in TerryCorp. Despite the tax advantages of the reorg, she should consult her business advisers to be sure that TerryCorp. fits her investment plans.

(4) Same as (3), except that Stella will receive $100 in TerryCorp. common stock and $400 in TerryCorp. debt obligations.

ANSWER TO (4)

Here, the continuity of interest is only 20% (*i.e.,* $100/$500). This is almost certainly too low a percentage. The deal will fail reorg status, and Stella will be taxed as in (1).

¶1005 ADVANCED PROBLEM

For a more advanced problem, *see* Problem C6 in Appendix C.

PART III
Taxing Partnership Income

CHAPTER 11

Valuation and *Realization* in Partnership Taxation

Introduction.	¶1100
A Little Bit of Terminology.	¶1101
Realization and the *Net Income* of the Partnership and Its Partners	¶1102
Basye and *Realization*	¶1103
Problem 11.1: Partnership Tax Basics.	¶1104
Business 101: What is a Partnership?	¶1105

¶1100 INTRODUCTION

Partnership taxation invites us to revisit the most basic problem of business taxation: *valuation*. As we saw in Chapter 1, an ideal system of income taxation would tax individuals every year on the change in market value of their business interests. But mark-to-market, we know, is impractical for reasons of *valuation* and liquidity. The IRS would struggle mightily to establish the value of every business every year, and the process would invite protracted litigation. Taxing business owners on valuation changes could also strain their finances: they'd be required to pay taxes even if the business had not yet paid them in cash.

The generic *valuation* problem goes exponential when it comes to the world of partnerships. Partnerships (as ¶1105 explains) are flexible and highly tailored to each particular situation. If you've seen one partnership agreement, well, you've seen one. The next one down the line will likely look completely different. Put another way, a partnership agreement is simply a contract. The parties can, quite literally, write in (nearly) anything they want.

From a business perspective, the flexibility of partnerships is a big advantage. Every business is unique, and the partnership form allows each deal to be tailored to the circumstances. By contrast, the corporate form is kind of clunky: state corporate law limits stakeholders to a relatively small number of interests, namely common stock, preferred stock, and debt.

But from a tax perspective, the flexibility of the partnership form is a headache, because it makes it especially difficult to understand and to value each partner's economic stake in the partnership. Valuing corporate stock in a closely-held company is hard enough, but at least in that case, every holder of, say, common stock, has the same rights and interests. In a partnership, by contrast, every single partner may have their own deal.

EXAMPLE 1. Andy and Beryl decide to go into business together. Andy will contribute land and a building in downtown Boston, and Beryl will contribute money and "sweat equity" to renovate the building as an upscale restaurant. Once the restaurant is up and running, Andy will be the chef and Beryl will manage the dining room and oversee the wait staff.

Like all business founders, Andy and Beryl face an uncertain future. The renovation may cost more (or, rarely, less) than they have budgeted. They may need to borrow money at some point. The restaurant may succeed or fail. One of the partners may want to sell out at some point. The business might eventually be sold at a profit or, at the other extreme, could wind up owing creditors a bundle.

The partnership agreement is the place where Andy and Beryl will hammer out all these scenarios. They will decide how to measure profits, how to share profits, and when partners may take cash out of the partnership. They will decide who is on the hook if the renovations run over budget and who has to co-sign a loan if needed. They will decide how to split profits if they sell the business and how to fund losses if they end up owing money to their creditors.

Now, Andy and Beryl might opt for the super simple approach, splitting everything 50-50. But, if you pause and think for a moment, that's unlikely. After all, the two brought very different types and amounts of assets and skills to the partnership. Andy, for example, might think that he should get a bigger share of the pie, since he contributed a valuable building in downtown Boston that he could have just rented out on the market. Beryl, for her part, might think that Andy should be on the hook if the building turns out to be in really bad condition. Andy might argue that any cost overruns should really be on Beryl's dime, since she's managing the renovation.

And there are many more issues to be resolved. What if a customer slips and falls in the restaurant and is awarded big damages? What if the restaurant is so wildly successful that a national chain buys it? What if the Boston real estate market goes crazy, and the partners sell the building at a profit?

We don't need to wade further into the details to see the big point: Andy and Beryl will either work out a deal that meets both their needs, or they'll walk away. But if they do go forward with their partnership, it is likely that they hash out a highly tailored deal, and one that will look very different in its particulars from other partnerships.

So you can see why a mark-to-market business income tax has been a nonstarter for partnerships. The IRS would not only have to value every partnership, but moreover parse every partnership contract to determine how much of that value should be allocated to each partner. The law instead makes the now-familiar move: to avoid the problem of *valuation*, it opts for *realization* instead.

But the move to *realization* doesn't entirely solve the tax problems created by the level of detail and customization we see in partnerships. We shall see that the partnership tax rules attempt to capture the nuance of individual partnership deals but often fall short. Looking ahead, we will see that the result is that partnerships can be used to achieve *tax deferral* and *income shifting* that could not be achieved in a corporate setting.

¶1101 A LITTLE BIT OF TERMINOLOGY

Partnership taxation has its own vocabulary, and before we dive in, we should clarify a few key terms. The first one is the word "partnership" itself.

In the tax world, a partnership is any entity taxed under the pass-through rules set out in Subchapter K of the Code. Put another way, the tax rules for "partnerships" can apply to entities that are not legally classified partnerships. They might be LLCs, or limited partnerships, or some other business entity created by state law.

To complicate matters further, not all pass-throughs are taxed under the partnership rules. Simplifying a bit, Subchapter K applies to *business* entities with multiple owners who elect into or default into pass-through treatment. (You may recall that the "check the box" regulations under Section 7701 govern whether an entity is taxed as a partnership or as a corporation.[1]). Some specialized pass-throughs have their own taxation regimes, and we will not consider them here.[2]

By contrast, the second key term, "partner," is fairly intuitive once you understand what a partnership is. When the code refers to partners, it means the people who are equity owners, akin to shareholders in the corporation. Of course, partnerships, like corporations, can have other stakeholders. A partnership can issue debt and hire employees. Creditors and workers are taxed just as they are in any other setting; it is only the taxation of partners that is defined by the rules of Subchapter K.

The third key term is distributive share. A partner's distributive share is the portion of partnership income and deductions that she must report on her own tax return. Very simply, if you and I were equal partners in the partnership, and if the partnership earned $100, we would each have a distributive share of $50. Since the partnership is a pass-through, I would pay tax on my distributive share, and you would pay tax on your distributive share.

---

[1] *See* Chapter 3, *supra.*

[2] For example, some investment vehicles are pass-throughs taxed under the Real Estate Mortgage Investment Conduit (REMIC) rules. (*See* Code Sec. 860A *et seq.*) Some trusts (but not all) are taxed on a pass-through basis. And there is a specialized tax regime for so-called "Subchapter S" corporations. These are entities classified as corporations but eligible to elect pass-through treatment because they have relatively few owners and a simple capital structure.

The confusing part here is that a "distributive share" has nothing to do with actual distributions from the partnership. So, although the two concepts sound similar, they are different for tax purposes. Think about it this way: a partner's distributive share, as we have seen, is her portion of partnership *income, whether or not the income is distributed*. By contrast, a distribution occurs when cash or other property exits the partnership and ends up in the partner's hands, *whether or not the partnership has earned any income*.

Consider what happens when the partnership does earn income. The partnership itself isn't taxable, as you know. That implies that somebody, namely the partners, must be taxed on a current basis. That is what the distributive share rules do; they identify the reportable income and deductions that are allocated to each partner. Continuing the simple example of the equal partnership, you can now understand that you and I each have a distributive share of $50 even if the partnership does not distribute any cash to us.

Now, you and I might be unhappy if the partnership hasn't distributed any cash to us. We might complain to each other that we don't have the cash to pay the tax. But the actual distribution of assets to partners may not happen until much later. (You might worry, at this stage, that partners will be taxed a second time when they receive cash distributions. But, never fear! We will see that the distribution rules are designed so that partners are not taxed a second time when they receive distributions of already-taxed income.)

The final key terms are "inside basis" and "outside basis." Inside basis refers to the partnership's basis in its assets, while outside basis refers to a partner's basis in her partnership interest. So, for example, if ABC partnership buys a building for $1 million, then the partnership has an inside basis of $1 million under Section 1012 (which states the familiar rule that basis equals cost). Every partner accounts for their own outside basis separately. So if Betsy buys a partnership interest for $100,000, then she has an initial basis of $100,000. The other partners in the same partnership will have their own outside bases, which most likely will be different than Betsy's.

Don't worry if your head is spinning a little. Even the effort to define terms requires us to learn a little about partnership tax, and you may understandably feel that you just don't know enough yet to grasp these distinctions. Your only task now is to watch out for these terms and register that they are specialized, technical terms. You can – and probably should – come back to this section a little later on, after you've learned some of the basics. These definitions will make more sense at that stage.

¶1102 *REALIZATION* AND THE *NET INCOME* OF THE PARTNERSHIP AND ITS PARTNERS

Now we can turn to the central task of partnership taxation: applying the realization rules to a business venture owned by multiple equity holders. Although partnership taxation has a reputation as being quite complicated (and we will shortly see why that is true), there are two pieces of good news to begin with. The basic *realization* rules are the same ones you learned in your first course on taxation. The partnership realizes income, for example, when it sells property, but not when it holds property. The realized income is then passed through to the partners to be taxed on their tax returns. Easy, right?

So, the complexity of partnership taxation doesn't reflect any new problems of *realization*. They're the same problems that you already know about. *Realization* permits taxpayers to choose the timing of income to some degree, and taxpayers, being rational creatures, often prefer *tax deferral*.

The second piece of good news is that the rules for determining net income are also pretty close to those that you already know. When a partnership engages in business, it earns gross income, which is then offset by business deductions. Partnership activities may also give rise to tax credits, which are subtracted from tax liability.

One new wrinkle, which is still pretty intuitive, is that partnerships generally pass through to the partners separate items of income, deduction, and tax credit. That way, partners can report those items on their own returns. Put another way, partnerships generally do not compute the *net income* of the partnership and then pass through shares of *net income* to the partners. Instead, the partnership measures gross income from different activities, and deductions that may be allowable, as well as any possibly applicable tax credits. The partnership then provides that information to each partner, cluing them in to the items of income they have to include, deductions they may be able to take, and tax credits they may be eligible to claim.

Why do partnerships take this complicated approach? It certainly seems as if it would be simpler for a partnership to compute its own *net income* and then just pass through a single, neat number to each partner, representing that partner's share of the pie. There are two reasons for passing through individual items of income and deductions, but they both reflect a single, overarching goal: the partnership rules aim to make the partnership transparent, that is, to measure partners' income as if they conducted the business directly, without any intervening entity at all.

More specifically, the first reason is that passing through individual items of income and deductions often better reflects the business deal of the parties. In simple classroom examples, we often assume a simple business deal, as in: "Anne and Betsy agree to share all profits and losses equally." That's fine for the classroom. But in the real world, it's common that the partners will hash out a more complicated deal that reflects their different investments, skills, and risk preferences.

> **EXAMPLE 2.** Let's return to the example of Andy and Beryl, whom we introduced in Example 1. The two partners intend to open a restaurant, but they have some work

to do before they can open. Andy contributed land and a building in downtown Boston, but the space needs to be renovated. Beryl agreed to fund and manage the renovation and to contribute "sweat equity" by doing some of the construction and decoration work herself.

Let's assume that Andy and Beryl initially agreed to share profits 60-40, but then Beryl raised an issue. The partnership's main asset is the Boston building, but the value of that building will go up and down in value with the Boston real estate market (and the Boston economy). Beryl points out that she came into the deal to start a restaurant, not to invest in real estate, and Andy agrees that that's a fair point. So the partners agree that if the partnership sells the building, any gain goes to Andy, and any loss will reduce his share of partnership profits.

So far, so good, except that Andy's lawyer chimes in to say that if Andy is on the hook for the ups and downs in the building's value, he should also get all the tax depreciation. Beryl agrees that that makes sense.

Whew! This is still a simple example by real-world standards, and yet it's getting complicated pretty quickly. The parties aren't deliberately trying to complicate matters, and they aren't (at this stage) engaged in any kind of fancy tax planning. They are just trying, very sensibly, to anticipate their joint future and to work out who is on the hook for what.

Now, back to the tax point. The deal between Andy and Beryl illustrates why it's a good idea for the partnership rules to allocate items of income and deduction to partners. Suppose that in a future year, the partnership earns $100 in profits from the restaurant but sells the Boston property at a loss of $10. (Maybe they've leased new space and don't need the building any more.) The total net income of the partnership is therefore $90 ($100 - $10). But it would be a mistake to tax Andy on 60% of that and Beryl on 40%. The terms of their bargain call for, in effect, attributing 100% of profits and losses from the building to Andy.

So a more accurate tax allocation would separate out the restaurant profits from the loss on the building. Beryl's share of taxable income should be 40% of $100, or $40. Andy's share should have two components. He should be allocated 60% of $100, or $60. And he should be allocated the $10 loss on the sale of the building.

The total amount included by the partners will still be $90 ($40 by Beryl and $50 by Andy). But the split no longer is an easy 60-40; it depends, instead, on a division of individual items of profit and loss.

The Andy-Beryl example also illustrates the second reason why partnerships pass through items of income, deduction, and credit one-by-one to their partners:

not all of these items are treated equally on each partner's tax return. Capital gains and losses, passive gains and losses, and nonrefundable tax credits may all have different values to different partners, depending each partner's tax situation.

> **EXAMPLE 3.** The upshot of Example 2 is that the partnership will pass through to Andy two different "buckets" of income and deductions. One bucket includes the income and deductions attributable to the restaurant. These will include ordinary income (from restaurant sales of food) and ordinary deductions (for waitstaff salaries and other expenses). The second bucket includes the loss on the sale of the building, which is likely a Section 1231 loss (*i.e.*, a loss on the sale of real property held more than a year and used in the trade or business).

Section 1231 requires each taxpayer to "basket" gains and losses on business property. If there is a net gain, it's a long-term capital gain and eligible for the preferential rate in Section 1(h). If there is a net loss, however, it is ordinary and so fully deductible against ordinary income.

The point is that we don't know whether Andy's $10 loss ultimately will be ordinary or capital, because it depends on whether he has other Section 1231 items and, if so, what the net gain or loss turns out to be. And there is no reason to suppose that the outcome of the Section 1231 basketing for Andy would be the same as for Beryl.

So the partnership rules allocate separate items to each partner so that the final taxation of each partner can abide by the normal rules that apply to individuals. Put another way, separate allocations serve the goal of taxing Andy, as much as possible, as if he owned the partnership property directly. The idea is that he shouldn't be better off or worse off, tax-wise, by operating via a partnership instead of by himself.

Taken together, these examples illustrate three aspirations of partnership taxation:

- First, the total amount of income allocated to partners should add up to the same amount that would be taxed if the business were conducted by one person. The formation of a partnership shouldn't reduce (or increase) total income.
- Second, each partner should be taxed on his appropriate share of income, no more and no less, so that all income is taxed at the correct person's marginal tax rate.
- Third, each partner should have tax timing and character that are the same (no better and no worse) than if she conducted the business directly.

These are noble aspirations. We will see that the law sometimes falls short, and, when it does, tax shelters pop up like weeds. But sometimes the law gets it right, as in the *Basye* case discussed in the next section.

¶1103 *BASYE* AND *REALIZATION*

A 1973 Supreme Court case illustrates how the *realization* rules apply to partners in a partnership. In particular, it illustrates that any income earned by a partnership must immediately be realized as income to the individual partners.

In *United States v. Basye*,[3] the issue was whether or not the partners had to include payments made by a third party into a pension fund. The case arose out of the formation of the Kaiser Permanente medical group, a famous, path-breaking HMO in Northern California. Kaiser, a corporation, ran the health plan, and Permanente was a partnership of physicians. By contract, the Permanente partnership agreed to provide physicians to Kaiser and its patients. Kaiser, for its part, agreed to pay a current fee of $2.60 per patient per month, plus an additional fee (of twelve cents per patient per month) to be contributed to a pension plan for those physicians.

It was the terms of the pension plan that led to the tax dispute. Every month, Kaiser contributed money to the pension plan. All the money in the pension plan would eventually be paid out to Permanente partners and employees. That is, Kaiser could not, under any circumstances, get its money back. But the pension plan incorporated a complicated vesting formula. Each physician would be entitled to a pension only if she reached retirement age, had accumulated 10 or more years of service, and met certain other requirements. If money set aside for a particular physician's pension was forfeited, it would go back into the total pool and would eventually fund retirement benefits for some other doctor in the Permanente group.

Complicating matters further, the pension fund was set up for the benefit of all the Permanente doctors. Some of these doctors were partners, but others were employees of the partnership. So not every dollar that Kaiser contributed to the pension fund would necessarily end up in the hands of a partner physician. Over the period at issue in the case, Kaiser contributed about $2 million to the pension plan.

The IRS took the position that all $2 million should have been included in the incomes of the Permanente partners, according to their percentage interests in the partnership. The partners protested: the money couldn't be income to them, they reasoned, because as individuals, they had no current entitlement to the money. The uncertainty would only be resolved years later, when they reached retirement.

Both the district court and the Ninth Circuit ruled for the doctors. But the Supreme Court reversed, upholding the IRS point of view. The key precedent, said the Court, was the assignment-of-income case, *Lucas v. Earl*.[4] In *Earl*, as you might (but probably won't!) remember from your basic tax course, a lawyer attempted to assign half his income to his wife. The Supreme Court there held

---

[3] 410 U.S. 441 (1973).
[4] 281 U.S. 111 (1930).

that the assignment of income was ineffective, because the income had been earned by Mr. Earl's efforts and could not be shifted to Mrs. Earl.

Applying *Earl* to the Permanente pension fund, the Supreme Court concluded that the partners should be taxed on all $2 million. Kaiser, after all, hadn't contributed the money out of the goodness of its (corporate) heart. The $2 million contribution was a bargained-for item in the contract that compensated Permanente for providing its physicians' services.

The Court acknowledged that individual partners, like Dr. Basye, could not know how much (if any) money they would eventually receive as a pension. But, said the Court – and here is the big takeaway for partnership tax! – the key is that the *partnership* had earned the money by its activities. Having earned the money, the partnership had no choice but to allocate the funds among its partners to be taxed. It was immaterial, the Court concluded, that the distributive share (*i.e.*, allocated taxable income) of any particular partner might not match her eventual pension payout:

> It should be clear that the contingent and unascertainable nature of each partner's share under the retirement trust is irrelevant to the computation of his distributive share. The partnership had received as income a definite sum which was not subject to diminution or forfeiture. Only its ultimate disposition among the employees and partners remained uncertain.[5]

Put another way, the Court held that the Permanente partners had to *realize* all $2 million of income now, even though later on they might receive less than that.

But don't feel too sorry for the Permanente doctors. The issue here really boils down to *tax deferral*. To see why, let's put some simple numbers on the *Basye* facts. Suppose that James is a partner in Permanente, with a 5% share of profits. Given the holding in *Basye*, he must include 5% of the $2 million Kaiser contribution (that is, $100,000) in his income now. Later on, James will encounter several possible scenarios:

(1) Some of the money taxed to James will be paid out to other Permanente doctors who are employees (rather than partners); James will then receive a deduction under Section 162.

(2) Some of the money taxed to James may be paid out to him; in that case, James won't be taxed again, since he's already paid the tax.

(3) All of the money taxed to James may be forfeited by him if he doesn't meet the conditions for a retirement pension; in that case, he receives a deduction in the year of forfeiture.

You can see why *Basye* is really all about timing. James is taxed *now* on the income, but he's never taxed again if he gets a payout of the money. And if he

---

[5] 410 U.S. at 456.

ultimately receives less than what he was taxed on, either because the money goes to an employee or is forfeited back to the pool, he gets a deduction. So, the Court in *Basye* was properly applying partnership principles. Permanente as a business had definitely earned the $2 million, and so the partners had to be taxed. Uncertainties in their actual payouts would be resolved later on.

This, as we have seen, is a fundamental principle of partnership taxation. Because a partnership is a pass-through, the system has to tax the partners on 100% of partnership income – there simply isn't anyone else to pay the tax. The *realization* doctrine thus operates as if the partners owned the business directly. If any individual had contracted to receive an irrevocable $2 million from a client, there'd be no doubt that it was taxable income. When the partnership receives such income, partners must be taxed just the same.

¶1104 PROBLEM 11.1: PARTNERSHIP TAX BASICS

Consider the tax consequences of the following transactions for the partnership and for each of the partners:

- Dahlia and Ewan form the DE Partnership ("DE"). Each contributes $200 in cash. The partnership buys a fast-food franchise, rents space, and hires workers.
    (1) In year one, DE earns gross income of $100. Depreciation expense is $20, and workers' salaries and rent total $35. How much must Dahlia and Ewan include on their tax returns?

ANSWER TO (1)

We know that the total income to be divided is $45 ($100 less ($20 + $35)). But we can't know how much each partner must report until we know more about the partnership agreement. It's possible that Dahlia and Ewan have agreed to split all profits and all expenses 50-50. In that case, each would report $50 of gross income and report deductions of $10 for depreciation and $17.50 for salaries. But it may well be that the two parties have agreed on a more complicated split that would affect their tax liabilities.

Section 704(a) expresses this general idea when it requires that each partner's distributive share be determined in accordance with the partnership agreement. (There are many exceptions and elaborations in the Code and regulations, but this is the bedrock principle.)

   (2) Suppose that the partnership agreement provides that no cash may be distributed to either partner before year five, and at that time, a distribution will be permitted only if DE has earned at least $1000 in net income. Would that provision change your answer to question (1)?

ANSWER TO (2)

Nope. This is a variant of the *Basye* case, which held that restrictions on (and uncertainty about) cash distributions do not excuse partners from including in current income their distributive shares of partnership income.

¶1105 BUSINESS 101: WHAT IS A PARTNERSHIP?

Many people use the term "partnership" to mean any joint venture. But in tax and business circles, the term has a more formal meaning. A partnership is a business entity with at least two owners, where their economic relationship is governed by a partnership agreement and by state law.

A partnership agreement is, basically, a contract that sets out the terms of the deal. The law typically permits partners wide latitude in drafting whatever terms they like; state partnership law mostly acts to recognize the entity and to fill in gaps if the partners are silent.

By contrast, a corporation (*see* "What is a Corporation?" in Chapter 2) is a more standardized business vehicle. Each stockholder has the same relation to the business as every other stockholder: their equity interests are standardized, and only the percentage interest varies. (Even a corporation with multiple classes of stock typically doesn't reach the degree of customization permissible in a partnership, and each holder of each class has the same rights as every other.)

Some partnerships have limited liability for some or all partners (that is, creditors may not claim the assets of the partners if the partnership fails to pay), but state law sometimes restricts the availability of limited liability.

A typical partnership agreement, then, covers the big contingencies that are likely to arise. Among these:

- Who contributes capital initially?
- Who must contribute more capital if needed later?
- Who must cover the debts of the partnership if the firm's assets are insufficient?
- Who receives distributions, and when?
- Who may exit the partnership, and who may buy their interest?

> **EXAMPLE 4.** Let's revisit Abbie and Brent, first introduced in the note on corporations. The two have decided to go into business together, running a restaurant to be called Farmstand.
>
> They form Farmstand Partnership under Connecticut law. Abbie and Brent sit down with their lawyers and hash out the terms of the agreement. Abbie will contribute most of the initial capital, but Brent will have to pony up an additional $100,000 if needed in the first five years. Abbie and Brent will both be liable for debts equally, if partnership assets are insufficient. And all profits will be retained by and reinvested in the partnership until there is a cushion of at least $200,000. After that, Abbie will receive 2/3 of all distributions, and Brent 1/3.

In Year Ten, a restaurant customer slips and falls on a wet floor. He sues Farmstand and is awarded a judgment of $500,000. Farmstand has no insurance and has assets of $200,000. Abbie and Brent must each pay 50% of the remaining $300,000 owed to the slip-and-fall victim.

CHAPTER 12

From Two Levels of Tax to One: The Basics of Partnership Taxation

Introduction . . . . ¶1200
Each Partner (Not the Partnership) Pays the Tax . . . . ¶1201
Partners Must Report Income Even Without Distribution . . . . ¶1202
Partners Adjust Their Bases to Ensure Income is Taxed Only Once . . . . ¶1203
Problem 12.1: Partnership Tax Basics . . . . ¶1204
Advanced Problems . . . . ¶1205

¶1200 INTRODUCTION

Getting your head around partnership tax is no small feat, for two understandable reasons. A first and obvious problem is that the rules are complex. (Just say "partnership tax" to even the most seasoned tax lawyer, and she may shudder, at least a little.) In later chapters, we'll unpack the conceptual problems that motivate the rules so that you can anchor the complex overgrowth of rules to a set of basic problems (mostly involving *tax deferral* and *income shifting*).

A second and less apparent problem is that the partnership rules require you to set aside much of what you know about business taxation and learn an entirely new kind of tax logic. To this point, the corporate tax has been our model for business taxation. If you've persisted in reading to this point, you've internalized (maybe more than you know!) double-tax concepts like an entity-level tax and a second-level tax on distributions. But partnership tax is going to unsettle many of the concepts you've learned. Fundamental building blocks like basis and distribution work very differently in partnership tax – because the system aims to collect just one tax and not two.

In this chapter, we will tackle that second problem first by introducing the mechanics of a one-level tax and contrasting the two-level rules of the corporate tax. In Chapters 13 through 15, we will go on to study the specifics and complexities of partnership tax in more depth. But having a mental picture of the basic structure will help you visualize what the technical rules are trying to accomplish.

We can boil down the mechanics of partnership tax into just three sets of rules. The three work together to ensure that partnership income is taxed once and at the partners' marginal tax rates:

- First, there is no entity-level tax; instead, partnership income is taxable to each partner at his or her marginal tax rate.

- Second, income is allocated to partners even if the partnership does not make a distribution.
- And, third, each partner's basis in their partnership interest increases to reflect income allocations and decreases to reflect loss allocations and distributions.

¶1201 EACH PARTNER (NOT THE PARTNERSHIP) PAYS THE TAX

Unlike a corporation, a partnership is not itself a taxable entity. The partnership certainly exists as a legal creation, of course, but the Internal Revenue Code does not impose income tax at the partnership level. This doesn't mean that the Code ignores the partnership entirely. If you take a course in partnership taxation, you will see that some tax administration takes place at the partnership level, and some items of income and deductions are aggregated at the partnership level. But, very generally speaking, tax is calculated at the partner level and collected from partners and not the partnership itself.

> **EXAMPLE 1.** *Pass Through of Income and Deductions.* John and Dora are equal partners in the JD partnership, which runs several vegan restaurants. In Year 1, the partnership earns gross income of $1,000,000. The business pays salaries of $500,000 and is entitled to deduct depreciation of $200,000 on its buildings and equipment.
>
> You know that a partnership is a pass-through (or "flow through") entity, and now we can make that concrete. The JD partnership has net income of $300,000: that's the gross income of $1 million less the $700,000 total deductions. But none of this is taxed to the partnership itself. Instead, the partnership divides up all of its tax-related items and allocates them to partners in accordance with the economics of their partnership agreement.
>
> In our simple example, John and Dora are equal partners. So, each one would report half of each partnership item. Specifically, John would report $500,000 in gross income, $250,000 in salary deductions, and $100,000 in depreciation. Dora would do the same.

The flow-through rules might at first seem to be a great deal of effort just to get to the same bottom line. After all, you could just as easily say that the partnership has net income of $300,000 and allocate half to each partner. But as we will discuss in greater depth in Chapter 14, the pass-through to the partners of separate items of income, gain, deduction, and loss serves an important purpose. Each item can then blend seamlessly into the individual partner's return. For instance, if, in some year the JD Partnership had a capital loss, that loss might have different effects for John and for Dora, depending on whether they also report capital gains (from some other investment) on their returns.

You can now see how the partnership rules manage to tax each partner at the appropriate marginal tax rate. If John has lots of other income that puts him in the 37% bracket, the net income from the partnership will be added on top and taxed at 37%. If Dora, by contrast, has lots of ordinary losses from other business endeavors, she may be able to offset her entire allocation of partnership income, paying tax at, in effect, a 0% marginal tax rate.

¶1202 PARTNERS MUST REPORT INCOME EVEN WITHOUT DISTRIBUTION

When we studied the corporate tax, distributions played a central role, and for a good reason: shareholders pay tax only when they receive a distribution. And so, the Code must contend with a range of issues including disguised distributions, stock redemptions, and stock dividends.[1]

By contrast, distributions are less significant in partnership tax. And again, there is a simple reason: in the partnership context, the timing and amount of income is not (generally) linked to distributions. Let's start with a simple example:

> **EXAMPLE 2.** *Partners' Income is Not Linked to Distributions.* Continue with John and Dora, the vegan restaurateurs from Example 1. They've formed the JD Partnership and intend to share all income and deductions 50-50. Suppose that, in their first year of operations, the partnership earns *net income* of $300,000. Dora and John are thrilled with their success, and they decide to expand by opening another restaurant. To fund the new venture, they decide to retain all their earnings and use them to buy and refurbish a new building downtown.
>
> As you can see, the example is engineered to show how a partnership might earn substantial amounts (here, $300,000) but make a business decision not to distribute those earnings. Put another way, a partnership, like a corporation, can retain earnings to reinvest in the business.
>
> But the tax consequences of retentions are very different for a partnership and for a corporation. If JD were a corporation, it would pay the 21% corporate-level tax on its $300,000 of earnings (and so would have $237,000 after taxes to invest in the new restaurant). As a partnership, JD pays no entity-level tax, and so it can invest the entire $300,000 in its business. But there's a big catch: John and Dora *must pay tax on their share of the partnership's earnings, even though they have not received any cash.*
>
> So, John reports $150,000 on his return and Dora does the same.

This tax result may at first seem harsh. Poor John and Dora – they have to report huge amounts of income on their tax returns and pay tax at their marginal tax rates, all without any extra cash at all to pay the tax. They will either have to dip into savings or borrow the money to pay the IRS.

---

[1] *See* Chapters 7 and 8, *supra.*

The result seems harsh because we filter it through our experience as workers – we would be in bad shape, indeed, as well as hopping mad, if we had to pay tax on wages we never received. But partners in a partnership are owners, not workers. Both John and Dora are better off by $150,000, measured by the value of their partnership interest. And so, it's appropriate for them to pay income tax on their earnings.

Think about it this way: since there's no entity-level tax on partnerships, the only possible taxpayers are John and Dora. If the Code permitted partners to defer paying their tax until earnings were distributed, then partnerships would be an amazing (and unwarranted) *tax deferral* device.

And any remaining sympathy you feel for John and Dora should evaporate when you realize that, as partners, they control partnership distributions. They can't protest that "the partnership" declined to distribute cash to them, since they are the partnership! You might worry that minority partners could be outvoted, but keep in mind that even small-stakes partners can (and should) negotiate distributions provisions when they join the partnership in the first place.

> **EXAMPLE 3.** *Partnership Tax Distributions.* After seven long years as an associate, Marlo has just been offered a BigLaw partnership. She will have a 1% interest in the firm's earnings, and she is thrilled to be stepping up to partner status. Knowing a good bit of partnership tax, Marlo reads the partnership agreement carefully and is pleased to see a "tax distributions" provision. That provision (which is common in professional partnership agreements) guarantees that the partnership will distribute to Marlo, each year, an amount at least sufficient to pay federal, state, and local taxes on her share of partnership income.

¶1203 PARTNERS ADJUST THEIR BASES TO ENSURE INCOME IS TAXED ONLY ONCE

The third key component of partnership taxation is the adjustment of partners' outside bases. The Code requires that partners *increase* their basis in their partnership interest ("outside basis") by allocated income and *decrease* their outside basis for distributions.

From the perspective of corporate tax, these basis adjustments seem odd – because there is no counterpart in corporate tax. But in the partnership context, these two basis adjustments – one for income earned and one for distributions – are critical to make sure that partnership income is taxed only once.

¶1203.01   PARTNERS' OUTSIDE BASIS INCREASES TO REFLECT ALLOCATED INCOME

To see the point, we can begin with a stylized example.

EXAMPLE 4. *Adjusting Outside Basis for Allocated Income.* Suppose that Kara and Lonnie form the K-L partnership, a new law firm, intending to split all profits 50-50. To keep the numbers simple, assume that they don't contribute any money to the firm – just the promise of future services. So, it makes sense that they each have an initial basis of zero in their partnership interest. (It makes sense because they haven't invested anything in the partnership yet; their future income will be taxable when and if it arises.)

Now suppose that the K-L Partnership earns $500 and distributes nothing. We know (thanks to ¶1202) that Kara and Lonnie must each report $250 on their own tax return. But think about where that leaves the partners. Each one now owns a partnership interest worth $250 (that's because the partnership as a whole has retained all $500). If the partners continued with their historic basis of zero, they would have a built-in gain of $250 each ($500 total). That can't be right, though, because they have already paid full tax on the $500.

To see the point another way, suppose that Kara's basis stays at $0 and she decides to sell her interest to Moira, a third party, for $250. Kara would report a $250 gain. That result would tax Kara twice on the same income, violating a key objective of the partnership tax rules – to tax partnership income just once.

To avoid the double tax result, the partnership rules increase partners' basis in their partnership interests by the amount of income the partnership allocates to them. In the example, Kara and Lonnie would report $250 each on their tax returns and increase their outside basis by the same amount. Kara, for instance, would then have a basis of $250 (zero initial basis plus $250 of allocated income). Thanks to the basis increase, Kara could sell her partnership interest for $250 without recognizing any gain. And that's the right answer.

If all this makes sense to you, great! You can move on to the next subsection on distributions. But if not, here's another conceptual way to get to the same point. When Kara pays tax on $250, but the partnership retains the money, we can recharacterize the transaction *as if* Kara received $250 in cash and then reinvested it in the partnership. When we see the transaction that way, the basis increase makes sense: Kara got the money, paid all taxes owed, and then reinvested the money in the partnership, creating $250 of basis in the process.

And if you're still not 100% there, here's a third way of understanding the basis increase. Basis is a fundamental part of the income tax because it creates the baseline for measuring when someone has made money on an investment. As you learned in your basic tax course, basis always reflects an investment of after-tax income, because that is the right baseline for judging future gains.

Concretely, then, if I put $100 into an investment, I get a basis of $100 because I have already been taxed on the $100. If I then get $105 from that investment, I have $5 of income, not $105, because the income tax targets only the incremental gain above what has already been taxed.

¶1203.01

These general principles underlie the partnership basis adjustment. When a partner like Kara pays tax on (say) $250 of partnership income, she should get basis for that amount to reflect the fact that she's already paid taxes on it. That way, when she sells her partnership interest for (say) $250, the tax system will recognize that she hasn't made any incremental gains.

¶1203.02   PARTNERS' OUTSIDE BASIS DECREASES TO REFLECT DISTRIBUTIONS

We've seen that partners' outside basis increases to reflect retained earnings. It follows that distributions of previously-taxed income should not be taxed again, and that basis should fall to reflect distributions of those retained earnings.

> **EXAMPLE 5.** *Adjusting Outside Basis for Distributions.* Recall Kara and Lonnie from Example 4. They each started with an outside basis of zero. They then increased their outside basis by $250 to reflect partnership income allocations. So, for the moment, each has an outside basis of $250.
>
> Now, suppose that a year has passed, and the partners have reconsidered their plan to reinvest the $500 in a new restaurant. Maybe the real-estate deal falls through or a competing restaurant opens up down the block. But for whatever reason, they decide just to distribute all $500 to the partners.
>
> When the partnership distributes $250 to each partner, neither should report any income, because they've already been taxed on that amount. Instead, each will decrease his or her outside basis by the amount of the distribution. Afterward, then, Kara and Lonnie will once again have a zero basis in the partnership.

Conceptually, we can understand the treatment of distributions as a portfolio reshuffle. The distribution of $250 to each partner doesn't create (or reflect) any additional economic income to the partners. Instead, it's just a change in the form of their holdings. Concretely, before the distribution, Kara had zero cash and a partnership interest worth $250 and with a basis of $250. After the distribution, Kara has $250 cash and a partnership interest worth $0 (we're assuming that the partnership has no value besides cash on hand). The $250 shouldn't be taxable to Kara, because she's already been taxed in the prior year. And cash always has a basis equal to face value, and so it makes sense that Kara's $250 of basis "migrates" away from the partnership interest and to the cash.

We can also understand the basis result as avoiding the creation of an unwarranted loss. Suppose that the Code did not adjust Kara's basis for distributions. She would then have a basis of $250 in a partnership interest worth zero. If she sold the partnership interest for zero, she could then claim a loss under Section 165 – even though she hasn't suffered an economic loss.

Looking at the same rules from a third perspective, we can see that outside basis serves as a measure of each partner's already-taxed income. Kara has a basis of $250 because she has already paid tax on that amount. So, if she gets distributions of up to $250, she shouldn't owe any more tax. (We will see that if she receives a larger distribution (say, $300), then she *has* made money and should report $50 of gain.)

¶1203.03 CONTRAST THE CORPORATE TAX RESULTS

At this point, you can begin to glimpse the elegance of the partnership system and the importance of adjusting outside basis for earnings and distributions. (It may take a few more examples and discussions to have a firm grasp, but that's just what the next few chapters will provide.) But that insight raises a new question: if these basis adjustments are such a great way to measure income, why doesn't the corporate tax use them too?

The answer lies in the logic of the double tax. The corporate tax can't incorporate these basis adjustments because it aims to collect two levels of tax on corporate income. If the corporate tax did adjust shareholder basis up by corporate earnings and down by distributions, the two-level corporate tax would collapse into a single-level (partnership) tax.

> **EXAMPLE 6.** *Single Tax vs. Double Tax.* Let's go back to Kara and Lonnie and see how they'd be taxed if they formed a corporation. Recall that they put $0 into the venture, and so they'd each have a stock basis of $0. When the corporation earns $500, it would pay corporate-level tax. The shareholders would be unaffected: they wouldn't report any of the income on their tax returns, and they wouldn't adjust their stock basis. The shareholders will be taxed when they receive distributions, and they will not receive any basis "credit" for previously-taxed corporate income.

¶1204 PROBLEM 12.1: PARTNERSHIP TAX BASICS

Suppose that Cassie and David form the C-D partnership, with each contributing $100. They intend to split all profits and losses 50-50. In the first year of the partnership, C-D earns $250 in *net income* and makes a distribution of $50 to each partner. In the second year of the partnership, C-D earns no additional *net income* and distributes $20 to each partner. What are the federal income tax consequences to all the parties?

ANSWER

Starting out, Cassie and David each have a basis of $100 in their partnership interest.[2] That makes sense, because each one has put $100 of capital into the deal.

---

[2] *See* Code Sec. 722.

When C-D earns $250, half will be allocated to Cassie, and half to David (since this is a 50-50 partnership). So, each partner will report $125 on her or his tax return and increase their basis in the partnership interest by that amount. The partners' basis is also reduced by the Year One distribution of $50 to each partner.[3] When the dust clears, each will have a basis of $175 ($100 +125 – 50).

You can double check to see if that result is sensible. At the end of Year One (*i.e.,* after the $250 is earned and the $50 to each partner is distributed), the C-D partnership is worth $350 ($200 original capital plus $250 earnings less $100 distribution). Half of $350 is $175. So, if either Cassie or David sold their partnership interest for fair market value, they would have zero gain or loss. That's the right answer, because they have been fully taxed on the C-D partnership's income.

In Year Two, there is no net income – only an additional distribution of $20 to each partner. The distribution is not taxable. (That makes sense, because C-D hasn't earned any additional income.) Instead, the distribution just reduces each partner's basis in their partnership interest by $20 to $155. And again, we can see that this is the right answer because the C-D partnership is now worth $310 (*i.e.,* last year's value of $350 – the $40 distribution). Half of $310 is $155, and so, once again, each partner could sell for FMV and have no gain or loss.

¶1205 ADVANCED PROBLEMS

For more advanced problems, *see* Problems P1 and P2 in Appendix C, which also contain material discussed in Chapter 13.

---

[3] *See* Code Sec. 705.

CHAPTER 13

Tax Deferral and Partnership Contributions

Introduction	¶1300
Tax Deferral and Partnership Contributions	¶1301
Tax Deferral at the Partnership Level	¶1302
Problem 13.1: Contribution Basics	¶1303
Income Shifting and Contributed Property: The Role of Code Sec. 704(c)	¶1304
Problem 13.2: Section 704(c) and Its Limitations	¶1305
Advanced Problems	¶1306

¶1300 INTRODUCTION

The tax rules on partnership formation are a gift to us all. I know that sounds odd, but they really are, because they (mostly) revisit and reconfirm concepts you already know from corporate formation. Chapters 5 and 6 introduced Section 351, which governs incorporations. Here, we'll focus on Section 721, which governs partnership formation.

You may recall three key points about Section 351, and these will do a substantial amount of work in the partnership context too. First, without any special provision, the formation of a business would be a *realization* event. After all, the business owner exchanges property (say, a piece of real estate) for an ownership interest in an entity (stock or a partnership interest), and those represent distinct legal entitlements sufficient to trigger *realization* under cases like *Cottage Savings*.[1]

Second, policy makers recognized that imposing *realization* of gain on business formation could have detrimental effects. Triggering tax could discourage people from forming businesses – probably not a great thing for a capitalist economy. Forcing a *realization* event in the absence of a sale poses *valuation* problems, because it often won't be obvious what the value of the business assets are. Finally, imposing tax on business formation could create hardships for business owners, because they'd have to pay tax even though they haven't sold anything for cash. All of these issues are pretty much the same in the corporate and partnership context.

And so, we reach the third commonality: the Code provides a special provision (Section 351 for corporations and Section 721 for partnerships) that awards

---

[1] *Cottage Savings Ass'n v. Comm'r*, 499 U.S. 554 (1991).

nonrecognition to many (though not all) business formations. In both settings, the goal is the same: the Code doesn't eliminate gains or forgive the tax permanently. Instead, it grants *tax deferral* using the mechanism of carryover basis.

In the rest of this chapter, we will see how these rules operate in the partnership context, and we will point out a few differences between corporate and partnership settings as we go.

¶1301 *TAX DEFERRAL* AND PARTNERSHIP CONTRIBUTIONS

Let's begin with contributions of cash to a partnership – the simplest case. When a partner contributes, say, $100 to a partnership and receives a partnership interest in exchange, the tax treatment is pretty intuitive. She has purchased something – here, a partnership interest – and so she should have a basis equal to the purchase price of $100. That would be the right answer under general tax principles (codified in Section 1012), and it turns out it's the right answer for a partnership contribution too, thanks to Section 722.

Contributions of property raise additional issues, of course, because the contributing taxpayer may have built-in gain or loss. Here is where Section 721 comes into play, awarding *tax deferral* to (most) contributions of property to partnerships. In return, Section 722 awards the contributing partner a carryover basis, which ensures that any built-in gain or loss will eventually be recognized and taxed.

> **EXAMPLE 1.** *Partnership Formation.* Ernie and Flannery form the EF Partnership. Ernie contributes $500 in cash, and Flannery contributes Greenacre, with a basis of $410 and a fair market value of $500. Ernie and Flannery plan to share income and loss 50-50.
>
> Section 721 applies to any contribution of property to a partnership, whether the deal involves a new partnership (as here) or an existing one. Ernie's situation is the easiest: he has no gain or loss and a partnership interest with a basis of $500. Flannery benefits from Section 721 here because she receives nonrecognition treatment for the $90 of built-in gain. Section 721 insulates her from the *realization* of any gain. And in exchange, Section 722 imposes a carryover basis in the partnership interest equal to $410. Thus, if Flannery turned around and sold the partnership interest to a third party for $500, she would then recognize $90 of gain, the appropriate amount. So, all is well with the world, and we can all sleep at night.

The carryover basis regime of Section 721 should feel familiar to you, because it reflects the same principles that govern corporate formations under Section 351 (and, incidentally, corporate reorganizations under Section 368).

Still, there are a few differences between the corporate and partnership contribution rules. Notably, Section 351 is more restrictive than Section 721; the former applies only if the 80% "control" test (set forth in Section 368(c) and discussed in Chapter 5) is met. Section 721 has no control test: it applies to any contribution by any partner at any time. (There are a few special exceptions, having to do with investment companies, foreign persons, and intangibles in Sections 721(b), (c), and (d), but we will overlook those for the sake of a general presentation.)

¶1302   *TAX DEFERRAL* AT THE PARTNERSHIP LEVEL

At this stage, we haven't yet said anything about the partnership-level treatment of contributions, and here things get a little more perplexing. The basic rule, which is sensible enough, is that the partnership takes a carryover basis in contributed property.

> **EXAMPLE 2.** *Partnership Basis in Contributed Property.* Continuing the example of Ernie and Flannery, Section 723 provides that the EF Partnership takes a carryover basis of $410 in Greenacre. Thus, if the partnership immediately sold Greenacre to someone for $500, the partners would have flow-through gain of $90. (In the next section, we will see that the gain would all be reported by Flannery under Section 704(c).)

You can probably see (or at least intuit) why carryover basis at the partnership level makes sense, but it may be less obvious why it also can reach the wrong result. Carryover basis at the partnership level ensures that individuals cannot use partnerships to achieve a level of *tax deferral* that they couldn't achieve directly.

To see the point, think about Flannery as an individual (before she joins any partnership). She could continue to enjoy *tax deferral* if she just held onto Greenacre. But she would have to *realize* the $90 gain if she wanted to sell Greenacre and reinvest in, say, the stock market. The carryover basis rule of Section 723 ensures that Flannery can't get a better tax result by forming a partnership. She can certainly continue to enjoy *tax deferral* as long as the EF Partnership holds onto Greenacre. But if EF sells Greenacre, the carryover basis rule ensures that the $90 of gain will be *realized*.

So far, so good. But you may have spotted the perplexity here: Giving a carryover basis to *both* the contributing partner and to the partnership seems to create the potential for double taxation of the same gain. The duplication of gain is familiar and correct in the case of corporate formation, as Chapter 5 notes. But partnership tax is supposed to collect one level of tax and not two! So how does the system avoid the double tax result on contributed property?

There are two scenarios that might result in double taxation. Let's deal with the easier one first, because it's a chance to see how the partnership tax rules elegantly avoid double taxation. The key, we will see, is the basis adjustments introduced in Chapter 12.

EXAMPLE 3. *What if the Partnership Sells Greenacre?* Suppose that EF immediately sells Greenacre for $500. The partnership *realizes* gain of $90, thanks to the carryover basis rule in Section 723. The $90 of gain (we will shortly see) will be allocated entirely to Flannery, the contributing partner. So, Flannery will pay tax on the $90 *and* will increase her basis by the same amount. Voilà! When the dust settles, Flannery will have a basis of $500 in her partnership interest ($410 carryover under Section 722 plus $90 basis increase under Section 705).

That's the right answer, because if Flannery turns around and sells her partnership interest for its fair market value of $500, she will *realize* no further gain. Thus, the pass through of gain to Flannery plus the adjustment of her basis work together to ensure just one level of tax. Once again, we can sleep soundly knowing that partners everywhere need not fear double taxation.

But there's another scenario that threatens double taxation, and unfortunately the partnership rules don't have quite the same kind of elegant solution.

EXAMPLE 4. *What if the Partner Sells Her Partnership Interest?* Now let's suppose that Flannery sells her partnership interest before the EF Partnership sells Greenacre. Flannery will *realize* and recognize a gain of $90 on the sale of her partnership interest. The buyer of her partnership interest (let's give him the creative name of Buyer) will have a basis of $500. *But EF itself still has a basis of $410 in Greenacre.* Thus, when EF sells Greenacre for $500, one or more partners (in this case, Buyer) will have to report and pay a second tax on gain of $90.

The source of the double-tax problem is that the inside (partnership) basis of Greenacre isn't automatically updated to reflect Flannery's *realization* of $90 of gain at the partner level. Accordingly, one way to avoid double taxation is to update the inside basis of assets when a partner realizes gain or loss. The problem is that updating basis can be complicated. The Flannery example is simple, of course: we can trace the problem to the basis of Greenacre, and we know we should update it to $500. But in a real-world setting, partnerships own lots of property, and partners may come and go frequently, making the task of updating a complex one.

Accordingly, the Code leaves the choice to the taxpayer. Sections 743 and 754 of the Code permit (but do not require) partnerships to update inside basis when partners sell interests in the partnership.

Finally, the (somewhat) good news is that even if a partnership does not update inside basis for sales of partnership interests, the double tax will eventually be reversed, thanks to our friendly neighborhood basis adjustments. Think about Buyer in the example. He starts with a basis of $500 and then, when the partnership sells Greenacre, he will be allocated he gain of $90. (This is another Section 704(c) result, discussed below.)

Buyer is going to feel aggrieved at this stage: he paid full value for his partnership interest, and yet he's saddled with $90 of gain thanks to a prior partner's transactions. But keep in mind that the basis of Buyer's partnership interest will rise by $90 to $590. He now has a basis of $590 in an asset (his partnership interest) that is worth only $500. And so, when he sells his own partnership interest for its fair market value of $500, he will *realize* a $90 loss.

This is all cold comfort for Buyer, of course. The loss is entirely artificial and may be long-deferred if the partnership sells Greenacre long before Buyer exits the partnership. But, mathematically, it all works out: Buyer has an artificial gain of $90 that will (eventually) be offset by an artificial loss of the same amount.

You might – and in fact, you should – worry that artificial gains and losses like these can spawn tax shelters. Taxpayers have shown considerable talent for turning these unintended results to their advantage. In one (in)famous case, called *Southgate*, the parties attempted to use the carryover basis rule of Section 723 to transfer a huge built-in loss from a non-U.S. party (which could not use the loss) to a U.S. taxpayer. The taxpayer ultimately lost the case when the court held that the partnership was a sham and that, in substance, the U.S. taxpayer had purchased the assets for cash (denying him the artificially high carryover basis he sought).[2]

¶1303 PROBLEM 13.1: CONTRIBUTION BASICS

Consider the tax consequences of the following transactions:
(1) D and E form the DE Partnership ("DE"). D contributes $200 in cash. E contributes undeveloped Greenacre (Basis=$110, FMV=$200). The partnership agreement gives each party a one-half interest in all profits and losses.

ANSWER TO (1)

Under Section 721(a), the formation of a partnership is a nonrecognition event. Under Section 722, D's basis is $200, and E's basis is $110. Under Section 723, the partnership takes a basis of $110 in Greenacre.

(2) In Year 1, DE earns $150 in net income.

ANSWER TO (2)

Per the partnership agreement (and Section 704), $75 is allocated to each partner. Each partner must pay tax on her share, and each increases the basis in the partnership interest by $75.[3]

---

[2] *Southgate Master Fund LLC v. U.S.*, 659 F.3d (5th Cir. 2011).
[3] Code Sec. 705.

(3) In Year 2, DE sells Greenacre for $230.

ANSWER TO (3)

DE recognizes gain of $120 ($230 - $110). Under Section 704(c)(1)(A), the first $90 of gain must be allocated to the contributing partner (E). The remainder of the gain ($30) is allocated, per the partnership agreement, equally between the partners (so $15 to each).

(4) In Year 3, DE distributes $100 to D and distributes Blueacre (purchased by the partnership for $75 and with a FMV=$100) to E.

ANSWER TO (4)

At this stage, outside basis (the partners' bases in their partnership interests) becomes relevant. D's basis is $290 (the original $200 plus $75 of income plus $15 of gain). E's basis is also $290 (the original $110 plus $75 of income plus $90 of gain plus $15 of gain). D pays no tax on her distribution of $100 and reduces her basis to $190.[4] E also pays no tax on the receipt of Blueacre; she takes Blueacre with a carryover basis of $75 and reduces her outside basis from $290 to $215.[5]

¶1304 INCOME SHIFTING AND CONTRIBUTED PROPERTY: THE ROLE OF SEC. 704(c)

Section 704(c) is one of the heroes of partnership taxation. Really. It's a workhorse that prevents a very easy and very destructive kind of tax shelter. Like all heroes, though, it has a tragic flaw, which we will get to shortly. But it also does a lot of good.

To see why we need Section 704(c), we need to travel back into the mists of time before 1984. You already know that, given the (legal) chance, taxpayers will leap at the opportunity to shift income. A dollar of income taxed at, say, 40% leaves only 60 cents for the taxpayer to spend, while a dollar taxed at 0% leaves $1. So, taxpayers are always on the lookout for legal ways to shift income from high-bracket taxpayers to low- (or zero-) bracket ones.

For example, suppose that Stella owns Greenacre, with a basis of $15 and a fair market value of $100. She'd like to sell Greenacre and reinvest in a portfolio of diversified securities, but a sale would trigger the *realization* of all $85 of gain. If Stella is in a high tax bracket, the taxes owed would take a big bite out of her capital. (At the 20% top capital gains rate, for instance, she'd pay taxes of $17 and have $83 left to reinvest. 100-(.2*85) = 83)

---

[4] Code Sec. 731(a)(1).

[5] Code Sec.s 732 and 733.

Enter the partnership. Before the enactment of Section 704(c), taxpayers like Stella could use partnerships to achieve income-shifting that isn't possible for an individual taxpayer. The basic idea is simple: a high-bracket taxpayer would form a partnership with a low- (or zero-) bracket partner and use the partnership rules to allocate gain to the low-tax party. Presto! The partnership could reinvest the money, and the taxes owed would be low (or zero).

> **EXAMPLE 5.** *Shifting Gains on Contributed Property (Before 704(c)).* Let's stay with the example of Stella, who has a basis of $15 in Greenacre, with a fair market value of $100. Stella has agreed to form an investment partnership with Big University, a tax-exempt institution. So, Stella contributes Greenacre, and Big University contributes $100 in cash. Thanks to Section 721, the formation of the partnership is tax-free to Stella, and the partnership takes a $15 basis in Greenacre.
>
> At this stage, Stella has maintained *tax deferral* on her $85 of gain, but that's not really objectionable, since she could get the same favorable result without a partnership. She could simply hold (and not sell) Greenacre and achieve the same degree of deferral.
>
> Instead, the opportunity for *income shifting* arises once the property has come to rest in the partnership. When the partnership sells Greenacre for $100, it *realizes* $85 of gain. Before the enactment of Section 704(c), the partners could agree to allocate that gain entirely to Big University. Big U. wouldn't care, because it's tax-exempt. But Stella would, in effect, be able to "borrow" the university's low tax rate: the partnership would have the full $100 to reinvest, and no partner would need a distribution to pay tax.
>
> Thanks to the partnership basis rules, this kind of income shifting produced only *tax deferral:* that is, eventually, Stella would cash out her partnership interest and would then pay the tax owed. To see why, recall that Stella's basis in her partnership interest would be $15 (not $100). Suppose that, at some point, Stella decided to withdraw her $100 contribution (measured in fair market value). At that stage, Section 731(a) would trigger *realization* of Stella's $85 gain. (The statute requires partners to recognize gain if they receive a distribution of money that exceeds their outside basis.)
>
> Still, *tax deferral* is nothing to sneeze at. In the meantime, which could be decades, Stella's partnership could reinvest the $100 over and over, deferring the tax on Stella's $85 gain until Stella withdrew her money.

Now, this whole transaction has a strong and fishy odor. The IRS might attack the deal on *substance over form* grounds. For instance, if the partnership doesn't result in any sharing of risk between Stella and Big University, the IRS might claim that there is no partnership at all.[6] But *substance over form* cases

---

[6] *See,* for example, the winning IRS argument in *Southgate Master Fund LLC v. U.S.*, 659 F.3d 466 (5th Cir. 2011).

¶1304

are difficult to litigate and to win, and savvy taxpayers can often throw in just enough reality to the deal to muddy the analysis.

Enter Section 704(c), cape billowing in the wind. It creates a bright-line rule that shuts down the possibility of *income shifting* by simply disallowing it. When a partner like Stella contributes appreciated property to a partnership, she is, in effect, "tagged" with the built-in gain. That gain will follow her around and may not be allocated to a different partner. Thus, the *income shifting* game is thwarted.

> **EXAMPLE 6.** *Application of Section 704(c).* Sticking with the example of Stella, let's see how Section 704(c) changes the tax result. Just as before, Stella can contribute Greenacre to the partnership without *realization*. And, just as before, Stella's outside basis and the partnership's inside basis are both $15.
>
> The critical difference is that, when the partnership sells Greenacre, the parties must allocate the $85 gain to Stella, the contributor of Greenacre. They may not allocate it to Big University, no matter what the partnership agreement may provide. And so, Stella must pay tax on the $85 of gain. In the end, she is no better off and no worse off than if she had sold the property herself. She can maintain *tax deferral* as long as she (or the partnership) holds onto Greenacre. But when it's sold, she must pay the tax due.

Section 704(c) applies to loss on property as well, and that makes sense, since parties can benefit from shifting losses as well as income. (Imagine what would happen if tax-exempt Big University could dump its losing investments in a partnership and shift the tax losses to high-bracket Stella.) You might think that the parties could avoid Section 704(c) by distributing the property to *another* partner, thus getting the property out of the partnership's ambit entirely. But Section 704(c) anticipates that gambit and applies to "tag" the contributing partner with the built-in gain if the partnership distributes contributed property to another partner.

This all seems pretty airtight, but, in fact, Section 704(c) has inevitable flaws because, in the end, it is stuck with the basic fact of the *realization* requirement. Section 704(c) does a great deal of good by linking built-in gain to the contributing partner. But the persistence of the *realization* regime means that taxpayers can still make use of partnerships to shift income as long as they avoid a *realization* event.

For example, a notable tax shelter case called *Southgate Partnership* actually made use of Section 704(c) to shift huge losses from the contributing partner to someone else.[7] A simplified version of the facts will illustrate how and why Section 704(c) wasn't sufficient to prevent *income shifting* using contributed property.

In *Southgate*, one partner (call him Owner) owned property (for now, just

---

[7] *Southgate Master Fund LLC v. U.S.*, 659 F.3d 466 (5th Cir. 2011).

call it Blueacre) with large built-in losses, say, a basis of $100 and fair market value of $5. Owner contributed Blueacre to a partnership. Owner then left the partnership, selling its interest to a high-bracket taxpayer. But – and here's the key – Blueacre remained in the partnership with its high carryover basis of $100. When the partnership then sold Blueacre, Section 704(c) could not operate to tag Owner with the $95 loss, because Owner had exited the partnership entirely. Instead, the rules operated to allocate the loss of $95 to Owner's successor, who was – by design –the high-bracket newcomer.

Southgate involves the shifting of losses from one party (Owner, who was not a U.S. taxpayer) to a newcomer (a high-bracket U.S. taxpayer). Section 704(c) was, in effect, a helpless bystander, because there was no *realization* event that could tag Owner with the built-in loss. The partnership didn't dispose of Blueacre until after Owner had exited. At that stage, the loss had to be allocated to someone, and so Owner's successor was allocated the losses.

This doesn't mean that Section 704(c) is useless. Far from it! But the *realization* doctrine often constrains how effectively a rote rule can measure economic income.

More generally, Section 704(c) can produce uneconomic allocations of income. Savvy taxpayers can then craft tax shelters that make use of the flawed allocations. In Chapter 15, we will see a tax shelter (in the *Castle Harbour* case) that follows exactly this script. In the meantime, the following problem illustrates the possibility for uneconomic results.

¶1305 PROBLEM 13.2: SECTION 704(c) AND ITS LIMITATIONS

Carolyn owns an apartment building with an adjusted basis of $0; she bought it fifteen years ago and has legally deducted the entire basis in depreciation. The building now has a fair market value of $10 million. Richard has $10 million in cash. Carolyn and Richard enter into a 50-50 partnership.

(1) How should Carolyn and Richard be taxed if the partnership immediately sells the building for $10 million? How would your answer differ if the partnership sold the building after a month at the (then) fair market value of $11 million? What if the building sold at that time for only $7 million?
(2) How should Carolyn and Richard be taxed if the partnership instead keeps the building and earns $1 million in rents annually?

ANSWER TO (1)

Section 704(c) would operate to allocate the tax gain of $10 million to Carolyn and zero to Richard. The two would then have tax basis = $10m = capital accounts, and everyone would be appropriately taxed. Section 704(c) *avoids the result of shifting any of Carolyn's gain to Richard*. If the building appreciates by $1 million, then the first $10m of gain goes to Carolyn, and then the remaining

$1m of gain is split 50-50. Afterwards, each has tax basis =$10.5m = capital accounts. The loss case is interesting: in theory, Carolyn has gained $10m and then both have lost 1.5m. But the basis of the asset is zero, and so there is $7m of GAIN, which all goes to Carolyn.

ANSWER TO (2)

So initially, Carolyn has basis = $0 and Richard has basis = $10m. Both have a capital account of $10m. So, the big issue is that basis (tax calculation) isn't equal to capital account (economic calculation). The split between economics and tax causes problems: the issue here is that the building is depreciating economically but not for tax purposes. Suppose that the building is depreciating (economically) by $1m/year. Economically, then, the Carolyn-Richard partnership is making zero profit. At the end of Year 1, both Richard and Carolyn would have capital accounts (economics) of $9.5m, because they have 50-50 ownership of a building with a FMV of $10m. But under the Code, no tax depreciation is allowed, because the basis of the building is $0. This is the "ceiling rule" in Reg. §1.704-3(b)(1) that is the heart of the *Castle Harbour*, discussed in Chapter 15. (*NB*: The ceiling rule still exists, although there is now an anti-abuse provision.)

Now, when you look at the result on an aggregate basis, taking all the partners together, the effect is to tax the partnership on too much income — $1m too much (*i.e.*, the partnership reports rental income of $1 million and zero depreciation deductions). But that is a familiar result of accelerated depreciation: the tax system awards "too much" depreciation (relative to economics) in the early years and then, when basis is exhausted, awards "too little" depreciation. The taxpayer gets the tax deferral in the meantime. Put another way, if Carolyn had just held onto the property, we wouldn't be offended by this result: she took accelerated depreciation and paid too little tax earlier; so now she is paying too much tax.

But in the partnership context, the ceiling rule imposes the wrong tax on BOTH parties. A is bearing too little of the over-taxation, and, in effect, B is bearing a portion of the too-high income from the property.

CHAPTER 13 | Tax Deferral and Partnership Contributions

	Economic View (Total)	Tax View (Total)	Economic (Partner-by-Partner)		Tax (Partner-by-Partner) with the Ceiling Rule		Corrected Tax (no Ceiling Rule)	
			A	B	A	B	A	B
Gross income (rents)	$1m	$1m	$500k	$500k	$500k	$500k	$500k	$500k
Depreciation	(1m)	$0	($500k)	($500k)	$0	$0	+$1m depreciation "recapture" ($500k) current dep	($500k)
Net income	$0	$1m	$0	$0	$500k	$500k	$1m	$0

¶1306 ADVANCED PROBLEMS

For more advanced problems, *see* Problems P1 and P2 in Appendix C, which also contain material discussed in Chapter 12.

CHAPTER 14

Income Shifting and Partnership Allocations

Introduction	¶1400
Valuation and Partnership Allocations	¶1401
Income Shifting and Partnership Allocations	¶1402
The Logic — and Limitations — of Code Sec. 704(b)	¶1403
Advanced Problems	¶1404

¶1400 INTRODUCTION

The taxation of partnership income initially seems straightforward. After all, Section 704(a) tells us that a partner's distributive share "shall, except as otherwise provided in this chapter, be determined by the partnership agreement." So, apparently, the parties just set down their tax allocations in the partnership agreement, and they're set.

But not so fast. Section 704(b), which at first glance doesn't look that daunting, tells us that distributive shares will instead "be determined in accordance with the partner's interest in the partnership" if "the allocation to a partner under the agreement of income, gain, loss, deduction, or credit … does not have *substantial economic effect*." (italics added)

Those three italicized words have motivated regulations that are, in all seriousness, probably the most complicated in the tax law. (Truly, if you ever want to scare a tax lawyer, just send an email saying you're about to send over a partnership agreement, and you want them to review the allocations for Section 704(b) compliance. They will first shrink in their chair and then dash away to hand off the assignment to the one person in the firm who understands that stuff.)

In this chapter, we won't attempt to map out the details of the substantial economic effect regulations. For that, you'll need a full course in partnership taxation. Instead, we will focus on the reasons why the Code must restrict partners' flexibility to allocate income among themselves. We first set the stage by highlighting the *valuation* problem that led policy makers to enact Section 704(b). From that point, the arc of the story is one you've seen before: *valuation* makes measuring economic income difficult, and so policy makers retreat to the *realization* requirement. But in retreating, they adopt an uneconomic approach, which creates unintended effects – and tax shelter opportunities.

¶1401 *VALUATION* AND PARTNERSHIP ALLOCATIONS

In Chapter 12, we saw that virtually any partnership poses a *valuation* problem for the tax law. Partnerships have different business models, of course. In addition, each partnership likely has individualized deals with many of its partners. The result is that it is often difficult for the IRS to value the rights that each partner has vis-à-vis the others. And so it is, practically speaking, impossible for the IRS to verify that a partnership's tax allocations are in accord with the underlying economic deal.

Classroom examples often aren't well-suited to illustrating the *valuation* problem, because professors design them for simplicity. So, when we say, for instance, that Alice and Burt form a partnership and agree to split all items 50-50, that doesn't seem to pose much in the way of a *valuation* problem. But real-world deals are typically far more complex and contingent. Here is an example from an article in *The Tax Adviser*:

Profit Allocations:

a. First, to reverse all cumulative allocations of net loss;
b. Second, to the partners in proportion to their percentage interests (as defined in section x) until each partner receives a preferred return of 12% on his or her unreturned capital;
c. Third, 75% to class A partners and 25% to class B partners until class A partners' capital account balances are increased to a level at which an immediate distribution of such capital account balance to a class A partner would cause a class A partner to receive a preferred return of 16%;
d. Fourth, the balance of 50% to class A partners and 50% to class B partners.[1]

This is, to put it mildly, more complex than the typical classroom hypo, and yet it's just a generic starting point. A real-world deal would need additional provisions on losses and on distributions. A real deal might well add additional detail on matters like depreciation and R&D credits. And it wouldn't be at all unusual to add contingencies (*e.g.*, if the business exceeds or falls short of targets) and customizations (*e.g.*, elections entitling partners to accelerate or defer their shares of items).

The complexity of partnership allocations isn't (necessarily) tax motivated. Sophisticated investors will use the flexibility of the partnership form to craft nuanced deals, and that's all for good reason – partnership law, like contract law, aims to permit contracting parties to memorialize pretty much any economic bargain they reach.

---

[1] Jennifer Seaton and Jeremy Henson, *Target or Waterfall: Partnership Allocations*, THE TAX ADVISOR, Apr. 1, 2009.

But the complexity of partnership allocations does pose a distinctive problem for the tax system. In principle, a mark-to-market tax system would tax each partner on the change in value of her partnership interest each year. But because partnerships are closely-held and highly-customized entities, the *valuation* problems inherent in mark-to-market would be prohibitive in the partnership context.

And so, in the by-now familiar compromise, the partnership rules do not attempt to determine the economic value of each partner's interest. Instead, the rules (initially at least, as expressed in Section 704(a)) follow the allocations set forth in the partnership agreement. But the Code can't stop there. Without any checks, the parties might well adopt tax allocations that benefit them at the expense of the Treasury. And so Section 704(b) attempts to limit taxpayer discretion by requiring that allocations have "substantial economic effect."

By the end of this chapter, you'll see why the Section 704(b) regulations must try to limit tax-motivated allocations. And you'll also see why the regulations are both complex and, in the end, limited in their reach, because they tackle what is essentially a *valuation* problem with *realization* tools. The predictable result is that the rules cannot close every loophole; indeed, it is well-known (at least to partnership experts) that the rules inevitably create gaps between economic income and taxable income.

¶1402 INCOME SHIFTING AND PARTNERSHIP ALLOCATIONS

Partnership allocations offer a tempting vehicle for *income shifting*, because they permit an almost infinite variety of allocations. Without Section 704(b), taxpayers could easily use partnerships to shift income and deductions between high- and low-bracket parties.

> **EXAMPLE 1.** *Income Shifting in the Absence of Section 704(b).* Suppose that Missy and Paul each contribute $100 to the MP Partnership. Missy is in the top tax bracket, while Paul has very little income. They include the following provisions in their partnership agreement:
>
> (1) *Tax allocations.* For tax purposes, 100% of all partnership income and gain will be allocated to Paul, while 100% of all partnership deductions and losses will be allocated to Missy.
>
> (2) *Distributions.* All distributions will be 50% to Missy and 50% to Paul.
>
> Without Section 704(b), these provisions would *shift income* by separating tax allocations from the economic deal. It's pretty clear from provision (2) that this is really a 50-50 partnership. But, without some limit in the Code, nothing would stop the parties from including provision (1) as well, with the intention of allocating taxable income to the low-bracket partner (Paul) and deductions to the high-bracket partner (Missy).

Now, the *income shifting* game here would be limited in time and amount by the partnership basis rules. These rules prevent a partner from claiming deductions in excess of their basis in the partnership, requiring excess deductions to be carried forward. Additionally, the rules typically tax distributions in excess of basis.

> **EXAMPLE 2.** *Loss Limitations and Distribution Rules Limit* Income Shifting *even without Section 704(b).* Missy has an initial outside basis of $100, and that amount will cap the losses she is permitted to deduct. (Section 704(d) provides that a partner may deduct losses only to the extent of her basis in her partnership interest; any unused losses carry over to the next year.)
>
> But that rule still permits Missy to deduct tax losses that aren't supported by the economics of the partnership. If, for instance, the partnership has a $100 salary deduction, it will all be allocated to Missy, even though, in economic terms, she is only "on the hook" for half of employee salaries (since she's a 50-50 partner).
>
> Eventually, to be sure, the misallocation of deductions will be cured by the distributions rules. Suppose, for instance, that the partnership operates for just two years and then liquidates. Over that time, the venture earns gross income of $450 (all allocated to Paul for tax purposes per Provision (1) of the partnership agreement) and pays deductible expenses of $100 (allocated 100% to Missy for the same reason).
>
> By the end of Year 2, then, Missy will have a zero basis in her partnership interest ($100 initial contribution minus $100 in allocated deductions). Paul will have a $550 basis in his partnership interest ($100 initial contribution plus income allocation of $450). At the end of Year 2, the partnership has assets of $550 ($200 initial cash plus $450 income less $100 expenses). So, per Provision (2), the partnership distributes half (or $275) to each partner.
>
> Under Section 731(a), Missy recognizes a gain of $275 on the distribution, while Paul recognizes a loss of $275. It is not an accident that the two amounts offset each other. *Income shifting*, after all, artificially allocates income and deductions between two parties. When they settle up economically – here, by liquidating the partnership – the artificial gains and losses will be reversed.
>
> To see the artificiality of the initial allocations and the way Section 731 corrects them, compare the economics of this partnership with the tax treatment:
>
> Economically, this partnership was a success: the partners invested $200 and earned *net income* of $350 ($450 gross income less $100 expenses), or $175 per partner, over the two years. And yet, Missy reported a loss of $100 for tax purposes. The Section 731 gain of $275 ensures that Missy is correctly taxed: in sum, she will have a loss of $100 and a gain of $275, for a correct total of $175 in income.

For his part, Paul has reported an artificially inflated income: he has been allocated $450 in income when, in the end, he earned only $175. The Section 731(a) loss of $275 evens the score (since $450 - $275 = $175).

But, as you know from the basic course in taxation, timing is everything. *Tax deferral*, especially over long periods, can be very lucrative for taxpayers. And so the drafters of the Code created special rules to target *income shifting* of the type Missy and Paul attempted.

¶1403 THE LOGIC – AND LIMITATIONS – OF CODE SEC. 704(b)

There's something endearing about the aspirations of Section 704(b). The Code just comes right out and says what it's after: partnership allocations must have "substantial economic effect." That's definitely the right goal, because it reflects a very basic Haig-Simons ideal: let's tax all taxpayers on their economic income.

The Missy-Paul example in the previous section confirms that Section 704(b) has its heart in the right place. In that simple example, we can readily see that Missy and Paul *really* have a 50-50 partnership, and so they ought to allocate income and deductions 50-50 down the line. They shouldn't be able to (mis) allocate all the income to Paul and all the deductions to Missy.

As I've mentioned, the regulations implementing Section 704(b) are long and complex. They require partnerships to keep capital accounts, to restore deficits, and to determine the substantiality of allocations, among other tasks. But, as a first approximation, we can boil down all these concepts to the appealing idea that partners' tax allocations should mirror eventual distributions of real assets. In the Missy-Paul example, the tax allocations fail to meet that standard: eventually, distributions will be strictly 50-50, because those are the terms of the (economic) deal.

Still, poor Section 704(b) is destined for heartbreak. Without a mark-to-market system, the Code cannot measure true economic income *on a current basis*. Instead, the Code will be anchored to *realization* events and (in the partnership context) distributions. The result may be that, despite the best efforts of the regulators, partners can still create uneconomic allocations that will permit *tax deferral* for some period.

Consider a simple example:

> **EXAMPLE 3.** Quentin and Rosa have an idea for a new iPhone app that will measure blood pressure, blood glucose levels, and other medical information based on the user's thumbprint. They've formed the Q-R Partnership to refine and market the app. The partners have a zero basis in the app, but they believe its fair market value at the time the partnership is formed is about $100,000. They believe that the app's value could increase to $10 million over the first few years after they refine the technology and market it effectively.

Using realization accounting, the Q-R partnership will predictably lose money in the first few years, since there will be no cash coming in but plenty of spending on research and development and marketing. By contrast, on a mark-to-market basis, the partners will likely be making plenty of money, at least if their idea pans out the way they expect it to.

Now, there's nothing new about the fact that the realization requirement mismeasures income. Either Quentin or Rosa, on their own, would benefit from the *tax deferral* (relative to a mark-to-market system) that results from the understatement of their economic income.

But a partnership offers Quentin and Rosa new avenues for maximizing the value of that tax goodie. Suppose that Quentin is in a high tax bracket, while Rosa is in a low bracket. Ideally, they'd like to allocate the early deductions to Quentin. How can they do that without running afoul of the Section 704(b) "substantial economic effect" rules?

The key is that the parties can (within bounds) predict the market value of their operations, but the IRS cannot. The only fact that is visible to the IRS is the *realization*-based calculation of income. For instance, suppose that Rosa and Quentin agree that the first few years of the partnership look like this:

Year	Value of the app	Taxable income (loss)
1	$100,000	($50,000)
2	$500,000	($50,000)
3	$10,000,000	$10,000,000

Glancing at the table, you can see that the app is steadily increasing in value, but the tax column shows only losses until Year 3, when the parties plan to sell the app for its then-market value of $10 million. Based on this pattern, Quentin and Rosa could write a partnership agreement that allocates all tax losses in the first two years to Quentin. They could provide that those tax losses would reduce Quentin's share of any distribution if the partnership winds up in the first two years. They would then provide that Quentin will receive a special allocation of $100,000 in income in Year 3, if (but only if) income for that year exceeds $1 million. After that special allocation, the provision would read, Quentin and Rosa would share 50-50 in income and losses.

¶1403

That provision would, on its face, look quite "real" in economic terms. Sure, Quentin is allocated a disproportionate share of losses in the first two years, but those losses would also reduce his payout if the partnership liquidates during that time. And, sure, the situation would change in Year 3, but only if the partnership earns income of more than $1 million. On paper, this all looks like a very real economic bet: Quentin is willing to take a greater downside risk than Rosa in the early years, but he expects to be compensated for taking that risk if and when the partnership's app makes big money. Only the partners know that, based on their economic projections, the deal is likely to have only tax effects and not real economic effects compared to a straightforward 50-50 split.

Now, it is possible that the scheme I've just created would not pass muster under the partnership regulations or, more generally, under the *substance over form* doctrine. The regulations under Section 704(b) do include the following, and it's worth quoting (in part):

> [T]he economic effect of an <u>allocation</u> ... is substantial if there is a *reasonable possibility* that the allocation... will affect substantially the dollar <u>amounts</u> to be received by the <u>partners</u> from the <u>partnership</u>, independent of tax consequences.[2]

These rules might be sufficient to catch out the Quentin-Rosa scheme. After all, in my hypothetical, I've imputed a high degree of knowledge and deliberation to Quentin and Rosa. And so, they may not be able honestly to say that there is a "reasonable possibility" that the allocation of losses to Quentin will "affect substantially" his payout from the partnership.

But you can see how tenuous the IRS position is. A real-world Quentin and Rosa will not know the value trajectory of their business with the certainty I've imputed to them. They may have a firm grasp of a range of values – indeed, they must do so in order to make confident business decisions! But they may not have the degree of probabilistic certainty required for the IRS to challenge the allocations under the "reasonable possibility" and "strong likelihood" standards.

And the same goes for a more general anti-abuse or *substance over form* challenge by the IRS. In my simple example, Quentin and Rosa know the future value of their app with certainty, and they are deliberately manipulating the partnership's tax allocations without altering the underlying economics of the deal. But in the real world, Quentins and Rosas will be operating on probabilities, not certainties, and they may be quite satisfied with a business deal that ultimately approximates 50-50 but contains enough "wiggle room" in the meantime to create a "realistic possibility" of real after-tax economic consequences.

---

[2] Reg. §1.704-1(b)(2)(iii) (emphasis added).

¶1403

And so the basic point still stands: when the tax law cannot take notice of market values, but instead must rely on *realization* to measure the taxpayers' situation, the taxpayer will have the upper hand. Perhaps a more sophisticated ploy would be needed, but it isn't too hard to imagine adding bells and whistles to the basic example. And the more you learn about the Section 704(b) regulations, the more you will see that very sophisticated taxpayers can still craft tax-advantageous partnership allocations.[3]

¶1404 ADVANCED PROBLEMS

For more advanced problems, which also contain material from Chapters 13 and 15, see Problems P3 and P4 in Appendix C.

---

[3] For a terrifically clear account of the Code Sec. 704(b) regulations and current issues that the regulations don't deal with very well, see Laura E. Cunningham & Noël B. Cunningham, THE LOGIC OF SUBCHAPTER K, A CONCEPTUAL GUIDE TO THE TAXATION OF PARTNERSHIPS (West Academic Publishing, 5th ed. 2017), Chapter 5.

CHAPTER 15

Substance Over Form in Partnership Tax

Introduction	¶1500
The Partnership Anti-Abuse Rule	¶1501
ACM Partnership v. Commissioner	¶1502
Castle Harbour	¶1503
Advanced Problem	¶1504

¶1500 INTRODUCTION

To this point, we've seen that partnership tax is particularly vulnerable to taxpayer efforts to engage in *income shifting* and *tax deferral*. The rules in Subchapter K make a valiant effort to anticipate tax avoidance, but they inevitably fall short. Just as in other areas of the Code, it's impossible for the drafters of the statute to predict exactly how taxpayers may take advantage of the rules. The flexibility of the partnership form has, if anything, multiplied the magnitude of this familiar problem.

Enter the *substance over form* doctrine. As you know, the doctrine gives the IRS and courts an additional weapon in defending against tax-motivated transactions. But, as we saw in Chapter 4, the doctrine has limited reach in the corporate context. There, the courts and the Service hesitate to look through the corporation to its shareholders, because corporate taxation is inherently formalistic. Legal fictions abound in the corporate realm, from the existence of the corporate entity itself to the independence of corporations and their shareholders, to the distinction between debt and equity.

The *substance over form* doctrine is used more expansively in partnership tax than in corporate tax. One reason may be the difference between a double tax and a single tax: the IRS has two levels at which it can collect a tax on corporate income, but just one shot at capturing partnership income. Another reason is that the partnership rules pass through losses, which corporations do not, and tax losses are a favorite target for tax planning and tax avoidance.

In this chapter, we will revisit the doctrine of *substance over form* to illustrate two points about partnerships. One is that the partnership rules lend themselves to opportunities for clever tax planning. A second point, however, is that the IRS and the courts have made fairly aggressive use of the *substance over form* idea in the partnership context. Faced with clever and sophisticated tax planning, the IRS and the courts have successfully struck back, challenging transactions and even partnerships themselves as lacking economic substance.

¶1501 THE PARTNERSHIP ANTI-ABUSE RULE

The IRS is, of course, well aware of the abuse potential inherent in partnerships, and so regulations in the partnership area often include anti-abuse rules. Indeed, there is an overarching partnership anti-abuse rule, found in Reg. §1.701-2, which applies to all partnerships at all times. The rule is worth quoting, because it offers a nice, self-contained summary of the *substance over form* doctrine as applied to partnerships by the IRS and courts:

(a) ***Intent of subchapter K.*** Implicit in the intent of subchapter K are the following requirements –
  (1) The partnership must be bona fide and each partnership transaction ... must be entered into for a substantial business purpose.
  (2) The form of each partnership transaction must be respected under substance over form principles.
  (3) ...The tax consequences under subchapter K ... must accurately reflect the partners' economic agreement and ... income...

(b) ***Application of subchapter K rules.*** The provisions of subchapter K ... must be applied in a manner that is consistent with the intent of subchapter K ... if a partnership is formed or availed of in connection with a transaction a principal purpose of which is to reduce substantially the present value of the partners' aggregate federal tax liability in a manner that is inconsistent with the intent of subchapter K, the Commissioner can recast the transaction for federal tax purposes, as appropriate to achieve tax results that are consistent with the intent of subchapter K... Thus, even though the transaction may fall within the literal words of a particular statutory or regulatory provision, the Commissioner can determine, based on the particular facts and circumstances, that to achieve tax results that are consistent with the intent of subchapter K –
  (1) The purported partnership should be disregarded in whole or in part, and the partnership's assets and activities should be considered, in whole or in part, to be owned and conducted, respectively, by one or more of its purported partners;
  (2) One or more of the purported partners of the partnership should not be treated as a partner;
  (3) The methods of accounting used by the partnership or a partner should be adjusted to reflect clearly the partnership's or the partner's income;
  (4) The partnership's items of income, gain, loss, deduction, or credit should be reallocated; or

(5) The claimed tax treatment should otherwise be adjusted or modified.

Commentators have had mixed reactions to the partnership anti-abuse rule. Some thought the rule does nothing more than summarize existing law. Others worried that the rule could lead to overreaching if the tax authorities (mis)interpret the regulation to authorize a more sweeping application of *substance over form*.

Ultimately, interpretation of the *substance over form* doctrine resides in the courts. While the IRS can challenge a transaction, it is judges who decide when and how to determine "substance." In the following sections, we will illustrate the application of the *substance over form* doctrine in two successful challenges to partnership transactions. All involve sophisticated tax planning; all rest on a colorable reading of the literal rules; and all raise questions about the proper balance between the rules of the Code and the powers of the courts.

¶1502 ACM PARTNERSHIP V. COMMISSIONER

ACM Partnership involves a complex transaction featuring international parties, a foreign partnership, a notional principal contract, an installment sale, and shifting ownership.[1] But we can radically simplify the facts to focus on the role of the partnership in producing the claimed tax benefits.

ACM Partnership was formed by three parties: Merrill Lynch (the now-defunct investment bank), a Dutch bank, and Colgate (yes, the U.S. toothpaste company). Merrill and Colgate were U.S. taxpayers, and Colgate was interested in obtaining a capital loss to offset a recently-recognized capital gain. Although the deal in question involved many moving pieces, we can focus on three elements of law that played a key role.

First, ACM involved a partnership because the flow-through of losses was critical. The aim was to generate an artificial gain at Time 1, which would flow through to a tax-indifferent party, followed by an artificial loss at Time 2, which would flow through to Colgate.

Second, the Dutch bank's role in the partnership reflected U.S. rules on the taxation of foreign parties. Since the Dutch bank was a foreign person not engaged in a U.S. trade or business, it would pay no U.S. tax on the artificial gain allocated to it at Time 1. After absorbing about 90% of the tax gain, the Dutch bank sold its partnership interest to Colgate. By Time 2, then, when the losses began to flow through to the partners, Colgate held 99% of the partnership (its initial 9% plus the 90% it bought from the Dutch bank). In return, the Dutch bank received a guaranteed return of its invested capital, along with a high interest rate.

---

[1] *ACM Partnership v. Comm'r*, 157 F.3d 231 (3d Cir. 1998).

Third, the parties were able to use the *realization* requirement to generate first an artificial gain and then an artificial loss. This will take a little more explaining, because the specific legal rules in question were found in regulations governing so-called contingent installment sales. But you'll quickly see the artificiality of the gains and losses at stake.

To begin, an installment sale is any sale in which the buyer makes payments over time. (You may have bought a car on the installment plan, paying for it in monthly installments over three or five years.) A contingent installment sale is one in which the buyer's payments are not fixed; rather, they are contingent on some set of events.

EXAMPLE 1. *Taxing a Simple Contingent Installment Sale.* Suppose that Dorothea, a recent law-school graduate, wants to buy a small-town law practice. Casaubon, the owner of the practice, is ready to retire and happy to sell to Dorothea, but they have a hard time setting a fair price. Casaubon is sure that his clients will stay with Dorothea, but she worries that the business may not flourish. In the end, they agree that Dorothea will pay Casaubon 10% of her earnings for the first ten years. That arrangement gives Casaubon a nice retirement income, if he's right about the business, and it ensures that Dorothea won't pay much if, in the end, the practice isn't lucrative.

A contingent installment sale poses a puzzle for the tax law. Under normal *realization* principles, the seller of property recognizes gain or loss measured by the amount realized and his basis. In a contingent installment sale, the seller knows his basis (it's whatever capitalized expenditures Casaubon has put into his law practice). But the amount realized cannot be known at the time of the sale, because it's, well, contingent.

At the time of *ACM Partnership*, the relevant regulations under Section 453 provided that the seller in a case like this should allocate his basis pro rata over the period of the contingency and then *realize* gain each year.[2]

Continuing the example, suppose that Casaubon had a basis of $100,000 in the law practice. Since the period of the contingency was 10 years, he would allocate 1/10 of his basis (or $10,000) to each year. Thus, if in Year 1, Dorothea ended up paying him $35,000, his gain in that year would be $25,000. He would do the same in each year, ending in Year 10.

The contingent installment sale rules made plenty of sense in a common scenario like the sale of a law or medical or dental practice. But, obviously enough, the rules don't rely on market *valuation* of the deal; instead, they're rules of thumb, created for ease of application. The result was that Merrill and Colgate were able to design a transaction that took advantage of the gap between market value and tax reporting.

---

[2] The current rules can be found in Reg. §15a.453-1.

EXAMPLE 2. *Simplified Version of ACM Contingent Installment Sale.* In the basic transaction, the partnership purchased securities for $100 and immediately resold them for a stream of payments with an expected market value of $100. Put in these terms, it was clear that the partnership had not made or lost money, and that was the parties' intent. But they were able to write a sales contract that fell within the contingent installment sale rules.

Using a financial contract called a "notional principal contract," the parties agreed to sell their $100 of securities for $90 in cash plus a series of five payments over five years, with the five payments to be determined by future interest rates. Both the buyer and the seller (ACM Partnership) knew that the expected present value of the series of payments was $100. But, formally, the contracts called for contingent payments, and so the deal was, Merrill and Colgate claimed, a contingent installment sale.

Applying the regulations, ACM (as the seller) would allocate its basis pro rata across the five years. It would then *realize* gain each year equal to the cash it received less its allocated basis. Here's what the allocations looked like, on the parties' assumption that each year's expected payment would be about $2 (for a total of $100 over time).

Year	Basis	Amount realized	Gain (loss)
1	20	92	72
2	20	2	(18)
3	20	2	(18)
4	20	2	(18)
5	20	2	(18)
Total	100	100	0

As the table illustrates, the parties expected the transaction to generate *zero* overall gain or loss over the five years. But the pattern of artificial gains and losses served their purposes. In Year 1, the Dutch bank would hold a 90% partnership interest and so would absorb 90% of the artificial gain. No U.S. tax would be paid, because the Dutch bank wasn't a U.S. taxpayer. The Dutch bank would then exit the partnership, selling its interest to Colgate, who would reap 99% (recall that it initially owned 9%) of the artificial losses that would flow through in Years 2 through 5.

The IRS challenged the transaction on *substance over form* grounds and won in both the Tax Court and the Third Circuit. The appeals court found that the purchase and sale of securities lacked economic substance, whether measured by the objective terms of the deal or the subjective intent of the parties. Accordingly, the court approved the IRS disallowance of the claimed losses.

The court emphasized that ACM expected to make no pre-tax profit on the purchase and sale of securities, and any slight profit would be more than offset by millions of dollars in transactions costs. And the court noted that the purchase and sale of securities had no business motive apart from its tax payoff.

¶1502

Still, we should not lose sight of the strength of the taxpayer's defense. Treasury regulations, when valid, have the force of law, and here, the taxpayer was relying on the law as stated. The contingent installment sale rules were not optional; they laid out a mandatory set of very detailed rules. (And, not coincidentally, the Treasury revised the rules after transactions like *ACM Partnership* came to light.)

As so often, then, the *substance over form* doctrine pits the literal language of the law against the broader spirit of the law. The Third Circuit in *ACM* held that Section 165 (which permits the deduction of losses) could not be used to deduct artificial losses – even though the IRS's own regulation seemed to authorize just that.

¶1503 CASTLE HARBOUR

The *substance over form* approach taken by the court in *ACM* is relatively familiar: the court determined that a transaction lacked economic substance. Another case, *Castle Harbour*, illustrates another use of the doctrine – to characterize the relationship between the parties as not a partnership at all.[3] But the District Court and the Court of Appeals disagreed, vehemently and repeatedly, about the application of the doctrine and the interpretation of the facts.

At bottom, the transaction at issue in *Castle Harbour* used an obscure rule in the regulations under Section 704(c) to *shift income* from one taxpayer (GE Capital) to another (surprise! A Dutch bank!). Simplifying quite a bit, the transaction looked like this:

> **EXAMPLE 3.** *Simplified Version of Castle Harbour.* GE Capital owned a fleet of airplanes which had been leased to airlines for, let's say, $100 per year. Each year, GE Capital would report the $100 in lease payments as income and would deduct depreciation on the planes. (Keep in mind that GE Capital, as the owner of the planes, was entitled to claim depreciation.)
>
> As time passed, the planes were eventually fully depreciated for tax purposes, but the planes were still flying, and the lease payments were coming in each year. Put another way, the planes had a tax basis of zero. Without any action, GE Capital would be in the position of paying tax on $100 each year, without any deduction for depreciation. (This is the expected effect of accelerated depreciation. When the Code permits owners of assets to deduct depreciation over a shorter period than the actual useful life of the assets, the result will be that, in the out years, depreciation will be exhausted before the end of the asset's economic usefulness.)

---

[3] *TIFD III-E, Inc. v. U.S.*, 666 F.3d 836 (2d Cir. 2012). TIFD III-E was a subsidiary of GE Capital and one of the partners in the partnership, Castle Harbour Limited Liability Company.

In an effort to shift that income off its tax returns, GE Capital formed a partnership, Castle Harbour, with a Dutch bank. Just as in *ACM Partnership,* the appeal of the Dutch bank was that it would pay no U.S. tax on partnership income allocated to it. The Dutch bank contributed cash, and GE contributed its airplanes, subject of course to the leases.

As you know, the contribution of property to a partnership is a nonrecognition event under Section 721. And so, Castle Harbour took a carryover basis of zero in the planes. Going forward, the partnership would report the $100 of income from the airplane leases and would deduct no depreciation (because the planes had a zero basis).

To this point, nothing even remotely objectionable has happened. As a package, the leased planes generated taxable income of $100 when held by GE Capital and now would do the same in the hands of the partnership.

But the key to *Castle Harbour* was the allocation of income between GE Capital, the U.S. taxpayer, and the Dutch bank, a party indifferent to U.S. taxes. Now, you might think that Section 704(c) makes this impossible. After all, the purpose of Section 704(c) is to allocate built-in gain at the time of contribution to the contributing party. But fully-depreciated property produced a different result under the Section 704(c) regulations, thanks to something called the "ceiling rule."

The ceiling rule seems obscure, but once you understand what it does, it seems quite sensible. In a partnership like Castle Harbour, the Section 704(c) regulations would normally require that the partnership allocate income and deductions to the Dutch bank (the noncontributing partner) based on the fair market value of the planes at the time of contribution. The ceiling rule provides, however, that the depreciation allocated to a partner cannot exceed the total amount of tax depreciation allowed to the partnership. The Castle Harbour deal deliberately involved property with a zero tax basis and, thus, zero depreciation in order to invoke the ceiling rule. The result was to inflate artificially the taxable income allocated to the Dutch banks – and to reduce artificially the taxable income allocated to GE Capital.

EXAMPLE 4. *Simplified Depiction of the Ceiling Rule.* Suppose that the airplanes contributed to Castle Harbour are expected to produce income (lease payments received) of $100 per year and are expected to suffer economic depreciation of $100 per year. In other words, suppose that the airplanes will produce exactly offsetting income and loss, for an economic profit of zero. (This assumption isn't necessary to the deal but makes the depiction easier.)

Normally, the Section 704(c) regulations would require that the partnership allocate economic depreciation to the noncontributing partner. The overall goal is to avoid shifting the pre-contribution tax attributes of property from the contributing to the noncontributing partner. And so, the regulations generally try to tax the

¶1503

noncontributing partner as if it had bought its share of the asset at market value at the time of formation of the partnership.

If that approach had worked in *Castle Harbour,* the result would be that the Dutch banks would report zero income or loss each year: their share of the $100 of income would be exactly offset by their share of the $100 of economic depreciation. And the result would be economically correct: after all, by assumption, the Dutch banks had acquired an interest in assets that, economically, were producing net income of zero.

But the ceiling rule distorted the income reported for tax purposes by overriding the economic depreciation rule and, instead, capping the depreciation deductions allocated to the Dutch bank at zero, the tax-permitted amount.

To maximize the distortion, the *Castle Harbour* partnership agreement allocated 98% of income and deductions from the planes to the Dutch bank. The table shows how the ceiling rule, in effect, *shifted income* – the lion's share of the taxable income from the planes was shifted away from GE Capital and to the Dutch bank.

	704(c) principles		Ceiling rule	
	GE Capital	Dutch bank	GE Capital	Dutch bank
Gross income	100	100	2	98
Depreciation	(0)	(100)	0	0
	100	0	2	98

Put in general terms, GE Capital structured the *Castle Harbour* deal to make use of the ceiling rule.

The *Castle Harbour* case initially went to the District Court, which ruled for the taxpayer on *substance over form* grounds. On appeal, the Second Circuit ruled for the IRS. And the case went back and forth several times as the parties litigated additional issues: each time, the District Court ruled for GE Capital, and the Second Circuit reversed.

The courts' disagreement turned on the judges' divergent views of the same facts. The District Court found it plausible that the Dutch bank faced economic risks as a *bona fide* investor in the partnership. By contrast, the Court of Appeals found that the deal created only the appearance, and not the substance, of risk for the Dutch bank. Instead of participating in Castle Harbour as a partner, the court ruled, the Dutch banks were nothing more than creditors. Without a partner, there is no partnership, and so Castle Harbour itself was disregarded under the appeals court's view. In substance, the court held, GE Capital had never disposed of the planes and so should be taxed as if Castle Harbour had never existed.

In *Castle Harbour,* as in *ACM,* the *substance over form* inquiry pits the literal requirements of the law (here, the ceiling rule in the regulations) against a broader commitment to taxing economic income. Like *ACM Partnership, Castle*

¶1503

Harbour is at once a satisfying victory for the government in a case of aggressive tax planning – and an exercise of government power that stands in tension with rule-of-law values like certainty and notice to taxpayers.

¶1504 ADVANCED PROBLEM

For a more advanced problem, which also contains material from Chapter 14, see Problem P4 in Appendix C.

APPENDIX A
The Basics of Writing an Issue-Spotter Exam

[Adapted from Anne L. Alstott, Taxation in Six Concepts, Second Edition (Wolters Kluwer 2018)]

Students sometimes feel at sea when they confront an issue-spotter in law school. College, it may seem, doesn't prepare us very well for this kind of professional exercise. None of my college exams involved stuff like estoppel, motions to dismiss, or the realization requirement.

But, in fact, a good issue-spotter exam follows the rules for any good essay. The three key elements are structure, legal judgment, and quality of expression. This section will discuss each in turn and will provide examples. For obvious reasons, the examples here focus on tax, but the insights should be more generally applicable.

I should add that professors differ. But if, like many of my students, you have received little or no guidance on how to write an exam, I hope this will be useful.

STRUCTURE

Begin with structure. Try to channel your best English teacher here — you know, the one who was tough but fair and helped you learn to write really well. Every good essay should have a thesis, should prove its thesis in an organized way, and should provide evidence for its assertions. A law school exam should follow the same model.

A thesis, in this context, is a clear and concise statement of what the issues are and how you will resolve them. Doing this is, of course, harder than it sounds. Typically, you will need to do your legal analysis first (in outline form or by jotting notes for yourself) and then go back and come up with a concise thesis. Please don't take the reader along for a ramble through the issues, thinking out loud. Instead, this is a moment for you to be the teacher: be organized and clear about where you are going.

For example, consider the issue-spotter question below, taken from one of my past exams. (This happens to be a short answer question, but a longer issue-spotter just involves more issues.)

> **EXAMPLE.** Pierre graduated from the Harvard Law School in 2004. From 2004 through April 2008, he worked at a corporate law firm as a litigator. His work consisted of defending products liability cases (*i.e.*, lawsuits alleging that his clients made defective products). In 2007-08, Pierre earned an LLM in International Law from NYU Law

School (attending night and weekend classes). In May 2008, Pierre took a job with the State Department negotiating international human rights treaties. Can Pierre deduct on his federal income tax return the tuition he paid to Harvard? To NYU? Please offer Pierre some brief advice.

A good answer would open by spotting the issue, relating it to the facts given, making reference to the relevant law, and giving a summary of your conclusions:

> The issue is whether Pierre's tuition payments to Harvard and to NYU may be deducted under section 162, must be capitalized under section 263, or are nondeductible under section 262. I conclude that Pierre may not deduct his Harvard tuition but has a reasonable (though not uncontestable) case for deducting his NYU tuition.
>
> [The answer then goes on and, in an organized way, discusses and addresses each issue]

A middling answer would dive right in without orienting the reader to the issues or the writer's legal conclusions. For instance:

> The question is about Pierre, who paid tuition to Harvard and NYU and probably would like to deduct his tuition on his tax return. Let's see if he can.
>
> [The answer then proceeds to spot issues in no particular order and address them piecemeal without cluing in the reader to where it's going.]

Another mistake is to open with the case law without orienting the essay to the facts given. For example:

> The main case on point here would be *Wassenaar v. Commissioner,* which held that a student could not deduct the costs of his LLM in taxation. Wassenaar had gone to law school and then went right to his LLM program.

The body of the essay should present the analysis in an organized way. The particular organization you choose should be driven by the issues, but the structure should be visible to the reader. In this issue-spotter, for instance, there is a question about the Harvard tuition and the NYU tuition, and so a logical organization would consider the Harvard tuition issue first and the NYU tuition issue second.

The body of the essay should also invoke relevant legal authorities. For example:

> The Harvard tuition is not deductible since the J.D. qualifies graduates for the (new) trade or business of being a lawyer. *See* Regs. §1.162-5(b).

APPENDIX A

A lesser answer might omit the authority or rely instead on secondary sources:

> I don't think Pierre can deduct the Harvard tuition. See Casebook at p. xx.[1]

LEGAL JUDGMENT

An issue-spotter should not only use good legal judgment but should demonstrate that judgment for the reader. The difference lies in the exposition: your task is to show and to explain your reasoning and to be clear about the judgments you are making and their justification.

A common mistake is to jump to a conclusion without portraying much of your reasoning. The conclusion may be correct, but it lacks the connections to the law and to the facts that will persuade your reader. For instance, a middling answer would state the issues and then simply say:

> The tuition Pierre paid for the LLM at NYU falls into a gray area in the law. Pierre's facts are better than those in *Wassenaar,* so I'm pretty sure he can take the deduction. It's worth a try anyway.

A better answer would explain how you've analyzed the relevant law:

> Pierre's LLM tuition falls into a gray area. Unlike *Wassenaar,* Pierre was clearly engaged in the practice of law before he attended NYU. But under Regs. §1.162-5(b)(3), the key issue is whether the LLM qualified Pierre for a new trade or business or provided the minimum qualifications for his profession.
>
> The norms of the profession should be relevant in determining the status of the LLM. In legal practice circles, being an international lawyer (or, even more narrowly, a human-rights treaty negotiator) is a different specialty from corporate litigation, but it is still recognized as the practice of law and may be done by people with the same legal training. Thus, Pierre might argue that "being a lawyer" is a single trade or business, as did the taxpayer in *Ruehmann.* Importantly, under professional norms, an LLM in international law is not generally a minimum requirement for practicing international human rights law; it is helpful but not necessary for any licensing requirement.

---

[1] It's fine to use the casebook and even to cite to the casebook if you reproduce its material verbatim, but please take the time to read what it says. Then look at the Code or the case and cite that. After all, your textbook isn't legal authority! Cite to relevant cases by name, just as you would in a brief or memo.

Given these professional norms, I conclude that Pierre has a good chance of success on the merits if the matter were litigated. But, as a matter of caution, I would want Pierre to be aware of cases holding that being a tax lawyer is a new trade. *See* Johnson v. United States, 332 F. Supp. 906 (E.D. La. 1971) (lawyer could not deduct the cost of an LLM in taxation because it prepared him for the new business of being a tax lawyer) (summarized in Casebook at 312). I believe that the *Johnson* precedent is distinguishable, because the tax law is a notoriously complex field and because many tax lawyers obtain an LLM as they enter the tax field. Still, the *Johnson* precedent suggests that this remains a gray area.

Note that this answer sticks closely to the facts of the issue spotter. It relates the case law and regulations to the question at hand. It does not fall into the trap of reciting the facts and analysis in relevant cases at length, which will tempt the professor to think that you are cutting and pasting the case briefs from your outline. For instance, a middling answer might say:

One case on point is *Wassenaar*. In *Wassenaar,* the taxpayer attended law school and then, after just one summer, attended NYU for an LLM. The court in *Wassenaar* analyzed whether the taxpayer's past employment in non-legal jobs could qualify as being engaged in the provision of services for compensation. The court also analyzed whether the taxpayer's work on the law journal and as a summer associate could qualify as performing legal work for compensation. The court put great weight on the fact that Wassenaar had not produced legal work as an attorney. The fact that Wassenaar was not a member of the bar before attending NYU was also dispositive.

This summary of *Wassenaar* isn't incorrect, but it tells the reader about the case rather than applying the case to the facts at hand.

A related mistake is the grand summary of the law, which — once again — will make the prof suspect that you are repeating what's in your outline:

The question of the deductibility of educational expenses is one that has occupied considerable time in the federal courts. Section 162 provides that a taxpayer may deduct ordinary and necessary business expenses, while Section 263 (as interpreted by *Indopco*) provides that a taxpayer must capitalize expenses that provide a lasting benefit. Adding to the mix, Section 262 disallows any deduction for personal consumption expenditures.

Higher education expenses tend to confound the tax law because they mix business purpose with personal edification, and they produce lasting benefits over time....

This wouldn't be a terrible opening to, say, a chapter on educational expenses deductions, but it isn't a precise way to address an issue-spotter. (*NB*: a policy question or a synthetic question calling for broad comment on the law might benefit from a bigger summary of the law; use your judgment.)

APPENDIX A

Another common mistake is the waffling answer. For example:

> Pierre might win his case or lose his case. Compared to *Wassenaar,* he had a much more solid track record as a practicing lawyer, and he had much more practice experience than the victorious taxpayer in *Ruehmann*. Still, there is the *Johnson* case, which held that being a tax lawyer is a new trade or business, so Pierre could lose if a judge put more weight on that case.

This answer applies the cases to the facts at hand but doesn't reach a resolution. By contrast, the answer above suggested an approach — consulting professional norms — that would enable a firmer answer, albeit one that is cautiously hedged. If you don't see the difference between the model answer and the waffle, ask yourself this: if you were the (non-lawyer) client, which answer would be more helpful to you?

Finally, your answer must deploy good judgment about what is important. If issues are small and easily-resolved, say so. Then spend your time on the hard issues. For instance, it is obvious that Pierre's Harvard tuition is nondeductible. Definitely say so, but do it crisply and move on. You could spend pages and pages on why the JD is nondeductible, but it's not a live issue. The LLM, by contrast, is a live issue with an uncertain resolution.

QUALITY OF EXPRESSION

Words are the tools of the law, and you will be judged on how well you use them. Writing well, even under time pressure, is a professional skill that is critical for practitioners, judges, and academics. Once again, your best English teacher had it right:

- Use active, not passive verbs when you can.
- Use parallel constructions when appropriate.
- Choose vivid and precise language but use adjectives and adverbs sparingly.
- Deploy appropriate transitions so that you communicate structure to the reader.

And so on. The best exams are a pleasure to read. You don't have to be Jane Austen (and please don't try!), but clear, precise expression reveals clear, precise thinking.

At the other end of the scale, poor spelling and grammar will definitely lose points. The occasional typo is not a big deal, but repeated mistakes suggest a lack of professional care. Issue-spotters are typically time-pressured exams, so (once again) you'll have to use your judgment in allocating your time between substance and exposition.

APPENDIX B
Advanced Strategies for Business Tax Exams

If you're reading this book, you're probably enrolled in an advanced course on corporate or partnership tax. Taking an issue-spotter exam in an advanced tax class can be daunting, because the transactions are intricate, and the tax laws are complex. But there are strategies you can use to bring order to the chaos, and in this Appendix, I offer suggestions that have worked for my students.

It goes without saying (but I will say it anyway) that your exam should follow the general guidelines for good exam-writing laid out in Appendix A. Here, I offer additional techniques that are geared to advanced tax classes.

The approach I recommend does require you to do some extra work ahead of time. You may already be working on a course outline, and that's a great way to learn the material and have the basics at hand. But I recommend creating an additional document that is devoted to issue spotting. It's a structured list of questions you can ask yourself as you read and analyze exam questions. (As a bonus, you can use the same approach when you're facing a complex deal in practice and need to spot the issues. It's incredibly comforting to have a structured "way in" to begin to analyze a transaction.)

Let's start with the five questions you need to ask about any tax fact pattern. (Bear in mind that these are the questions you must ask and answer *before* you write your answer. The answer should be a coherent essay, as I discuss in Appendix A.) I'll first lay out the five questions, and then I'll go through a detailed example.

1. *Who are the parties, and what kind of entities are they?* These facts will help orient your analysis. If a C corporation is involved, you need to be attuned to corporate tax. If individuals are involved, they may face different tax consequences than corporations. And partnerships, of course, face partnership tax issues. The question also reminds you to be aware of the tax issues for *all* parties. Even though your client will be only one of these parties, it may be highly relevant (for bargaining and structuring purposes) to be aware of the tax stakes for the other players in the deal.
2. *What is the transaction?* As you now know, the tax law tends to operate by putting transactions into categories. In corporate tax, for instance, we study formations, distributions, redemptions, and so on. So, very early on in your analysis, you want to make sure that you have identified what the key features of the transaction are. For instance, if a C corporation has distributed land to its shareholders with respect to their stock, then you know that the tax category will be either an ordinary distribution (taxed under Section 301) or a liquidating distribution (taxed under Section 331 or 332).

3. *What are the key issues for that type of transaction?* This portion of the list will differ from subject to subject, but you can prepare ahead of time. For instance, if the transaction is an ordinary (*i.e.*, nonliquidating) distribution of property by a C corporation, then your list of questions would include:
   – What is the fair market value of the property? (Section 301(b))
   – Does the shareholder assume any liabilities? (Section 301(b))
   – Is the property appreciated or depreciated? If so, the distributing corporation will recognize gain but not loss. (Section 311(b))
   – What is the corporation's accumulated and current E&P? (Section 312)
   – What portion of the distribution will be a dividend, a return of basis, and gain? (Section 301(c))
   – What is the shareholder's basis in the property? (Section 301(d))
4. *Are there substance over form issues?* It's always a good idea to ask this question. Sometimes we get so focused on the formalities that we forget to step back and think about possible challenges by the IRS based on the interdependence of different pieces of the transaction and the business purpose (or lack thereof) of the deal.
5. *What are the tax consequences of the analysis for the parties?* By the time you get to the fifth question, you should be feeling very much in control. Having identified the transaction and analyzed the issues, you can run through the major tax consequences, which should include:
   – Do the parties realize and/or recognize income, deduction, gain or loss?
   – If gain or loss, what is the character?
   – If parties have received property, what is its basis?

To illustrate how you might use the five questions in an exam setting, let's take an example from one of my Corporate Tax exams. Here is the question:

> **EXAMPLE.** In December 2020, Susan and Edmund incorporate Aslan Enterprises Corporation ("AEC"), a C corporation incorporated in Delaware. The siblings plan to sell a line of organic food for animals. Susan contributes Blueacre, a parcel of undeveloped land with a fair market value of $100,000, which Susan bought in 2015 for $85,000. Edmund contributes $100,000 in cash. In exchange, each receives 50 shares of the single class of common stock in AEC. In February 2021, Narnia Enterprises Limited ("NEL"), an unrelated partnership, agrees to provide management services to AEC for three years in exchange for an additional 50 shares of AEC common stock.

To stay organized, I like to use a table to answer the five questions. A table allows me to jot down notes and to look at the range of issues all at once. I can quickly address any issues that are easy, while leaving blank space for issues that require a more extended analysis of the law or the facts. Here's what my notes for this exam question might look like:

… APPENDIX B | Advanced Strategies for Business Tax Exams   175

1	2	3	4	5
Parties	Transaction	Specific issues	Substance over form	Consequences
Susan (individual/sister) Edmund (individual/brother) AEC (C Corp.) NEL (unrelated partnership)	December 2020 corporate formation February 2021 management services contract in exchange for stock	a. Realization? Yes, under *Cottage Savings*, because S and E are exchanging property or services for AEC stock. b. Nonrecognition under Section 351? (Issues include contribution of property, contribution of services, and control) Seems to apply to the Dec. 2020 transfer taken in isolation: both parties transfer property and the two together have 100% control afterwards. Section 351 would not apply to the Feb. 2021 deal, b/c NEL transfers services, not property. So full realization and recognition for NEL. Cite *James*. Big issue: will Dec. 2020 and Feb. 2021 be integrated? If so, Susan and Edmund will not qualify under Section 351, b/c they have only 67% of the stock (100 shares total out of 150). *See* Section 368(c)	The issue (see 3.) is whether the December 2020 and February 2021 transactions will be integrated. The short time period (three months) suggests strongly yes, unless there are facts (not included in the hypo) suggesting that NEL's participation was separate and unanticipated. Discuss *Intermountain Lumber* on the interdependence issue. There doesn't seem to be a binding contract here, but the time gap is very short.	If, as seems likely, the two transactions are integrated, then the transaction will not meet the requirements of Section 351, and Susan will realize and recognize all gain and loss. Susan will have $15,000 of gain, likely capital under Section 1221 since this is undeveloped land (unless Susan is a dealer in land). She has held the land for more than one year, and so the gain is long-term capital (Section 1223). Her stock basis will be FMV ($100,000). Though unlikely (see 4.), if the December 2020 deal did qualify for Section 351, Susan would not recognize any gain, and she would take a basis of $85,000 in her AEC stock. Edmund contributed cash, so no gain/loss realized, and he takes a basis of $100,000 in his stock whether or not Section 351 applies. Whether or not the two transactions (in Dec. 2020 and Feb. 2021) are integrated, NEL cannot qualify for nonrecognition under Section 351, because it is not a transferor of property. It realizes and recognizes ordinary (compensation) income equal to the FMV of the 50 shares in AEC. (The FMV is presumably $100,000, since Edmund and Susan paid that amount shortly before.) NEL will have a FMV basis (likely $100,000) in its AEC stock. AEC recognizes no gain or loss. If the two transactions are integrated, Section 351 does not apply, and AEC takes a FMV basis ($100,000) in Blueacre. (Section 1012) If, though unlikely, Section 351 did apply to Susan's transfer in Dec. 2020, then AEC takes a carryover basis of $85,000 in Blueacre.

APPENDIX C

Advanced Problems

The following problems (and answers) draw on material from different chapters. The answers are printed after the question.

CORPORATE TAX

C1. *Anna and Burt Start a Business.* In 2019, Anna and Burt agree to form a new firm called AB, Inc. ("AB"), a Delaware corporation. Anna contributes undeveloped land with a basis of $95,000 and a fair market value of $100,000 in exchange for 100 shares of AB Class A common stock. Each share of Class A common stock has one vote on corporate matters. At the same time, Burt contributes a fleet of delivery trucks with a basis of $80,000 and a fair market value of $100,000 in exchange for 100 shares of Class B common stock. Each share of Class B common stock has one vote on corporate matters. The Class B common is identical to the Class A common, except that Class B is convertible at any time, at Burt's option, into (non-voting) bonds of AB with a principal amount of $110,000, stated interest of 8%, and a maturity date of December 31, 2020.

Please analyze the federal income tax consequences of these transactions for the corporation and its investors.

ANSWER TO C1.

The transactions here involve transfers of property to a corporation in exchange for instruments labeled stock. If we respect the form of the transaction, and in particular the designation of Burt's interest as "stock," then Section 351 applies to both Anna and Burt, because both transfer property in exchange for stock, and (together) they own 100% of the AB stock afterward. However, there is reason to question whether Burt's interest will be treated as stock rather than debt.

If Section 351 applies, then neither Anna nor Burt recognizes any gain. Anna's basis in her AB stock will be $95,000, and Burt's will be $80,000. [Section 358] AB will take a basis of $95,000 in the land and $80,000 in the fleet of trucks. [Section 362]

But there are reasons to question whether the "common stock" issued to Burt will be respected as stock for tax purposes or whether, instead, the instrument will be treated as debt. If the instrument is considered to be debt of AB rather than stock, then Burt's transfer will not qualify under Section 351, and he will realize and recognize his $20,000 built-in gain. In that case, he will take a basis of $100,000 in his stock under Section 1012, and AB will take a basis of $100,000 in the fleet of trucks. (Note that the disqualification of Burt's transfer will not affect the tax treatment of Anna, because she would still be a transferor of property and would own 100% of the AB stock afterward, because Burt's "stock" would not be treated as stock.)

Applying the multi-factor tests drawn from the case law, the "stock" issued to Burt has both equity and debt features. The Class B common stock appears to have typical equity features, including voting rights and full participation in the upside potential of the company (through the possibility of unlimited dividends and liquidating distributions). It is significant that the Class B common stock gives Burt 50% of the total voting rights of the company – a substantial stake.

The conversion feature is the primary problem: by exercising, Burt can turn his stock into a straightforward debt instrument with an approximately one-year maturity, permitting him to cash out of the venture very easily and to recover his full investment at the end of 2020. With a principal amount of $110,000, the debt would lock in a minimum profit of $10,000 for Burt (plus interest on the whole $110,000) after about a year. Still, if Burt converts, he loses his 50% voting rights in the venture as well as the upside potential associated with the common stock.

Although it is difficult here (as in any debt-equity case) to reach a definitive answer, Burt should know that there is a significant risk that the "stock" will be treated as debt, with the consequence that he does not qualify for Section 351 nonrecognition. The parties would do better to clarify their deal and structure an instrument that is more clearly debt or equity for tax purposes.

* * *

C2. *Missy and Norm Change up their Investments.* In 2020, Missy and Norm each owned 50 of the outstanding 100 shares of L Corporation, a C corporation. At the end of 2020, L Corporation redeemed all of Missy's stock for $50,000. At the end of 2021, L Corporation redeemed 10 shares of Norm's stock for $10,000. Missy and Norm are unrelated, and each had an initial basis of $35,000 in the L Corporation stock. L Corporation has ample E&P. Please comment on the federal income tax treatment of these transactions for Missy and Norm.

ANSWER TO C2.

The transactions here are redemptions of stock governed by Section 302. As detailed below, the redemption of Missy's stock will be treated as an exchange, but the redemption of Norm's stock will be treated as a distribution and, ultimately, as a dividend.

When L Corporation buys back all of Missy's stock for $50,000, the redemption qualifies under Section 302(b)(2) (disproportionate redemptions) and under

Section 302(b)(3) (complete termination of interest). Because Missy and Norm are unrelated, none of Norm's stock is attributed to Missy, who thus owns 50% of the stock beforehand and 0% afterward. Accordingly, Missy's redemption will be taxed as an exchange. (Note that the restrictions of Section 302(c)(2) are irrelevant, because Missy and Norm are unrelated, and therefore no waiver of the Section 318(a)(1) attribution rules is needed. [*See also* Section 302(b)(6)])

Missy will therefore realize and recognize gain of $15,000. The gain is capital under Section 1221, because Missy is almost certainly an investor in L (and not a dealer with respect to the L stock). We do not know Missy's holding period.

The redemption of Norm's stock, by contrast, is not an exchange. He is now the sole stockholder of L Corporation, and so he owns 100% before and after the redemption. He cannot qualify under Section 302(b)(2) (no reduction in proportionate interest) or Section 302(b)(3)(not a complete termination). Under *Davis*, a sole stockholder cannot obtain exchange treatment on a redemption under Section 302(b)(1) either. (We have no facts indicating that Section 302(b)(4) on partial liquidations might be relevant.)

Thus, Norm's redemption will be treated as a distribution under Section 302(d). The facts state that L Corporation has "ample" E&P, implying that the entire $10,000 will be a dividend under Section 301(c). Norm will report the dividend as ordinary income, possibly eligible for taxation at the capital gains rate if the requirements of Section 1(h)(11) are met.

* * *

C3. *Thomas Corporation Alters its Stock Structure.* Thomas Corporation is a closely-held C corporation with two classes of stock, common and preferred. The preferred stock is nonvoting. In 2020, Thomas Corporation distributes a one-for-one common stock dividend on the common stock. (That is, the distribution is one additional share of common stock for each outstanding share of common stock.) At the same time, Thomas Corporation pays its regular 5% cash dividend on its outstanding preferred stock. Thomas Corporation has ample E&P. Discuss the federal income tax consequences of these transactions.

ANSWER TO C3.

The transactions here are a stock distribution and a distribution, implicating Sections 305 and 301, respectively. The analysis should begin with the distribution on the preferred stock, since the application of Section 305(b)(2) can depend on whether there is a "companion distribution." The distribution on the preferred stock would be a dividend, given that Thomas Corporation has "ample" E&P. [Section 301(c)]

The common-on-common stock dividend will, however, not be taxable as a distribution under Section 305(b)(2). The cash distribution on the preferred fulfills the condition under Section 305(b)(2)(A) that some shareholders receive property. But the common-on-common stock dividend does not fulfill the second condition under Section 305(b)(2)(B), because the common stockholders do not increase their proportionate interest in the corporation. Before and after the redemption, the common stockholders hold 100% of the residual interest in the corporation, subject to the senior claim of the preferred stock. [*See* Reg. §1.305-3(e), Ex. 2]

* * *

C4. *Harriet Leaves in a Hurry.* Harriet and Peter are married and the sole shareholders of Wimsey Corporation, a C corporation. Each owns 50 shares (50%) of the common stock, and each has a basis of $230,000 in the stock. In 2020, Harriet decides to leave the company in order to concentrate full-time on her fiction writing. Wimsey Corporation is short on cash, but it has an unused parcel of undeveloped land, Greenacre, worth $450,000. Wimsey Corporation purchased the land years ago for $410,000. Wimsey also owns Treasury bonds with a basis of $65,000 and a fair market value of $50,000. Harriet agrees to accept Greenacre and the Treasury bonds in exchange for her Wimsey Corporation stock. Peter requests that Harriet remain on the Wimsey Corporation Board of Directors, and she agrees. Please advise the parties on the federal income tax consequences.

ANSWER TO C4.

The transaction is a redemption that will be treated as a distribution to Harriet. The distribution to Harriet of Greenacre will also result in the realization of gain by Wimsey Corporation.

Beginning with Harriet, the key fact is that she is giving up all of her stock in exchange for a package of consideration with a fair market value of $500,000. This would be a complete termination of interest under Section 302(b)(3), except for the fact that Harriet and Peter are married. Under the attribution rules of Section 318(a)(1)(A)(i), one spouse is considered to own the stock owned by the other spouse. Accordingly, Harriet is considered to own 100% of the Wimsey Corporation stock before and after the redemption, foreclosing the application of Section 302(b)(2) and, per *Davis*, Section 302(b)(1).

Harriet cannot qualify for the waiver of the Section 318(a)(1) attribution rules in Section 302(c), because she will continue to hold a position as a Wimsey Corporation director. [*See* Section 302(c)(2)(A)]

Accordingly, under Section 302(d), the redemption is treated as a distribution to Harriet. The amount of the distribution is $500,000 [Section 301(b)(1)]. Depending on Wimsey Corporation's E&P, the distribution will be taxable to Harriet as a dividend, as a return of basis, or as a (capital) gain. [Section 301(c)]

Wimsey Corporation will be treated as having made an in-kind distribution. Under Section 311(b), it will realize and recognize the $40,000 gain on Greenacre but will not be able to recognize the $15,000 loss on the Treasury bonds. The gain on Greenacre is likely capital under Section 1221 (assuming that Wimsey Corporation is not a dealer in undeveloped land).

* * *

C5. *Carlco Says Goodbye to the Entertainment Business.* Carlco, Inc. ("Carlco") is a C corporation. It has two shareholders, Damon and EarthCorp (another C corporation). Damon owns 15% of the Carlco stock, and Earthcorp owns 85%. Years ago, Carlco had a profitable business in DVD rentals and sales. But with changing times, the DVD market has dried up, and Carlco can no longer compete with Netflix and other streaming options. Accordingly, on July 1, 2020, Carlco adopts a plan of liquidation. Carlco distributes $150,000 in cash to Damon and distributes its remaining asset, an empty strip mall in Texas, worth $850,000, to Earthcorp. Carlco bought the strip mall in 2020 for $805,000 and has not claimed depreciation. Please outline the federal income tax consequences of these events.

ANSWER TO C5.

The transaction in this case is a corporate liquidation. Section 331 will require recognition of gain and loss related to the distribution to Damon, but Section 332 will apply nonrecognition rules to the distribution to Earthcorp.

Under Section 331, Damon recognizes gain or loss based on the difference between his basis (unspecified in the problem) and the $150,000 in cash he receives. The gain will almost certainly be capital gain under Section 1221 and *Arkansas Best* (unless Damon is somehow a dealer in the Carlco stock). Damon's holding period is not specified.

Section 332 will apply to the liquidating distribution by Carlco to Earthcorp if (as appears to be true on the facts given), Earthcorp meets the 80% ownership requirement and the timing requirements of Section 332(b). Accordingly, Earthcorp recognizes no gain or loss on its stock disposition in the liquidation and takes a carryover basis of $805,000 in the strip mall under Section 334. Carlco also recognizes no gain on the distribution of the strip mall. [Section 337]

* * *

C6. *Delia Sells her Company.* XYZ Corporation, a C corporation, manufactures cardboard boxes in a factory in Rochester, NY. Delia, the sole shareholder of XYZ, would like to sell the company and retire to Florida. Boxes Inc. ("Boxes"), a large C corporation, has expressed interest in purchasing the factory for $10 million. XYZ's basis in the factory is $2 million. Delia's basis in her stock is $1 million.

The management of Boxes is open to a stock acquisition or an asset acquisition. Delia needs some cash for her retirement but would "prefer to pay as little in taxes as possible." What advice would you give her?

ANSWER TO C6.

This is an open-ended planning problem that invites you to contrast taxable and tax-free corporate acquisitions.

A taxable stock sale would impose one level of tax: Delia would realize and recognize the $9 million gain on her stock. The character would be capital under Section 1221. Delia's holding period is not given (but, on these facts, seems likely to be more than one year, and so the gain would be long-term capital under Section 1222).

By contrast, a taxable asset sale would trigger the realization and recognition of two levels of tax: a gain of $8 million to XYZ and $9 million to Delia.

If the parties can agree to structure the deal as a statutory merger under Section 368(a)(1)(A), an "A" reorganization would permit Delia to obtain some cash while deferring some gain. As Chapter 10 discusses, the judicial continuity of interest requirement would require Boxes to furnish at least 40% (or so) of the consideration in Boxes stock. Assuming that Delia is happy with a 60-40 mix of cash and stock, she could obtain tax deferral on a portion of her gain.

PARTNERSHIP TAX

P1. *Luca and Jane Start a Boutique.* In 2018, Luca and Jane decide to open a clothing boutique (to be called "Belles Fleurs," French for "beautiful flowers") and to do so, they form the LJ Partnership ("LJ"). LJ is formed under New York law and (because Luca and Jane do not elect otherwise, per the check-the-box rules) is taxed as a partnership under Subchapter K. The two partners agree to share all income and losses 50-50. Luca contributes a building with an attractive storefront space (basis = $95 and fair market value of $100). Jane contributes a computer system (basis = $80 and fair market value of $60) plus $40 in cash. Belles Fleurs opens its doors on January 1, 2019. In 2019, the boutique incurs a net loss of $30. In 2020, the boutique earns net income of $110. LJ makes no distributions until January 1, 2021, when it distributes $50 to Luca and the same amount to Jane. Please discuss the federal income tax consequences of these events for all three parties (Luca, Jane, and LJ).

ANSWER TO P1.

The transaction is the formation of a partnership. The initial formation is tax free under Section 721. Luca takes an initial basis in his partnership interest of $95, and Jane takes an initial basis in her interest of $120. [Section 722]

In 2019, the boutique incurs a net loss of $30. Accordingly, Luca and Jane each report an ordinary loss of $15 on their individual tax returns, and each reduces the basis in the partnership interest by that amount. [Section 705] After doing so, Luca's outside basis is $80 ($95 - $15), and Jane's is $105 ($120 - $15).

In 2020, the boutique earns net income of $110. Luca and Jane must each report half that amount ($55) on their individual tax returns. Adjusted for the 2020 income, Luca's basis is now $135 ($80 + $55), and Jane's is $160 ($105 + $55).

The 2021 distribution of $50 to each partner is not taxable and reduces outside basis. [Sections 731 and 733] After the distribution, then, Luca's basis is $85 and Jane's is $110.

* * *

P2. *Terence and Tabitha Take a Business Risk.* In 2019, Terence and Tabitha start a French coffee shop (called "Café Café" or "Coffee Café" in French). Each founder contributes $200 in cash and will co-manage the café day-to-day. The two entrepreneurs choose a Delaware limited liability company for their business, and they agree to split profits and losses 50-50. Unfortunately, Café Café is plagued by difficulties and never makes a dollar of profit. In fact, the café loses $350 in the first year. Discouraged and broke, Terence and Tabitha agree to liquidate the partnership at the end of 2019. Each receives a final distribution of $25. Please discuss the federal income tax consequences of these transactions.

ANSWER TO P2.

The problem does not specify that Café Café is taxed under Subchapter K. We can infer that, but it is worth spelling out our assumptions (in the real world, determining the tax status of the venture would be critical; if we get the form wrong, our tax advice will be way off). The organizational form is a Delaware LLC, which is not a mandatory C corporation. The entity is closely-held, and the facts do not mention any tax election. Accordingly, the venture will be taxed by default under the partnership rules of Subchapter K, unless there are facts not specified in the problem.

Under Section 722, Terence and Tabitha each take an initial basis of $200. The partnership's one-year loss of $350 is allocated $175 to each partner, and each partner deducts that amount on his or her individual return. [Section 701] Each reduces his or her outside basis by that amount, leaving each with a basis of $25. [Section 705] The final distribution is not taxable; instead, it reduces the basis of each founder to zero. [Sections 731 and 733]

* * *

P3. *Johanna and David Design Video Games for Fun and Profit.* In 2019, Johanna and David form a new start-up venture, GameTrends Limited ("Game Trends"). Game Trends is a partnership formed under Connecticut law, and it is taxed under Subchapter K as a partnership. Johanna contributes $100 in cash, and David contributes a computer system (basis = $80 and fair market value = $100). In 2019, GameTrends earns $500 in net income from sales of its first video games. Flush with profit, on January 1, 2020, Johanna and David sell the old computer system for $100 and buy a new one for $250. Please discuss the federal income tax consequences of these events.

ANSWER TO P3.

We know (per the facts) that GameTrends is taxable as a partnership. Under Section 721, the formation of the partnership is non-taxable, and Johanna has an initial basis in her partnership interest of $100, while David has an initial basis of $80. [Section 722] GameTrends' earnings of $500 must be reported by the partners. [Section 701 and *Basye*, 410 U.S. 441 (1973)] The facts do not specify how the partners' distributive shares will be determined, and so under Section 704(b), allocations will be determined based on the facts and circumstances.

Let's assume for the moment that the partners intend a 50-50 split. If so, Johanna and David must each report $250 in ordinary income on their tax returns. Johanna's outside basis is then $350, while David's is $330. [Section 705]

When GameTrends sells its computer system in 2020, it realizes a gain of $20 (assuming no depreciation has been claimed in 2019). The gain will be ordinary under Section 1221(a)(2) *but* may qualify for Section 1231 treatment if it meets the one-year holding period. See Section 1223 for tacking rules relevant to holding periods. Under Section 704(c), all of the gain is allocated to David. Accordingly, he reports $20 on his individual tax return, and his outside basis increases to $350.

* * *

P4. *Gemma and Harry Cook Up a Scheme.* For nearly a decade, Gemma has run a small grocery store (called "Gemma's Groceries"). Gemma would like to update the store with new fixtures and appliances but is short on cash. She sends her friend Harry the following email:

> Hey, Harry! Hope you're doing well. I have kind of a big favor to ask, but I think it'll be worth your while. I need $1 million to do a total revamp of Gemma's Groceries, and I just don't have the cash. That's where you come in, haha! If you will invest the $1 million, you can be a 50-50 partner in the business with me. And, even better, I can guarantee you $1 million in tax deductions very fast. Everything I am putting in the store will be depreciable (that means "deductible") over one year under something called Code Section 168(k). And I will agree in writing that you will be allowed to claim all $1 million of that depreciation on your own tax return. (I won't claim any.) The depreciation is really just a tax gift – it won't in any way affect our 50-50 business deal. So if we make a profit, we'll distribute half to you, and if we sell or liquidate the business, you'll get half. So how about it?

Harry knows that you know something about tax. He shows you Gemma's email and asks you if she is correct about the tax part of the proposed deal.

ANSWER TO P4.

Harry is smart to seek tax advice. Gemma's proposal would likely lack substantial economic effect under Section 704(b), because it purports to allocate tax deductions (depreciation) to one partner without affecting his 50% share of profits and liquidation proceeds. The purpose of the Section 704(b) rules is to prevent the parties from sharing tax items divorced from economic consequences, and that is just what Gemma seems to be proposing.

Case Table

All references are to paragraph (¶) numbers.

ACM Partnership v. Comm'r, 157 F.3d 231 (3d Cir. 1998)...303, 1502, 1503

ASA Investerings Partnership v. Comm'r, 201 F.3d 505 (D.C. Cir. 2000)...303

Baumer v. U.S., 580 F.2d 863 (5th Cir. 1978)...801

Castle Harbour—see TIFD III-E, Inc. v. U.S...1304, 1305, 1503

Comm'r v. Bollinger, 485 U.S. 340 (1988)...303, 304

Comm'r v. Duberstein, 363 U.S. 278 (1960)...804

Cottage Savings Ass'n v. Comm'r, 499 U.S. 554, 111 S. Ct. 1503, 113 L. Ed. 2d 589 (1991)...500, 501, 901, 1300

Cullinan v. Walker, 262 U.S. 134 (1923)...501

Eisner v. Macomber, 252 U.S. 189 (1920)...802-804, 1001, 1002

Exacto Spring Corporation v. Comm'r, 196 F.3d 833 (7th Cir. 1999)...801

Gregory v. Helvering, 293 U.S. 465 (1935)...1000

Indmar Products v. Comm'r, 444 F.3d 771 (6th Cir. 2006) ...402, 403

Intermountain Lumber Co. & Subsidiaries v. Comm'r, 65 T.C. 1025 (1976)...504

James v. Comm'r, 53 T.C. 63 (1969)...603

Johnson v. U.S., 332 F. Supp. 906 (E.D. La. 1971)...App A

LeTulle v. Scofield, 308 U.S. 415 (1940)...1002

Lucas v. Earl, 281 U.S. 111 (1930)...1103

Lyon, F. v. U.S., 435 U.S. 561, 98 S. Ct. 1291, 55 L. Ed. 2d 550 (1978)...500

Marr v. U.S., 268 U.S. 536 (1925)...501, 1001

Moline Properties, Inc. v. Comm'r, 319 U.S. 436 (1943)...303

Paulsen v. Comm'r, 469 U.S. 131 (1985)...1003

Pinellas Ice & Cold Storage Co. v. Comm'r, 287 U. S. 462 (1933)...1002

Roth Steel Tube Co. v. Comm'r, 800 F.2d 625 (6th Cir. 1986)...402

Southgate Master Fund LLC v. U.S., 659 F.3d 466 (5th Cir. 2011)...1302, 1304

TIFD III-E, Inc. v. U.S., 666 F.3d 836 (2d Cir. 2012)...1503

U.S. v. Basye, 410 U.S. 441 (1973)...1102-1104, App C

U.S. v. Phellis, 257 U.S. 156 (1921)...501

Table of Code, Regulations and Rulings

All references are to paragraph (¶) numbers.

Code Sections

1…102
1(a)-(d)…401
1(g) … 200
1(h)…1102
1(h)(11)…102, 201, 202, App 2-1, 401, 703, App C
1(j)(2)(C)….102
11…102, 201, 401, 500
83…603
102…804
162…1003, App A
163(a)…401
163(j)…App 2-1, 401
165…1203.02, 1502
168(k)…App C
199A…102, 201-203, App 2-1
199A(b)(2)…203
199A(d)…203
199A(d)(1)…102
243…703, 902
246(c)…703
262…App A
263…App A
301…701, 703, 705, 802-804, 902, App B, App C
301(b)…App B
301(b)(1)…702, App C
301(c)…701, 702, App B, App C
301(d)…702, App B
302…704, 705, 802, App C
302(a)…705
302(b)…705
302(b)(1)…705, App C
302(b)(2)…705, App C
302(b)(3)…705, App C
302(b)(4)…705, App C
302(b)(5)…705
302(b)(6)…App C
302(c)…App C
302(c)(2)…App C
302(c)(2)(A)…App C
302(d)…705, App C
305…802, 803, App C
305(a)…803, 804
305(b)…803

305(b)(1)…803, 804
305(b)(2)…803, App C
305(b)(2)(A)…App C
305(b)(2)(B)…App C
305(c)…803
311(b)…702, App B, App C
312…702, 703, App B
316…702, 703
316(a)…702
317(a)…803
318… 704, 705
318(a)(1)…App C
318(a)(1)(A)…705
318(a)(1)(A)(i)…App C
331…902, 904, App B, App C
332…902, App B, App C
332(b)…App C
334…App C
337…App C
351…502-504, 600-604, 900, 903, 1300, 1301, App B, App C
351(a)…502-504, 602-604
351(b)…601, 602, 604
351(b)(1)…601
351(g)…602, 604
354…903.02, 1000
356…1000
358…503, 601, 1000, App C
358(a)…503, 601, 602, 604
361…903.02, 1000
362…502-504, 601, 903.02, 1000, App C
362(a)…503, 601, 604
368…903, 903.01, 1000, 1002-1004, 1301
368(a)(1)(A)…903.01, 904, 1000, 1002, 1004, App C
368(a)(1)(B)…903.01, 1003, 1004
368(a)(1)(C)…903.01, 1003
368(a)(1)(D)…903.01
368(a)(1)(G)…903
368(c)…503, 504, 903.01, 1301, App B
453…1502

701…App C
704…1303
704(a)…1104, 1400, 1401
704(b)…1400-1403, App C
704(c)…1302, 1304, 1305, 1503, App C
704(c)(1)(A)…1303
704(d)…1402
705…1204, 1302, 1303, App C
721…1300, 1301, 1304, 1503, App C
721(a)…1303
721(b)…1301
721(c)…1301
721(d)…1301
722…1204, 1301-1303, App C
723…1302, 1303
731…1402, App C
731(a)…1304, 1402
731(a)(1)…1303
732…1303
733…1303, App C
743…1302
754…1302
860A et seq. …1101
1001…501-503, 702, 704, 705
1012…501, 902, 1101, 1301, App B, App C
1014…App 2-1, 603
1015…502, 603
1032…501, 502
1060…902
1211…500, 703
1212…500
1221…702-705, 902, 904, 1004, App B, App C
1221(a)(2)…501, 502, App C
1222…App C
1223…App B, App C
1231…501, 502, 1102, App C
1272 et seq. …401
7701…1101
7704… 301, 302, 304

Regulation Sections

1.162-5(b)...App A
1.162-5(b)(3)...App A
1.305-3(e), Ex. 2...App C
1.316-2(a)...702
1.368-1(e)...1002, 1003
1.368-1(e)(2)(v), Ex. 1...1003

1.368-2...903.01
1.701-2...1501
1.704-1(b)(2)(iii)...1403
1.704-3(b)(1)...1305
15a.453-1...1502
301.7701-2...301

301.7701-2(a)...302
301.7701-2(b)...302
301.7701-3...301
301.7701-3(a)...302
301.7701-3(b)...302

Rulings

Rev. Proc. 2019-44, 2019-47 IRB 1093...102
Rev. Rul. 83-98, 1983-2 C.B. 40 (1983)...402

Index

All references are to paragraph (¶) numbers.

A

ACM Partnership ... 1502

Acquisitions. See Corporate acquisitions, realization and tax deferral in

Advanced problems ... App C

Allocations among partners. See Partnership allocations

Anti-abuse rule ... 1501

Asset sales ... 901–902

B

Basye ... 1103

Baumer ... 801

Bollinger ... 303

Business entities, choice of. See Income shifting, tax deferral, and choice of business entity; specific types of entities

Business tax exam advanced strategies ... App B

Buybacks of stock ... 706

C

Castle Harbour ... 1503

Check-the-box rules ... 301–302

Choice of business entity. See Income shifting, tax deferral, and choice of business entity

Code sections. See also Table of Code, Regulations and Rulings
  199A ... 102
  301 ... 701
  302 ... 704
  305 ... 802–803
  351 ... 502, 601–602, 604, 1300
  358 ... 601
  368 ... 1002
  704(b) ... 1400, 1402–1403
  704(c) ... 1304–1305, 1503

Compensation for services ... 603

Continuity of interest ... 1002–1003

Corporate acquisitions, realization and tax deferral in ... 900–906
  asset sales ... 901–902
  corporate acquisition, defined ... 905
  liquidation ... 901
  overview ... 900
  reorganizations and taxable acquisitions ... 904
  reorganizations and tax deferral ... 903–903.02
  Section 368 ... 903.01
  sellers ... 901
  stock sales ... 901–902
  structures ... 901
  targets ... 901
  taxable acquisitions ... 902

Corporate distributions and redemptions ... 700–707
  dividends ... 702–703, 706
  overview ... 700
  realization and distribution rules ... 701
  Section 301 ... 701
  Section 302 ... 704
  stock buybacks ... 706
  substance over form ... 704

Corporations
  acquisitions ... 900–906. See also Corporate acquisitions, realization and tax deferral in
  advanced problems ... App C
  corporate control, defined ... 505
  defined ... 204
  distributions and redemptions ... 700–707. See also Corporate distributions and redemptions
  formation. See Tax deferral and corporate formation
  partnership tax compared ... 1203.03
  pass-through taxation vs. ... 201, 203
  S corporations ... 201

Cottage Savings ... 501

D

Debt vs. equity ... 400–405
  debt, defined ... 404
  Indmar ... 402
  overview ... 400
  Roth Steel ... 402
  taxes ... 401

Definitions
corporate acquisition ... 905
corporate control ... 505
corporation ... 204
debt ... 404
distributive share ... 1101
dividend ... 706
inside basis ... 1101
outside basis ... 1101
partner ... 1101
partnership ... 1101, 1105
preferred stock ... 605

Disguised dividends and stock dividends ... 800–805
Baumer ... 801
disguised dividends ... 801
Exacto Spring ... 801
independent investor test ... 801
Macomber ... 802–803
overview ... 800
Section 305 ... 802–803
stock dividends ... 802–803

Distributions. *See* **Corporate distributions and redemptions**

Distributive share, defined ... 1101

Dividends
corporate distributions and redemptions ... 702–703
defined ... 706
disguised. *See* Disguised dividends and stock dividends
income shifting ... 703

Double taxation, partnership avoidance of ... 1203.01, 1203.03

E

Entity choice ... 300–304. *See also specific types of entities*
Bollinger ... 303
check-the-box rules ... 301–302
overview ... 300
taxation ... 304

Equity vs. debt ... 400–405. *See also* **Debt vs. equity**

Exacto Spring ... 801

Exams
advanced strategies ... App B
issue spotter exam writing ... App A

Expression, quality of ... App A

I

Income reporting by partners ... 1202

Income shifting, tax deferral, and choice of business entity ... 200–205
corporation, defined ... 204
corporation vs. pass-through ... 201, 203
dividends ... 703
entity choice math ... App 2–1
overview ... 200
partnership allocations ... 1400–1404. *See also* Partnership allocations
partnership contributions ... 1304
quantifying value ... 202
S corporations ... 201

Independent investor test ... 801

Indmar ... 402

Inside basis, defined ... 1101

Intermountain Lumber ... 504

Issue spotter exam writing ... App A

J

James ... 603

L

Legal judgment ... App A

LeTulle ... 1002

Liquidation ... 901

Loss limitations and distribution rules limit for partnerships ... 1402

M

Macomber ... 802–803

Marr ... 1001

Mergers. *See* **Corporate acquisitions, realization and tax deferral in**

Multiple tax rates ... 102

N

Net income, partnership ... 1102

Nonqualified preferred stock ... 602

INDEX 193

O

Outside basis
    adjustment for allocated income ... 1203.01
    adjustment for distributions ... 1203.02
    defined ... 1101

P

Partnership allocations
    income shifting ... 1400–1404
    loss limitations and distribution rules limit ... 1402
    overview ... 1400
    Section 704(b) ... 1400, 1402–1403
    valuation ... 1401

Partnership taxation ... 1500–1504. *See also* **Tax deferral and partnership contributions**
    ACM Partnership ... 1502
    advanced problems ... App C
    allocations ... 1401
    anti-abuse rule ... 1501
    bases adjustments ... 1203
    basics ... 1200–1205
    Castle Harbour ... 1503
    ceiling rule ... 1503
    corporate tax results compared ... 1203.03
    distributions ... 1202
    income reporting ... 1202
    outside basis adjustment for allocated income ... 1203.01
    outside basis adjustment for distributions ... 1203.02
    overview ... 1200, 1500
    payment by partner (not partnership) ... 1201
    Section 704(c) ... 1503
    single tax vs. double tax ... 1203.01, 1203.03
    Treas. Regulations 1.701-2 ... 1501

Partnership valuation and realization ... 1100–1105. *See also* **Tax deferral and partnership contributions**
    Basye ... 1103
    distributive share, defined ... 1101
    inside basis, defined ... 1101
    net income ... 1102
    outside basis, defined ... 1101
    overview ... 1100
    partner, defined ... 1101
    partnership, defined ... 1101, 1105
    terminology ... 1101

Pass-through taxation ... 201, 203
    partnerships ... 1201

Paulsen ... 1003
Pinellas Ice ... 1002
Preferred stock, defined ... 605
Proprietary interest continuity ... 1002–1003

R

Realization
    corporate acquisitions. *See* Corporate acquisitions, realization and tax deferral in
    corporate distributions and redemptions ... 701
    distribution rules and ... 701
    incorporation ... 501
    partnerships. *See* Partnership valuation and realization
    reorganizations ... 1001

Redemptions. *See* **Corporate distributions and redemptions**

Reorganizations
    LeTulle ... 1002
    Marr ... 1001
    Paulsen ... 1003
    Pinellas Ice ... 1002
    proprietary interest continuity ... 1002–1003
    realization ... 1001
    Section 368 ... 1002
    substance over form ... 1000–1005
    taxable acquisitions ... 904
    tax deferral ... 903–903.02

Roth Steel ... 402

S

S corporations ... 201

Southgate Partnership ... **1304**

Stock. *See also* **Disguised dividends and stock dividends; Dividends**
    buybacks ... 706
    nonqualified preferred stock ... 602
    preferred stock, defined ... 605
    sales ... 901–902

Substance over form doctrine
    corporate distributions and redemptions ... 704
    corporate formation and tax deferral ... 504, 603
    debt vs. equity. *See* Debt vs. equity
    disguised dividends and stock dividends. *See* Disguised dividends and stock dividends
    entity choice and. *See* Entity choice
    Indmar ... 402

SUB

Intermountain Lumber ... 504
partnership contributions and tax deferral ... 1304
partnership tax. *See* Partnership tax
reorganizations and. *See* Reorganizations
Roth Steel ... 402
tax challenges ... 304, 400–405

T

Targets of corporate acquisitions ... 901

Tax challenges
debt vs. equity ... 401
multiple tax rates ... 102
partnerships. *See* Partnership valuation and realization
substance over form ... 304, 400–405
valuation of business income ... 101

Tax deferral and corporate formation ... 500–506. *See also* **Income shifting, tax deferral, and choice of business entity**
boot ... 601, 604
compensation for services ... 603
corporate acquisitions. *See* Corporate acquisitions, realization and tax deferral in
corporate control, defined ... 505
Cottage Savings ... 501
Intermountain Lumber ... 504
James v. Commissioner ... 603
limitations ... 600–605
nonqualified preferred stock ... 602
overview ... 500

preferred stock, defined ... 605
realization and incorporation ... 501
reorganizations and ... 903–903.02
Section 351 ... 502, 601–602, 604
Section 358 ... 601
substance over form ... 504, 603

Tax deferral and partnership contributions ... 1300–1306. *See also* **Partnership taxation; Partnership valuation and realization**
basics ... 1303
basis in contributed property ... 1302
cash ... 1301
income shifting ... 1304
overview ... 1300
property ... 1301
Section 351 ... 1300
Section 704(c) ... 1304–1305
Southgate Partnership ... 1304
substance over form ... 1304

V

Valuation of business income ... 100–102
income shifting ... 202
multiple tax rates ... 102
overview ... 100
partnership allocations ... 1401. *See also* Partnership valuation and realization
tax challenges ... 101